The errors on the following pages were not detected prior to publication: 3, change *Robert Haldeman* to *H. R. Haldeman;* for Leonard Garment, change *Assistant* to *Counsel;* 31, delete sentence *re* prominent men; 39, the actual name of the Watergate Committee was "Senate Select Committee on Presidential Campaign Activities"; 43, witnesses other than Dean disclosed Hughes gift to Rebozo; 104, change *Special Prosecutor* to *Special Counsel;* 183, change *John Haldeman* to *H. R. Haldeman;* 192, delete sentence *re* pending trial; 199, change *Jim Thornton* to *Ray Thornton;* 222, change *1973* to *1993.*

WITHOUT
HONOR

WITHOUT HONOR

HONOR

CRIMES OF CAMELOT

and the

IMPEACHMENT OF PRESIDENT NIXON

Jerry Zeifman

Former Chief Counsel, House Judiciary Committee

THUNDER'S MOUTH PRESS

Copyright © 1995 by Jerome Zeifman
All rights reserved

First edition
First printing, 1995

Published by
Thunder's Mouth Press
632 Broadway, 7th Floor
New York, NY 10012

Zeifman, Jerry
    Without Honor: crimes of Camelot and the impeachment of
President Nixon / by Jerry Zeifman.—1st ed.
        p.   cm.
    Includes index.
    ISBN 1-56025-128-X
    1. Impeachment. 2. Government—United States.
3. President Richard M. Nixon. I. Title

    Library of Congress Catalog Card Number 95-062422

    Printed in the United States of America

    Distributed by Publishers Group West
            4065 Hollis Street
        Emeryville, CA 94608
            (800) 788-3123

To Marianne

CONTENTS

ACKNOWLEDGMENTS

I would like to thank the many people whose help and support during the writing of this book meant so much, starting with my wife Marianne and our family: Timothy, Vivien, Cassandra, Sara, Lisa, John, Emma, Molly, Lydia, Clara, and Timothy John.

A special debt of gratitude is owed to several persons who were my mentors and friends and who are now deceased: David Burliuk, Emanuel Celler, Bess Dick, Samuel Goldberg, Balcomb and Gertrude Greene, Marjorie Royce Hubbard, Katherine Miller Johnson, Thomas "Tip" O'Neill, William Phillips, Byron Rogers, and Edwin E. Willis.

Others who have been of help and encouragement include Jeunesse Beaumont, Francis Board, Irma Cavat, John Dean, Donald Dinan, Maureen Dyer, James Farr, Mark Jackson, Marita Lorenz, Sarah McClendon, James McGrath, David McMichaels, Charles Morgan, Jr., Neil Ortenberg, Franklin Polk, Vicki Rosenberg, Michael Snyder, Wayne Thevenot, Patricia Wait, and John Wentzell.

Finally, I gratefully acknowledge the help, good humor, and patience of Robert Weisser, whose extraordinary literary sensitivity and editorial skills have been invaluable.

FOREWORD

When Richard Nixon resigned from the presidency on August 9, 1974, for most people it marked the end of a nightmarish episode in the history of our country. At the time, the House Judiciary Committee had voted to recommend to the full House that Nixon be impeached. An impeachment trial in the Senate might well have brought out some of the causes of the contagion that ended the Nixon presidency. But Nixon's resignation closed this door into his high office, as well as public evaluation of the impeachment process itself.

Jerry Zeifman has now reopened this long-closed door. Using his detailed contemporaneous diary of the impeachment inquiry proceedings and other materials that have since come to light, Jerry provides unique, often startling insights into the incomplete impeachment of Richard Nixon. I found this fascinating book to be a real page-turner: Jerry brings to life the players in the drama, provides a mass of important information concisely, and supports his assertions convincingly. The book provides missing information that cannot be ignored by students of the period, the Nixon presidency, Watergate, and Congress.

I had lost track of Jerry, who was a colleague and friend from our days together on the staff of the House Judiciary Committee. When Jerry tracked me down, we had not spoken for more than two decades. The last time we saw each other, I was testifying as a key witness before the Judiciary Committee during the impeachment inquiry. Jerry thoughtfully made his office available to my attorney and myself during breaks.

Since Jerry's call, we have had many long discussions about what occurred during the impeachment inquiry. As we talked, I realized that Jerry had answers to many of the questions that have long surrounded those extraordinary proceedings. As the Judiciary Committee's top staff attorney, he was like a thirty-ninth member of the committee because of his quiet influence on the members, who respected his views and looked to him for guidance. As the committee's Chief Counsel, he had a unique vantage point from which to analyze, criticize, and contribute to the proceedings, and the observations in his diary—not only about the impeachment inquiry but also about American politics in general—are breathtaking and disquieting.

An impeachment inquiry by the Judiciary Committee has been compared to the proceedings of a grand jury. The committee determines whether an indictment or charge is appropriate, and whether to recommend a Bill of Impeachment to the full House. But in the case of Richard Nixon, unlike with a grand jury, those in charge of the day-to-day inquiry decided not to undertake their own investigation. Indeed, when I first met with the inquiry staff's Special Counsel, John Doar, before I testified, I was struck by how restrained his curiosity about what I knew seemed. At the time, I thought that perhaps his restraint was appropriate—perhaps the Democrats were not out to skewer Richard Nixon, but merely intended to sift through the charges to determine if an impeachable offense had been committed. Jerry Zeifman, however, indicates that much more than that was going on.

During the summer of 1973 I had testified before the Senate Watergate Committee chaired by Senator Ervin. Although I answered questions for a week, I considered my testimony little more than an outline. While I had provided additional information to the Watergate Committee staff, I thought Doar and the impeachment inquiry staff would have endless questions. To the contrary, they only wished to make a limited review of what I had already said to the Senate. My appearance before the Judiciary Committee seemed designed to make me available to the President's attorney, James St. Clair, for cross-examination rather than to elicit information about my knowledge or areas for further investigation. Now, after reading Jerry's book, these puzzling events are beginning to fall into place.

Jerry's often-pointed analysis is provocative. Hopefully, his book will provoke a more complete look at the legal, constitutional, and ethical issues that the truncated impeachment inquiry left in its wake.

John W. Dean III
November 1995

WATERGATE PERSONALITIES

Spiro T. Agnew: Vice President of the United States
Carl Albert (D-Oklahoma): Speaker of the House
Bernard Barker: participant in Watergate break-ins
Hale Boggs (D-Louisiana): House Majority Leader ·
Lindy Boggs (D-Louisiana): widow of Hale Boggs and successor in House of
    Representatives
Robert Bork: U.S. Solicitor General, later Acting U.S. Attorney General
Patrick Buchanan: Special Assistant to President Nixon
Warren Burger: Chief Justice of the Supreme Court
Alexander Butterfield: Deputy Assistant to President Nixon
Charles Colson: Special Counsel to President Nixon
John Connally: Secretary of the Treasury and advisor to President Nixon
Archibald Cox: Watergate Special Prosecutor
John Dean III: Counsel to President Nixon
John Ehrlichman: Assistant to President Nixon for Domestic Affairs
Sam Ervin, Jr. (D-North Carolina): Chairman, Senate Watergate Committee
Gerald Ford (R-Michigan): House Minority Leader, later Vice President
    and then President of the United States
Leonard Garment: Assistant to President Nixon
L. Patrick Gray III: Acting FBI Director
General Alexander Haig: White House Chief of Staff
Robert Haldeman: White House Chief of Staff
Bernard Hellring: personal counselor to Peter Rodino
Richard Helms: Director of the CIA

Lawrence Houston: former Chief Counsel to CIA

E. Howard Hunt, Jr.: participant in Watergate break-ins

Tom Charles Huston: Associate Counsel to President Nixon

Leon Jaworski: Watergate Special Prosecutor

Herbert Kalmbach: personal attorney to President Nixon

Henry Kissinger: Secretary of State, National Security Advisor

Richard Kleindienst: U.S. Attorney General

Baruch Korff: Chairman, National Citizens Committee for Fairness to the President

Philip Lacovara: Counsel to the Special Prosecutor

Melvin Laird: Secretary of Defense

G. Gordon Liddy: participant in Watergate break-ins

Jeb Stuart Magruder: Deputy Director, Committee for the Re-election of the President

John Mitchell: U.S. Attorney General, Chairman of Committee for the Re-election of the President

Sun Myung Moon: Korean evangelist, supporter of President Nixon

Charles Morgan, Jr.: Washington Director, American Civil Liberties Union

Richard Nixon: President of the United States

Thomas "Tip" O'Neill (D-Massachusetts): House Majority Leader

Henry Petersen: Assistant Attorney General, Criminal Division

Charles (Bebe) Rebozo: financier and personal friend of President Nixon

Elliott Richardson: U.S. Attorney General

William Ruckelshaus: Deputy Attorney General

James St. Clair: Special Counsel to President Nixon

John Sirica: Judge, U.S. District Court for the District of Columbia

Lieutenant General Vernon Walters: Deputy Director of CIA

Rose Mary Woods: personal secretary to President Nixon

Ronald Ziegler: White House Press Secretary

Members of the House Judiciary Committee

Peter Rodino, Jr. (D-New Jersey): Chairman

Edward Hutchinson (R-Michigan): Ranking Minority Member

Jack Brooks (D-Texas)

M. Caldwell Butler (R-Virginia)

William Cohen (R-Maine)

John Conyers, Jr. (D-Michigan)

George Danielson (D-California)
David Dennis (R-Indiana)
Harold Donohue (D-Massachusetts)
Robert Drinan (D-Massachusetts)
Don Edwards (D-California)
Joshua Eilberg (D-Pennsylvania)
Hamilton Fish, Jr. (R-New York)
Walter Flowers (D-Alabama)
Lawrence Hogan (R-Maryland)
Elizabeth Holtzman (D-New York)
William Hungate (D-Missouri)
Barbara Jordan (D-Texas)
Robert Kastenmeier (D-Wisconsin)
Delbert Latta (R-Ohio)
Trent Lott (R-Mississippi)
Robert McClory (R-Illinois)
James Mann (D-South Carolina)
Joseph Maruziti (R-New Jersey)
Wiley Mayne (R-Iowa)
Edward Mezvinsky (D-Iowa)
Carlos Moorehead (R-California)
Wayne Owens (D-Utah)
Tom Railsback (R-Illinois)
Charles Rangel (D-New York)
Charles Sandman (R-New Jersey)
Paul Sarbanes (D-Maryland)
John Seiberling (D-Ohio)
Henry Smith III (R-New York)
Ray Thornton (D-Arkansas)
Jerome Waldie (D-California)
Charles Wiggins (R-California)

Permanent Staff of the House Judiciary Committee
Pearl Chellman: Executive Secretary to Chief Counsel
Garner Cline: Associate General Counsel
Daniel Cohen: Counsel
William Dixon: Counsel

Franklin Polk: Chief Minority Counsel
Jerry Zeifman: Chief Counsel

Staff of the Impeachment Inquiry
Richard Cates: Senior Associate Special Counsel
John Doar: Special Counsel
Samuel Garrison: Chief Minority Counsel
Albert Jenner: Minority Counsel
Bernard Nussbaum: Senior Associate Counsel
Hillary Rodham: Counsel

WATERGATE CHRONOLOGY

1969 January 20   Nixon inaugurated President.

       May 12   First of seventeen illegal wiretaps installed on
                      reporters and White House aides after *New
                      York Times* discloses bombing of Cambodia.

1970 April 22   House Majority Leader Hale Boggs denounces
                      FBI and other agencies for wiretaps and sur-
                      veillance of members of Congress.

       July 23   President Nixon approves illegal Huston plan
                      for political intelligence gathering.

1971 June 13   "Pentagon Papers" released by Daniel Ellsberg;
                      published in *New York Times*.

       September 3   White House aides E. Howard Hunt and
                      Gordon Liddy and others burglarize office of
                      Ellsberg's psychiatrist.

1972 June 17   Hunt, Liddy, McCord, and others burglarize
                      Watergate office of Democratic National
                      Committee.

       June 20   Nixon and Haldeman discuss Watergate arrests.

       June 23   Nixon directs Haldeman to urge CIA Director
                      Helms to impede Watergate-related investi-
                      gations.

       October 22   Hale Boggs disappears in small plane over
                      Alaska.

       November 7   Nixon reelected in a landslide.

1973	January 8-30	Trial of Watergate burglars. All defendants enter guilty pleas except for Liddy and James McCord, who are found guilty by the jury.
	January 20	Ninety-third Congress convenes. Charles Morgan begins "Impeach Nixon" movement.
	February 6	Senate Select Committee on Campaign Activities with Senator Sam Ervin as Chairman is established to investigate Watergate.
	May 18	Elliott Richardson becomes Attorney General; appoints Archibald Cox as Watergate Special Prosecutor.
	June 25-29	John Dean, in testimony before Ervin Committee, accuses Nixon of participation in Watergate coverup.
	July 13	White House tapes discovered by Ervin Committee.
	July 23	Cox subpoenas tapes of nine presidential conversations.
	October 10	Under criminal indictment, Vice President Agnew resigns.
	October 13	House Judiciary Committee begins hearings to confirm Gerald Ford as Vice President.
	October 20	"Saturday Night Massacre": Cox fired, Richardson and William Ruckelshaus resign.
	October 23	House Judiciary Committee begins impeachment inquiry.
	November 27	Ford confirmed as Vice President.
	December 20	After two month search, John Doar is chosen as Special Counsel in charge of the Judiciary Committee's impeachment inquiry staff.
1974	April 11	Judiciary Committee issues its first subpoena for White House tapes.
	May 11-June 21	At the insistence of Doar and Rodino, the Judiciary Committee holds secret hearings to hear evidence.
	July 2-17	Judiciary Committee interrogates nine witnesses, including John Dean.

July 24-30	In nationally televised debate, the Judiciary Committee adopts three articles of impeachment: obstruction of justice, abuse of power, and noncompliance with subpoenas.
August 5	Nixon complies with Supreme Court order to release some White House tapes. "Smoking gun" tape of June 23, 1972 reveals Nixon's participation in coverup.
August 9	Nixon resigns. Ford is sworn in as President.
August 20	House of Representatives accepts Judiciary Committee Impeachment Report by a vote of 412 to 3.
September 8	President Ford pardons Nixon for any and all prior criminal acts, known or unknown.

Seas without fish.
Forests without trees.
Women without virtue.
Men without honor.
　　　　—from Dante's *Inferno*

PROLOGUE

In January 1974, Yale Law Professor Burke Marshall placed calls to two of his most trusted former students. Marshall had formerly been Assistant Attorney General under Robert Kennedy, and he would later become Ted Kennedy's principal Chappaquiddick advisor. At Yale, the students and faculty considered him "the Attorney General-in-waiting of the 'Camelot government-in-exile.'" He advised them to send their resumes to John Doar, Special Counsel to the House Judiciary Committee. Doar, who was heading the impeachment inquiry of President Nixon, had been Marshall's most trusted deputy in the Kennedy Justice Department.

The two Yale alumni were Hillary Rodham and Bill Clinton.

On Marshall's recommendation, Doar offered staff jobs to the two neophytes, who were then only a year out of law school. At the time, though, Clinton was planning a run for public office in Arkansas, where President Nixon had tremendous support. Fearful of becoming identified with the impeachment movement, Clinton turned down Doar's offer.

A decade before, Hillary Rodham had been a "Goldwater Girl," but had long since shed much of her conservativism. She had developed ties to Peter Edelman, who had been one of Robert Kennedy's top aides. Edelman had married Hillary's close friend, social activist Marian Wright. Encouraged by the Edelmans, Rodham accepted Doar's offer.

In a temporary office in the former Congressional Hotel, Rodham was assigned to work under the supervision of Bernard Nussbaum, Doar's Senior Associate Counsel and another former member of the Kennedy Justice Department. Under the tutelage of Marshall, Doar, and Nussbaum, Rodham was soon to receive a unique indoctrina-

11

tion into presidential and congressional politics that would eventually be reflected in her actions as First Lady.

Twenty years later, Marshall described Rodham's responsibilities to the then-First Lady's biographer: "The job required basic legal skills of analysis in an area that was quite unexplored. It also required somebody who would keep her work to herself, or within the work of the group." Rodham performed her job admirably.

Twenty years later, Nussbaum became the chief White House counsel to President Bill Clinton—with an office close to the First Lady's. Subsequently, Nussbaum was subpoenaed by the Whitewater grand jury—and cited in *New York Times* editorials entitled "Slovenly White House Ethics" and "White House Ethics Meltdown." President Clinton eventually forced him to resign.

Watergate's "cancer on the presidency" did not begin—or end—with Nixon.

On August 9, 1974, Gerald Ford was sworn in as President of the United States. After Chief Justice Warren Burger administered the oath of office, Ford made a short inaugural address; in it were these now-famous words: "My fellow Americans, our national nightmare is over. Our Constitution works: our great republic is a government of laws and not of men. Here the people rule."

The evening before Ford's momentous speech, President Richard Nixon had announced that he would resign. Ultimately, he had been done in by the "smoking gun" tape—the recording of the June 23, 1972 conversation in the Oval Office that clearly incriminated him in the Watergate coverup. In his televised speech, Nixon had said, "It has become evident to me that I no longer have a strong enough political base in the Congress. . . . Therefore, I shall resign the presidency effective at noon tomorrow."

On August 20, the report of the House Judiciary Committee containing the articles of impeachment was brought to the floor of the House and accepted by a vote of 412 to 3. This, for the entire nation to see, was the final word on the Watergate scandal. The public believed that the system had worked. The old era of political warfare, enemies lists, and paranoia was over; a new era of conciliation and healing had begun. The Congress had done its work. Nixon had been removed from office, and we were all saved from tyranny.

We now know it was all a sham.

Not until after Nixon's resignation were we to learn that the "cancer on the presidency" that John Dean referred to—that criminal conduct by government officials and their agents can be condoned in the "national interest"—was not touched. Indeed, the months-long investigation of the Nixon administration was seemingly designed to cover up malfeasance in high office throughout the Cold War: political assassinations around the world, sponsorship of coups to overthrow governments, illegal wiretaps on American citizens.

The "smoking gun" tape hinted at untold evidence of these crimes. The transcript of that tape revealed Nixon directing Robert Haldeman to have CIA Director Richard Helms influence the FBI to back off the Watergate investigation. As Nixon said to Haldeman: "When you get the CIA people in say, 'Look, the problem is that this will open up the whole Bay of Pigs thing again.' So they should call the FBI in and for the good of the country don't go any further into this case. Period."

Nixon also instructed Haldeman that, to further influence Helms to cooperate, he should remind Helms of "this Hunt, that will uncover a lot of things. You open this scab there's a hell of a lot of things. This involves those Cubans, Hunt, and a lot of hanky-panky that we have nothing to do with ourselves." Nixon concluded his instructions with, "We protected Helms from one hell of a lot of things."

In 1953 the CIA executed a coup in Iran led by CIA operative Kermit Roosevelt, the son of Theodore Roosevelt. The coup overthrew the government of Premier Mohammed Mossadegh, which had had the temerity to nationalize the Anglo-Iranian Oil Company, and restored Shah Mohammed Reza Pahlavi to power. For this success, Roosevelt was awarded the National Security Medal and personally praised by President Eisenhower.

The next year, the agency also orchestrated a coup in Guatemala, overthrowing President Jacobo Arbenz's regime by putting together an army and bombing Guatemala City. Arbenz had made the mistake of trying to make agrarian reform a reality in his poor country, and had expropriated some unused land that was owned by the United Fruit Company, distributing it among 100,000 Guatemalan farm families. He had paid the American owners of the company what he thought was a fair, if ironic, price—the value that the owners themselves had placed on the land for tax purposes.

At that time, CIA General Counsel Lawrence Houston, who had been with the CIA since its inception in the Truman administration, became concerned that CIA operatives might be detected by the FBI and prosecuted for the felonies that they were now committing. He negotiated an illegal secret agreement with the Department of Justice to shield CIA operatives from criminal prosecution. The agreement was first negotiated between Houston and then-Deputy Attorney General William Rogers—who eventually became Secretary of State under Nixon and later headed a commission to investigate the Iran-Contra scandal during the Reagan administration.

The Rogers-Houston agreement unlawfully delegated the Attorney General's authority to the Director of the CIA in cases involving crimes committed by CIA operatives. This agreement gave the CIA the power to direct the Justice Department not to prosecute or even investigate known criminals.

As revealed in a stunning 1976 cross-examination of Houston by Bella Abzug, chair of the House Subcommittee on Government Operations, this policy acted as a shield for government-sponsored murder. Abzug asked Houston whether under his agreement with Rogers the CIA could "get away with murder."

HOUSTON: It would depend on the nature of the sensitivity of the information.
ABZUG: In other words, this memorandum of understanding in your judgment gave authority to the CIA to make decisions, to give immunity to individuals who happened to work for the CIA for all kinds of crime, including possibly murder.
HOUSTON: It was not designed to give immunity to individuals.
ABZUG: Was that not the effect of the actual interpretation made by the CIA and their advisors?
HOUSTON: It could have that effect, yes.
ABZUG: Did it not have that effect?
HOUSTON: In certain cases it did.

The Houston-Rogers agreement and the policies that it reflected remained in effect for more than two decades, through the Eisenhower, Kennedy, Johnson, and Nixon administrations. (They were rescinded by President Ford.) In 1960 and 1961, CIA-supported assassination attempts were made on Patrice Lumumba, premier of the Congo; the CIA also supported plots in the Dominican Republic that caused the murders of President Rafael Trujillo and General Rene Schneider. In 1963, a CIA-sponsored coup in South Vietnam resulted in the assassination of Ngo Dinh Diem, president of that country. The Chilean government of Salvador Allende Gossens was overthrown in a 1973 coup supported by the CIA, and Gossens was assassinated.

Perhaps the most sensationalized example of this policy involved assassination attempts against Fidel Castro. The idea, which constituted criminal conspiracy to commit murder, was hatched with the approval of Vice President Nixon and CIA Director Allen Dulles in 1960, at a time when Nixon was campaigning for the presidency. The illegal plan contemplated that Sam Giancana and the Mafia would help the CIA assassinate Castro, and that regardless of whether Nixon or Kennedy won the election the mob would resume control of gambling and prostitution in Cuba. During the campaign, Kennedy was briefed on the plans, and the two candidates secretly agreed not to discuss American policy toward Castro. Instead, their televised foreign policy debate concerned the defense of Quemoy and Matsu, two relatively insignificant islands off the coast of Communist China.

John Kennedy won the election amidst charges of ballot box improprieties and Mafia involvement. Robert Kennedy, who had cut his political teeth as Senator Joseph McCarthy's aide during the Red Scare of the 1950s, took over the Justice Department. The fear of Castro at the highest levels of government was heightened, and the joint CIA-Mafia plots against Castro went forward. Although there may be some doubt as to whether high-ranking officials of the Kennedy Justice Department were actually shown a copy of the Houston-Rogers memorandum of understanding, the policy was implemented during the Kennedy administration during the Justice Department tenures of Archibald Cox, Burke Marshall, and John Doar.

Why did the CIA turn to the Mafia for assistance? Because they had been doing it successfully for years. During World War II, the Office of Strategic Services (OSS, forerunner of the CIA) recruited the anti-Mussolini Sicilian Mafia leader Don Colegro Vizini and his organization to help liberate Sicily—and later to help with the Allied occupation of Italy. When the war was over, the OSS recruited Mafia members to fight communist labor organizers in Italy.

I was there. I was a coding officer of highly classified messages for OSS Navy Captain Roscoe Hillenkoetter, who was part of a joint naval-diplomatic mission to Italy with Secretary of State James

Byrne. The mission's covert duty was to foster anti-communist sentiment in Italy, and to ensure that Prince Umberto's fledgling government stifled communist influence. Another young officer assigned to help the Italian government in this struggle was Army Captain Peter Rodino.

In 1947, Hillenkoetter, by then an admiral, became Director of the CIA under President Truman. He was charged with setting up a wide range of covert activities to prevent the communists from gaining control of Italy in the 1948 parliamentary election.

In 1973, Rodino, by then a senior congressman from Newark, New Jersey, became chairman of the House Judiciary Committee. He was charged with investigating the Watergate coverup.

PART ONE

PRELUDE TO
IMPEACHMENT

*[Secrecy] in a popular government is but a
Prologue to a Farce, or a Tragedy, or perhaps both.*
—James Madison

1

THE NEW CHAIRMAN

On a cold late-January day in 1973, the body of former President Lyndon Johnson lay in state in the rotunda of the Capitol. As the line of mourners filed by his casket, another ritual was taking place in the chamber of the House of Representatives. As it did at the beginning of each new Congress, the House was electing the chairs of its standing committees. In keeping with the seniority system, House members automatically cast their votes for the representatives who had served the longest.

Nine months before, the stooped chairman of the Judiciary Committee, Emanuel Celler—who was first elected to Congress in 1922—had made a politically fatal speech. Opposing the Equal Rights Amendment, Celler had asserted, "There is as much difference between a man and a woman as between lightning and a lightning rod—and between a chestnut horse and a horse chestnut." Soon after that, Celler was deposed in a primary in his Brooklyn district by a political newcomer, the young feminist Elizabeth Holtzman.

With Holtzman now occupying Celler's former congressional seat, Peter Rodino became chairman of the Judiciary Committee.

With twenty-four years in Congress, Rodino now enjoyed a lavish suite in the House Office Building, the edifice named for Lyndon Johnson's mentor, Sam Rayburn of Texas. Like the building itself, Rodino's office was furnished in Texas Baroque, an opulence restrained only by the limits of political good taste. The most prominent feature of his office was a large bronze of the she-wolf suckling Romulus and Remus, the legendary founders of Rome

Like most congressmen, Rodino sat in a high-backed leather chair behind a large walnut desk. Behind him on the right stood the

19

American flag, with heavy golden tassles; on the left stood the New Jersey state flag.

Peter was then in his sixties, his thick black hair already well-silvered. A short man, he wore elevator shoes. He was trim and impeccably dressed, always wearing a well-tailored pinstriped suit and an elegant Italian silk tie. On his lapel was a small silk insignia attesting to his membership in the Knights of Malta, a centuries-old secret society.

Rodino often talked effusively about his father, who left the small village of Avalino to come to work in a foul-smelling leather factory in Newark. Baptized as Pelligrino Rodino, Jr.—later anglicized to Peter Wallace Rodino, Jr.—the immigrant's son grew up in a roach-infested apartment over a slum candy store. When he was five years old his mother died of tuberculosis. With his father at work in the factory, motherless Peter was exposed to crimes and vice on the streets of Newark's Little Italy.

As an adolescent Peter was traumatized by viewing the naked corpse of a hoodlum who had been garotted and castrated for seducing the daughter of a mob leader. With the naked corpse draped over a wire fence, the dead man's genitals were tucked partially into his slit-open anus. The sight was to return to Peter in recurrent bad dreams for years. But with the encouragement of his hard-working father he rose out of Newark's slums. He excelled in high school and then worked his way through college and law school by taking such jobs as railroad laborer, insurance salesman, factory hand, and social worker. During World War II he enlisted in the army, received a commission as a captain and served in a unit that helped liberate Italy. Returning home to New Jersey he won election to Congress in 1948—unseating Republican Fred Hartley, co-author of what Rodino described as the "iniquitous antilabor Taft-Hartley Act."

Now at the height of his political power, Rodino faced a crisis. Because of recent scandals in New Jersey, he feared he would be a one-term chairman.

Rodino's closest friend and political ally was Hugh Addonizio, who had represented a district adjoining Rodino's. For many years Addonizio and Rodino had shared a Capitol Hill apartment. In the privacy of the Democratic cloakroom, their colleagues spoke of them as the "gold dust twins."

In 1962, Addonizio left Capitol Hill to run for Mayor of Newark. Tip O'Neill—who became House Majority Leader in 1973—related this story: When he asked Addonizio why he was leaving Congress, "Hughie" said, "Christ, do you know what the budget for the City of Newark is? Take one percent of that and I'm going to have something."

Hughie got his one percent during his two terms as mayor, but he also got something else—a conviction for racketeering and extortion in 1970 and a ten-year prison term. Out of loyalty to the disgraced mayor's family, Rodino had put Addonizio's son, "Little Hughie," on the congressional payroll. Many of Rodino's former supporters feared that, like Addonizio, Rodino had Mafia ties.

In addition, the early 1970s were particularly scandalous years for New Jersey's Democratic congressional delegation. In 1970 Cornelius Gallagher, a senior congressman from Bayonne, had been charged with taking kickbacks, and was in prison after being convicted of income tax evasion. In 1971 a magazine story depicted Gallagher as a front for gangsters.

Large numbers of New Jersey's Italian Americans were beginning to register as Republicans. To add to Rodino's worries, his Tenth District was being racially polarized. For the first time, blacks held a majority in the district. Imamu Amiri Baraka, a prominent Black Muslim author, was organizing a campaign to replace Rodino with a black representative. At the same time, many of the Italian Americans who remained registered Democrats were rallying behind Rodino's racist rival Anthony Imperiale, who was getting national media coverage by chaining himself to fences of integrated housing projects and denouncing Rodino as a bleeding-heart liberal who was betraying the white race. To avoid facing the brickbats of both sets of extremists, Rodino frequently canceled his usual weekend trips home to Newark.

Rodino often turned for advice on his political and personal problems to Bernard Hellring—the Harvard-trained criminal defense lawyer who had also represented Addonizio. Portly, with rosy cheeks and white hair, Hellring had a jovial Friar Tuck demeanor. He represented racetrack owners, gambling casino operators, and other clients suspected of ties to organized crime.

Once, Bernie invited my wife and me to a party of his clients and associates at Laurel Racetrack in Maryland. Quite a number of the other guests were known to have ties to organized crime. Besides the fact that Bernie really knew how to entertain, I remember the party for one guest in particular whom we were introduced to: William Casey, a well-heeled lawyer from New York, later to become head of the CIA and chief keeper of government secrets.

Rodino's closest confidantes also included Lois D'Andre—officially his secretary but in reality Peter's eminence grise. She was the only member of his staff permitted to call him by his first name. A recent graduate of American University, Lois appeared mature beyond her years. She had Anna Magnani-like features and was always tastefully dressed. Not only was she a very big woman— much larger than Rodino—but she had the habit of watching over everyone's shoulder. Behind her back other staff members referred to her as "Big Mama."

Hellring and D'Andre shared confidences with each other. They generally agreed in advance on any advice they gave Rodino on sensitive political or personal matters. They also had common perceptions that Rodino's greatest strength—as well as his greatest weakness—was his caution. In the inner sanctum of Rodino's office one of Hellring's joking but affectionate descriptions of Rodino was that he was the kind of person who would usually bet on the favorite in a race—to place. D'Andre's observations were, "Peter has the cleanest mind in Washington, he changes it so often" and "Peter believes in making love—and not war. If he ever had to lead troops into combat, his battle cry would be, 'Forward men! I'm right behind you.'"

Never being out in front of any legislation—other than a bill to make Columbus Day a national holiday—was probably one key to Rodino's longevity in Congress. He rarely publicly said or did anything that angered his constituents. He had his staff scrutinize Newark publications for news of births, baptisms, communions, bar mitzvahs, marriages, deaths, funerals, wakes, and every other form of testimonial ceremony. Rodino would either attend the ceremonies himself or send a warm, hand-signed note on official stationery.

This cultivation of his constituents resulted in an episode that haunted Rodino for his entire political career. When he was a young congressman, Newark was the site of the famous wedding of Johnny Dio's daughter—the wedding that served as the model for the opening scene of Mario Puzo's *The Godfather.* Anyone who was connected to behind-the-scenes power in New Jersey and the Northeast was invited, and most of them attended. So did Rodino. Later, whenever anyone wrote an article or opened an investigation about organized crime, one of the first documents hauled out was the guest list from that wedding.

Before his official installation as Judiciary Committee chairman, Rodino summoned me to his office to offer me the job of chief counsel to the committee. By then I had already served the committee for eleven years, the last six as counsel to the Subcommittee on Civil Rights, chaired by Representative Don Edwards. I had reservations about leaving the subcommittee, even though it meant a large step up the career ladder for me. First, I had great respect for Edwards and the other members of the subcommittee, both Democrats and Republicans. Second, I really enjoyed my work with the subcommittee, because it had been at the focus of the most explosive issues Congress had to deal with—voting rights, school desegregation, forced busing, discrimination in jobs and housing, and others. This was exciting labor.

Third, I regarded Rodino as a weak and indecisive congressman. (Some members of the Judiciary Committee nicknamed him "The Leader"—not because of his heroic stands on the issues, but because he loved to lead congressional junkets to foreign countries.) A joke told by his staff compared him to a character played by Gina Lollabrigida in a great Italian film, *The Good Old Days.* She played a Sicilian prostitute being tried for murdering her mother-in-law. When she is asked how she could have sex with so many men, she replies, "I can never say no to a Christian." Peter Rodino had a hard time saying no to lobbyists who curried his favor.

And fourth, although I enjoyed his friendship and had often worked closely with him, there were other things in his personality, even beyond the allegations of ties to organized crime, that made me uncomfortable. For instance, the way he sometimes treated servants left much to be desired. I once accompanied him on a Congressional delegation that toured NATO countries. In England, Rodino and I were chauffeured around in a Jaguar driven by a man whom we knew only as James. During conversation, James revealed himself to be an intelligent, well-informed gentleman. At one point, Rodino said to him, "James, I don't understand how someone with your obvious intelligence and ability is content to be a chauffeur all his life. Haven't you ever thought it would be a good idea to better yourself?" Sitting in front, I saw the slight, almost condescending smile that played on James's lips as he replied, "I was brought up to believe that it is better to be a good driver than a poor prime minister."

When we got out of the car, Rodino appeared crestfallen. He seemed to sense that the driver had put him down. He turned to me and said, "What the hell did he mean by that crack?" Knowing the British well (having been married to an Englishwoman), I recognized that James was talking about pride in one's work, no matter one's social status. But this was lost on Rodino.

When he offered me the job as chief counsel, Rodino showed me a handwritten memo headed "Hot Potatoes" in which he had listed what he perceived as the most explosive political issues before the committee: abortion, the death penalty, crime, drugs, school prayer, and whether to make Martin Luther King's birthday a national holiday. Fearful that a mishandling of any of the inflammatory issues might further endanger his chances of reelection, he made it clear that my role would be to juggle the hot potatoes and help shield him from their heat. Knowing of my Navy service during World War II, he jokingly compared me to a navigator who avoided minefields and dangerous storms. Placing his hand on my shoulder he said, "You're the best man for the job. A majority of the committee members have recommended you. Lois and Bernie Hellring are looking forward to working closely with you."

I looked at the handwritten memo again. Although revelations about the Watergate break-in were starting to come out with astonishing rapidity, the scandal was conspicuously absent from the list.

What ultimately changed my opinion was the advice of Don Edwards. Although acknowledging my concerns, he suggested that all of the civil rights issues that we had been working on in subcommittee would be advanced with me as chief counsel to the entire committee. I called D'Andre the next day and accepted the post.

To be able to work closely with Peter Rodino, two proclivities were essential—to admire things Italian and to enjoy after-dinner conversations. It helped that one of my great-grandmothers was Italian and that I could speak a little of the language.

When we dined together, Rodino would regale me over and over with the colorful stories of his life. However, there was one topic about which I always enjoyed hearing—opera. Very often, the conversation would turn to the famous opera star Maria Jeritza. The first time Rodino mentioned Jeritza to me, he was delighted to learn that I too was one of her fans and that I agreed with him—before Maria Callas, Maria Jeritza was the greatest diva of our century. Her most famous role was as Salome—the temptress who enticed Herod to bring her John the Baptist's head on a platter. Once, after a few glasses of wine, Rodino said, "When I first saw the great Jeritza and heard her sing I was very young—and she was much older. But her age didn't matter, I fell in love with her *immediatamente* and completely. But of course, although I have known her personally for many years, my love for her has always been pure—*innocente*—like Dante's love for Beatrice in the *Divine Comedy*. You can understand that, can't you?"

On the day that Rodino officially became chairman of the Judiciary Committee, no one could have predicted that in the near future an aged and wrinkled Maria Jeritza, her eyes still lustrous with mischief, would invite the famous chairman to her box at the Metropolitan Opera and teasingly suggest that he deliver the head of Richard Nixon to her on a platter.

2

THE ATTORNEY GENERAL AND THE GHOST OF GYP DECARLO

There is no sport more exotic on Capitol Hill than the courting of political favors. Although each party has its own style of courtship, many political leaders tend to follow their own fancy. Most conservative Republicans, like the elephant that symbolizes their party, are slow to mate. Richard Kleindienst, who was Attorney General at the time of Watergate, was an exception. Politically, he was a fast worker.

Just a few days after Peter Rodino became chairman, the Attorney General called to arrange an appointment, purportedly to request a postponement of a hearing we had scheduled on a routine bill. For a cabinet member to visit a congressional office is like the mountain coming to Mohammed, and I had already advised Kleindienst's secretary that we would agree to such a postponement. Rodino and I suspected that Kleindienst had something more important on his mind.

Our suspicions were confirmed when Kleindienst arrived by himself, for normally an Attorney General came to Capitol Hill with a retinue of aides. He greeted Rodino warmly: "Pete, how the hell are you? It's good to see you. How's Anne and the kids?" Then he added in seriocomic fashion, "I hope that all of your new duties are not going to weigh to heavily on you. Jesus, I know what that can be like ... But anyway, Pete, I want you to know that all of us at the Department of Justice will do everything we can to ease your burdens."

Then came a teaser: "The President sure is fond of you, Pete. If you want any help from us, just tell me. What can I do to help you out?"

Rodino's eyes brightened, and with the same good humor he

26

said, "Dick, it's good to see you too. It's nice of you and the President to want to help me. Gee, if all of the Democrats and Republicans around here could get along as well as we do, it would be great." Then, coyly, "But gee, Dick, I'm doing fine. I really enjoy being a chairman. It's no great burden, and I'm looking forward to working with you and the President."

In a less-jocular, but still lighthearted manner, Kleindienst repeated his offer: "Pete, you're a great guy. But come on, there must be something we can do for you."

Like a tango dancer, Rodino gracefully turned the conversation to his problems in Newark. "Well, Dick, maybe you could prosecute LeRoi Jones—you know, that Black Muslim writer who now calls himself Imamu Baraka. He's opening a Black Muslim center in a mansion in one of the best residential sections in my district. There's a lot of questions about where the money is coming for that. Yeah," Rodino said laughingly, "I suppose you could find something to prosecute him for."

Kleindienst chuckled loudly. "Hey, Conyers, Rangel, and Jordan would love jumping on my ass for that, wouldn't they?" (John Conyers, Charles Rangel, and Barbara Jordan were the three black members of the Judiciary Committee.)

Then, making his own tango move, the Attorney General turned the discussion to Watergate. "Lemme tell you Pete, I got some people in my own department on my ass already—about Watergate! Hey, every Friday night when I come home from the office I tell my wife, 'Well darlin', we got through another week without getting indicted.' Christ, Pete, if I can get out of this Watergate mess with my skin intact, I'd be willing to go back to Phoenix and pump gas for a living!"

After dropping this bombshell, Kleindienst looked at his watch and excused himself. Rodino and I had been party to countless such conversations, but this one left us stunned. Peter sat down at his desk, looking pale and pensive. We both understood Kleindienst's unspoken message—if Rodino wanted any help from the White House in getting reelected, he would have to help the administration reduce the political fallout from Watergate.

Just a few days after our meeting with Kleindienst, Rodino received a call from a young Justice Department lawyer who owed his lower-echelon job to Rodino's recommendation. The young man requested a private after-hours meeting, and Peter asked me to be there.

Late that evening, Lois D'Andre admitted the young man. Visibly trembling, he sat by Rodino's desk, unable to begin. To put him at ease Rodino said compassionately, "It's good to see you again. What can I do for you?"

The young man looked up with a start: "Pete, you should run for President. The country needs you. You're the best Democrat we got!"

"You're very kind," Rodino replied.

The young lawyer's next words came out in a rush. "Pete, you're a great man and I want to help you. I came to warn you. You're in danger."

Now chain-smoking and perspiring profusely, the young man explained that President Nixon had recently given a pardon to a convicted Newark gangster named Gyp DeCarlo. DeCarlo subsequently died under mysterious circumstances. But before his demise, DeCarlo had supposedly given Kleindienst incriminating evidence that Rodino had Mafia connections. Rambling on, the distraught young man said that DeCarlo had also given Kleindienst evidence that President Kennedy and his brother had recruited Mafia leaders to hire hitmen to assassinate Fidel Castro . . . and various other fantastic allegations.

Rodino seemed unperturbed by the young man's warning. After he left, Peter explained to me that he knew the young man's parents, who had told him that their son had had a nervous breakdown and was still undergoing psychiatric treatment. Rodino advised me to attribute the young man's bizarre charges to his mental instability.

In the coming months, Kleindienst's offer appeared more and more like a political carrot—and the warning of the young lawyer possibly a stick—to induce Rodino to sanitize the investigation of Watergate. Soon after the impeachment proceedings began, the *Washington Post* ran a feature on Rodino which brought up Rodino's ties to the convicted Addonizio and pointed out that Rodino represented "a region where organized crime is entrenched and political corruption common." But the Nixon-appointed prosecutor who led the case against Addonizio gave Rodino a boost: "There's never been an inquiry about Rodino, never the slightest anything. In my opinion Pete Rodino is an honest man and a fine public servant."

Around the same time, Rodino related to me that columnist Jack Anderson, one of the best-informed journalists in the city, had told him there was a scheme afoot in the Justice Department to begin criminal investigations of himself and three other Democratic representatives.

The warnings were turning out to be more prophetic than paranoiac.

3

CANCER ON THE PRESIDENCY

Peter Rodino had long enjoyed cordial relations with President Nixon. But the one person at the White House whom both he and I knew best and trusted most was Nixon's counsel, John Dean III.

In the early 1960s the Judiciary Committee's Republicans had hired Dean to be my counterpart on the minority staff. In those years there was a bipartisan comity on the committee that was reflected in our dealings with Dean. Although we were often political adversaries, we developed a high degree of trust and respect for each other. We worked together daily, and in a political sense we were mirror images.

John's principal boss was Bill McCullough, the ranking Republican on the Judiciary Committee. McCullough was elderly and generally conservative, but he had the same commitment to civil rights as my principal boss, the elderly Democratic chairman of the committee, Manny Celler. Following John Kennedy's assassination, the alliance forged by McCullough and Celler and their staffs was essential to the passage of the Civil Rights Act of 1964 and the Voting Rights Act of 1965.

Celler and McCullough had different political agendas, and both had strong personalities but they had high regard for each other. They helped each other whenever possible, and were wise enough to deal with each other honestly and openly. This attitude was imbued in their staff, as well. Thus, both Dean and myself served our political apprenticeships under politicians who, though crafty, realized that their political stock in trade was their word and their reputations for good-faith negotiation.

Dean and I had also shared some personal pains. Both of us had been divorced at about the same time—a process that we both felt was like having surgery without anesthesia. Each of our wives had left us for more prominent men. We both became workaholics—drowning our despair in the blended elixirs of law and congressional politics.

When I first met Dean I learned that, like his father and grandfather, he was named after John Wesley, who rebelled against the Church of England and became the founder of Methodism. Aside from his name, one of his notable features was the earnest innocence of his "boy scout" demeanor. Thus I was not surprised when years later Attorney General Kleindienst often referred to Dean as "junior," while some of Dean's White House detractors derisively nicknamed him "Pretty Boy."

When Dean was chosen to be White House Counsel, Rodino, myself, and his other Judiciary Committee friends were pleased. He had attained his position after years of intense devotion to the combined crafts of law and politics. Envied by other, less-skilled executive branch lawyers, Dean had become an extraordinarily clear-eyed legal and political counselor. He was much more a "counselor" than an "advocate"—he avoided clashes of personality, and disagreed without being disagreeable. In this he was markedly different from Haldeman, Ehrlichman, Colson, Liddy, and other Nixon advisers, who were proud of their adherence to Leo Durocher's maxim "Nice guys finish last." Dean wanted to finish first, but he still wanted to be known as a nice guy.

Because of our regard for Dean, both Rodino and I were dismayed when the April 17, 1973 *Washington Post* devoted half of its entire front page—the most space yet to a Watergate story—to an article targeting Dean as a felon. A sensational lead by editor Ben Bradlee stated that:

> Former Attorney General John Mitchell and White House Counsel John W. Dean III approved and helped plan the Watergate bugging operation, according to President Nixon's former Special Assistant, Jeb Stuart Magruder. Mitchell and Dean later arranged to buy the silence of the seven convicted Watergate conspirators, Magruder has also said.
>
> Magruder, the deputy campaign manager for the President, made these statements to federal prosecutors Saturday, according to three sources in the White House and the Committee for the Re-election of the President.

It was inconceivable to me that Dean had originated the Watergate break-ins, and I told Rodino that I couldn't believe these claims. The John Dean I knew was too smart, too professional, and had too much pride and self-respect to jeopardize his career in such a way. That the President was now seemingly throwing his two closest legal advisors to the wolves indicated to me that he was passing the buck downwards. I was tempted to phone Dean, but Rodino thought it more prudent to wait to hear how he responded.

We did not have to wait long. Before noon, Dean issued a statement from his office at the White House. He said: "Some may think that I will become a scapegoat in the Watergate case. Anyone who believes that does not know me, know the true facts, nor understand our system of justice." I suspected that my friend may have had me specifically in mind.

In June, Dean was subpoenaed by Senator Ervin's Watergate Committee to tell what he knew of the Watergate coverup. His much-anticipated televised testimony was explosive. He admitted his own role in the coverup, but attributed the whole plan to Nixon—who Dean said had personally ordered him to "keep his fingers in the holes" and pay hush money to Howard Hunt and the other burglars. Recalling dates and events in meticulous detail, Dean described a "cancer on the presidency" and said that the White House had "lost its moral compass."

The next morning, Tip O'Neill sat down to a breakfast meeting with Rodino and me. The House Majority Leader muttered, "Dean refuses to be the fall guy. My guess is that in fingering Nixon, he's telling the truth. Hey, Nixon ran the dirtiest campaign in my lifetime. He talks out of both sides of his mouth, whistles through the middle. He's a liar. What do you think?"

Having worked closely with Dean over a number of years, I told O'Neill that he "would never have stuck his neck out to cover up Watergate without at least enough authority from Nixon to be sure that Nixon would give Dean the credit."

It was clear to O'Neill, as it was to me, that if Dean had committed a felony under Nixon's orders, then the President himself was a conspirator, and thus a felon! O'Neill said: "Impeachment is going to hit this Congress and we'd better be ready for it!" Encouraged by O'Neill, Rodino agreed to let me start discreetly preparing for impeachment, "just in case."

That is how I found myself flying to London during the next congressional recess to do research tracing impeachment proceedings all the way back to Edmund Burke's 1786 prosecution of Warren Hastings in Parliament, one of the most famous such proceedings in Western law. My work made the ironclad case that a president who has committed a felony can be removed from office by Congress without first being prosecuted in the courts.

As members of Congress entered the House chamber for their daily prayers and debates during the hot summmer of 1973, anyone who had the temerity to call for Nixon's impeachment was held in about as much regard as a mad dog. The first of these to find his way into the office of the House Clerk to register as a lobbyist was Charles Morgan, Jr. from Birmingham, Alabama.

In the 1960s Morgan was one of the few white lawyers to defend victims of civil rights violations in the Deep South. In and out of courthouses from Alabama's black belt to the U.S. Supreme Court, he was renowned for his defenses of Muhammad Ali (for his conscientious objection to the draft), Dr. Howard Levy (the Army physician who refused to train Green Berets to fight in Vietnam), Julian Bond (who was denied a seat in the Georgia legislature for antiwar statements), and Daniel Ellsberg (who was prosecuted for leaking the Pentagon Papers).

Morgan first moved to Washington in 1972 to head the ACLU's Capitol Hill office. While there, he became the personal attorney for Spencer Oliver, a member of the Democratic National Committee. As head of an organization of state Democratic chairmen, Oliver occupied one of the offices that were bugged by the Watergate burglars. Since Oliver was a victim of the burglary, Judge Sirica allowed him to be represented by Morgan in the criminal case against the burglars.

The portly, rumpled Morgan soon won new renown as Washington's most loquacious anti-Nixon advocate. Led by Morgan's calls for impeachment, for the first time in its history the ACLU—traditionally a defense-oriented organization—lobbied for the prosecution.

By the spring of 1973, Morgan was in high dudgeon. He was being shunned by many in government, and even a number of Democrats feared him as a madman—and some had good reason to. Angered at the weak efforts to investigate the Watergate scandal, he would rail against "the limousine liberals who strike only at Nixon's capillaries—and are too candy-assed to go for the bastard's jugular."

Rodino and I had always treated the ACLU lobbyists—including Morgan—with respect out of concern that the organization might support the movement in Newark to replace Rodino with a black congressman. Rodino was pleased to have their endorsement and we often worked together openly—and sometimes behind the scenes—to defeat bills promoting school prayer, right to life, right to work, capital punishment, and other issues dear to conservatives. Perhaps as a result of this, Morgan was more tolerant with us at this time, as shown in his recollection of our first meeting about impeachment:

> Zeifman had spent years in Washington, but a belief in democracy still lurked within him. First we talked about the general corruption of the Justice Department. Then we talked about Nixon. Too polite to ask if I had lost my mind, Zeifman listened as I asked him to move against the most senior law-firm partner in the Western World. I told Zeifman that . . . I believed that Nixon could be impeached. . . .

At that time, Morgan also explained to me that he was particularly skeptical of Ted Kennedy, and was especially distressed that the senator had sponsored an amendment to the resolution establishing the Senate Watergate Committee that precluded the committee from investigating presidential misconduct. Kennedy's private life had been documented in a secret dossier that Howard Hunt had prepared. (John Dean had removed the dossier from a White House safe, and FBI Director Patrick Gray had illegally burned it.) Morgan was certain that Nixon had such intimidating dossiers on the whole Kennedy family, and he was concerned that the Massachusetts senator was being blackmailed by Nixon.

In May, Richard Kleindienst resigned as Attorney General and pleaded guilty to a criminal charge of refusing to answer pertinent questions of a Senate committee. When Nixon chose Elliot Richardson to be the new Attorney General, Morgan was even more skeptical. Although the White House portrayed Richardson as a strait-laced Boston patrician, Morgan considered him to be "King Richard Nixon's best-dressed courtier front man."

After Nixon chose him to be the new Attorney General, Richardson made a courtesy call on Rodino that I was invited to attend. The meeting was perfunctory. Richardson arrived accompanied by several aides in plain gray suits with regimental ties. In contrast, the Attorney General wore a tailored Savile Row suit, a starched white collar, and a flaming crimson necktie. In a pained voice, he enunciated his "personal commitment to restoring public confidence in the Department of Justice." After a visit of no more than a few minutes he shook Peter's hand, tapped me on the shoulder, and was gone.

After Richardson left, Rodino asked for my impressions. At that time Morgan, Rodino, and I all regarded Richardson with skepticism. Along with his aristocratic demeanor, he had a fondness for fashionable Georgetown cocktail parties, and a proclivity to leave hard policy decisions to others.

During President Nixon's first term, Richardson had been shifted from one prestigious figurehead position to another. In each of three different federal agencies, he had permitted his Nixon-appointed subordinates to be supervised by the White House staff. Previously, as Under Secretary of State Richardson had supported extending the Vietnam War. As Secretary of Health, Education and Welfare he supported the administration's "southern strategy" by reducing the enforcement of civil rights laws. As Secretary of Defense he had defended the secret bombing of Cambodia.

As we saw it, Richardson's career had become so intertwined with the Nixon administration that the new Attorney General had a self-interest in saving Nixon from prosecution and impeachment. As a result, Rodino and I supported the intensive lobbying campaign of Morgan and the ACLU to require Richardson to appoint an independent prosecutor in the Watergate case. When Richardson complied by appointing Harvard professor Archibald Cox, Morgan became even more skeptical.

Morgan had had prior dealings with Cox, who had served as solicitor general during Robert Kennedy's negotiations with Alabama governor George Wallace during the school desegregation crisis in 1962. Morgan considered Cox and Richardson to be "Look-alike, think-alike, political lawyers who both suffered from Harvard elitism—a crippling liability that anesthetizes the sense of right and wrong."

When Nixon first nominated Richardson, Senator Kennedy was opposed, but Kennedy's opposition to Richardson evaporated as soon as Richardson agreed to appoint Cox as independent prose-

cutor. As a result, Morgan feared that Cox would strike a deal with
Richardson to keep Nixon in office and help pave the way for the
election of Senator Kennedy to the presidency in 1976. I advised
Rodino that I shared Morgan's fears.

Cox's first days as independent prosecutor tended to confirm
Morgan's suspicions. One of his first acts was to urge the Senate to
postpone its hearings until after he completed the criminal prosecutions of the Watergate cases. As Morgan saw it, Nixon's presidency would have been saved by Cox had not Senator Sam Ervin
stood firm. His eyebrows aflutter with anger, the North Carolinian
told Cox, "The American people are entitled to find out what actually happened without having to wait while justice travels on leaded
feet!"

Stymied in this, Cox tried another end run around the intentions
of the Senate. He called a meeting of the original team of Watergate
prosecutors. Since the Senate had insisted that Cox be independent,
the prosecutors—all employed by the Justice Department—arrived
in Cox's office with their letters of resignation in hand. To their surprise, Cox urged them to stay on the case in the interest of "conti-
nuity." With this stroke, Cox preserved the very connection with the
Nixon Justice Department that Ervin and the Senate had expected
to be terminated.

Adding to this tangled web was a more personal connection
which, if Morgan knew at the time, he did not bring to light. Cox's
brother Maxwell was a senior partner of Cox and Davis, a Wall
Street law firm that represented Howard Hughes. As Special Prosecutor, Archibald was charged with investigating a gift of $100,000
in cash that Hughes had given to Nixon's close friend, millionaire
Bebe Rebozo.

As part of my efforts to begin preparing for possible impeachment,
Rodino agreed that I should meet discreetly with Cox and Sam
Dash, Senator Ervin's counsel. The main objective of the visits
would be to find out the extent to which Cox's investigation, as well
as the Senate's, included the President.

Since all of the actions of the primary Watergate figures were
now being followed closely by the media, we kept the meetings
secret to avoid stirring up swarms of reporters. The last thing
Rodino wanted was front-page speculation that the Judiciary Committee was preparing for impeachment. Thus, I decided to set up

the meetings personally rather than allow even my secretary to know the plans.

When I called Cox's office, I was momentarily stunned by the receptionist's pronouncement—"To talk to anyone in this office you must give permission for your call to be recorded." I thought, what foolishness—discouraging potential witnesses who might want to cooperate with the prosecutors. Curious as to how strictly Cox's staff would enforce the policy, I replied, "I'm the chief counsel of the Committee on the Judiciary of the House of Representatives. I would like to talk to Mr. Cox on official business without having my conversation recorded."

Without a pause, the receptionist said there could be no exceptions. Feeling no need for combativeness, I agreed to be taped and made an appointment with Cox. Next I called Dash's office and made arrangements to meet with him a few days later. When I finished the phone calls, I reflected a minute on Cox's taping policy, but then filed it away in my mind.

On the day of the meeting with Cox, to avoid the appearance of partisanship, I invited Frank Polk, the Judiciary Committee's minority counsel, to come with me. It was one of that year's hottest days, and Frank and I arrived at Cox's office mopping the sweat from our foreheads. There were armed guards outside the door. We identified ourselves to them, went through an elaborate security process, and were finally ushered into Cox's office.

I had last seen Cox several years earlier when he had been the Justice Department's second-in-command under Robert Kennedy. He had not aged well—his crewcut hair was turning white. He was in his shirtsleeves, and wore a thin bowtie of scotch plaid that had been fashionable at Harvard in the 1940s. He greeted us with a thinly veiled indifference, which was also characteristic of Harvard professors of his generation.

I began the conversation by telling him formally that we had a mandate from the chairman and ranking minority member of the Judiciary Committee to inquire about the scope of the Watergate prosecutions. As I had thought might happen, he promptly said he was not free to disclose any evidentiary information, and that he would only discuss procedural matters relating to his scope of authority.

I then asked directly whether he believed he had sufficient legal authority to investigate the President. His reply was curt.

"I am not investigating the President."

He reminded us that Attorney General Richardson had once been his student at Harvard Law School, and then proceeded to explain that "Elliot" had delegated to him "all of the discretion allowed prosecutors by the Constitution." Then he added:

> Elliot and his legal team are of the opinion that a sitting President is not indictable until after he is out of office. I disagree with their interpretation of the Constitution. But even if the President is indictable, it would not be inappropriate for me to exercise prosecutorial discretion in favor of not indicting him—and deferring to the impeachment power of the House of Representatives.

Pressing him on this remarkable statement, I asked what he would do if he unintentionally discovered evidence that might tend to incriminate the President. "Why, if I were to get even a whiff of presidential culpability," he replied, "I would waltz right up to Capitol Hill and tell the Speaker of the House of Representatives—and if you gentlemen have any recommendations as to other members of Congress in whom I should confide, I shall be pleased to consider them."

In the cab back to the Rayburn Building, Frank and I reflected for a while in silence. Cox's revelations had rattled us. Most of the President's top aides—including Haldeman, Ehrlichman, Mitchell, Dean, and Kleindienst—had resigned under a cloud, and many of them were being investigated for felonies. Convicted Watergate burglar James McCord charged that witnesses had committed perjury at the Watergate trial and that the defendants had been pressured to plead guilty and remain silent. John Dean's testimony before the Ervin Committee had given the whole world more than a "whiff" of presidential culpability. Yet Cox had in effect told us, "I don't smell anything! And even if I did, I have the authority to ignore it."

As we drove past the White House, Frank broke the silence. In a resigned tone, he muttered, "Washington has become the city of the absurd."

Sam Dash had at least two things in common with Archibald Cox. Both had worked in the Kennedy Justice Department. Both had left the Justice Department to become professors and were now on limited assignment with temporary select committees. Unlike Cox, however, Dash seemed disorganized and unsure of himself. With his outer office filled with reporters, Dash kept us waiting for more than an hour.

When we finally got into his office, our meeting was perfunctory. In response to my question about the scope of his investigation, Dash said, "The only thing I can tell you is that officially we are barred from investigating presidential misconduct as a result of an amendment to our Committee's authorizing resolution sponsored by Senator Kennedy."

Officially, he was telling the truth. The actual name of the Watergate Committee was "Senate Select Committee on Campaign Activities." The resolution establishing the committee restricted it from looking into misconduct by the executive branch, the FBI, or the CIA in the investigation of the Watergate matter. In a staged dialogue between Senators Kennedy and Ervin that occurred on the Senate floor when the resolution was debated, Ervin had stated, "I thought that the committee should confine itself to the investigation and study of the conduct of any group of individuals or committees or organizations that may have participated [in the Watergate break-in] and not include in the investigation the action of investigatorial or prosecutorial agencies." (Such a rehearsed dialogue, called a *colloquy,* is an accepted practice in the Senate. Recalling the colloquy many years later, Morgan told me, "Kennedy was more concerned about what the Watergate Committee ought not to investigate than about what it should investigate.")

And yet the committee had taken John Dean's testimony. Somewhat incredulously, I pointed out that Dean's testimony certainly indicated presidential misconduct, but Dash cut me off: "I can't talk to you unless I have the approval of Senator Ervin. I suggest that you have Chairman Rodino write a letter to Senator Ervin formally requesting that the Senate provide such information to the House Judiciary Committee." End of discussion.

Back in Rodino's office, Peter and I reviewed these two meetings. His reaction to Dash's statement was, "I certainly am not going to send Sam Ervin a letter like that. It would immediately get leaked to the press and reported as the beginning of an impeachment effort."

As to the meeting with Cox, I advised Rodino that I suspected Cox was in league with Richardson to shield Nixon from being indicted as a co-conspirator. Peter agreed that Cox's reliance on prosecutorial discretion to avoid indicting Nixon was inspired more by politics than by academic legal analysis. He made no further specific comments.

Feet firmly planted on both sides of the fence, Peter's last instruction to me as I left his office was to keep expanding my confidential file of impeachment materials, "just so we have it ready if the need arises."

4

SECRET TAPES, DEEP THROAT, AND THE CIA

In 1973, the thirteenth of July fell on a Friday. It was an ill-fated day for President Nixon, for it was then that Senate investigators learned the President had been taping his conversations in the Oval Office. Thousands of hours of secret tapes comprised a history of the entire Nixon presidency. The revelation sent shock waves throughout Washington and the country. If investigators could get their hands on a tape that corroborated John Dean's testimony, the President's guilt for conspiring to obstruct justice could be proved beyond doubt!

Just a few days before, Frank Polk and I had had our eye-opening meetings with Cox and Dash. For both of them now to demand access to the White House tapes was somewhat inconsistent with their prior assurances. However, to fail to do so would have aroused the ire of the public, which would have regarded them as party to the coverup.

Concern about public opinion won out. Both Cox and Dash quickly modified their positions, and on July 23 Richard Nixon became the first American president to be served with congressional and judicial subpoenas—two from the Senate Watergate Committee and one from the United States District Court. They demanded that the President produce tapes relating to Watergate.

By having his office bugged, Nixon may well have been the architect of his own downfall. But his fall must also be credited to the *Washington Post,* which played a major role in sealing his fate.

When Rodino and I first learned of the secret tapes, we assumed from Dash's accounts that two junior Senate staffers, Scott Armstrong and Don Sanders, had stumbled on their existence while interviewing Alexander Butterfield, a fairly low-level White House aide. Much later we learned that the discovery had resulted from a lead given to Dash's staff by *Post* reporter Robert Woodward, who purportedly learned about the tapes from a confidential source he called "Deep Throat."

Sensational revelations attributed to Deep Throat were eventually published by Woodward and Carl Bernstein in their book *All the President's Men*. The book revealed that Deep Throat had targeted Butterfield as a source of useful information to Woodward—who in turn passed the lead on to unidentified "friends" on Dash's Watergate Committee staff. Mindful of the restrictions of the Kennedy amendment, Dash was apparently reluctant to interrogate Butterfield, whose role did not involve campaign activities within the scope of Dash's authority. He had to be prodded at least three times by Woodward's contacts before he finally authorized Butterfield's interrogation.

For a reporter who had been working for the *Post* for less than a year prior to the Watergate break-ins, Woodward played an extraordinary role in the fall of Nixon. But it has since come out that Woodward had more than good reportorial skills and good luck.

Woodward had been a high school classmate—and later roommate and close friend—of Scott Armstrong, who played a key role in the discovery of the presidential tapes. Armstrong was best man at Woodward's wedding. He was hired as an investigator for the Ervin Committee largely on the basis of Woodward's recommendation and the *Post's* contacts.

In the context of the access that Woodward and the *Post's* had to anonymous sources in the government, a rereading of *All the President's Men* with the advantages of hindsight is now interesting for facts which were either not uncovered by the *Post's* reporters or if known to them were not reported.

Even before the Watergate break-in, it was commonly known that Democratic National Chairman Larry O'Brien, whose Watergate offices were burglarized, had come to Washington years earlier as a top aide to President Kennedy—and later became manager for Robert Kennedy's 1968 presidential campaign. After Robert Kennedy's assassination, O'Brien became a high-paid Washington representative for Hughes.

Woodward's biography on the cover of *All the President's Men* stated that, prior to becoming a reporter, he had served as a naval communications officer. In this position, he presumably had access to highly classified information. We now know that during Woodward's Navy tenure, Hughes was CIA, as was later confirmed by a recording of convicted Nixon aide Charles Colson: "The Hughes interests, Summa Corporation [was] the biggest single contractor of the CIA. They do a lot of their contract-out work like . . . satellites, this new Global Marine, this *Glomar Express*, this new oceano-graphic vehicle is CIA."

There were also several other pertinent facts about Hughes that were publicly known. During the 1960 presidential campaign, the *Post's* reported a shady, unsecured loan of $205,000 from Hughes to Nixon's ne'er-do-well brother Donald—a scandal which helped Kennedy in an extremely close race. It was also common knowledge that the Hughes interests gave substantial campaign contributions to both Republicans and Democrats.

As the Watergate scandals began to unravel, John Dean and others disclosed to the Watergate Committee and its staff that Hughes had secretly given $100,000 cash to Nixon's close friend Bebe Rebozo. Yet these facts too were absent from *All the President's Men*.

In addition, there were several other facets of the Hughes-O'Brien connection that either were not uncovered by the *Post's* reporters or were simply not published at the time. We now know that O'Brien lost his job as a Hughes lobbyist when the Nixon administration insisted that the CIA-controlled Hughes Enterprises use Robert R. Mullen & Company, a Washington public relations firm which had long provided a cover for CIA agents in Europe and Asia. The president of Mullen was CIA operative Robert F. Bennett, who later became senator from Utah.

After a recommendation from CIA Director Richard Helms, Mullen had hired Howard Hunt after Hunt had retired from the CIA to become one of the White House plumbers. (Helms was later convicted of committing perjury by lieing under oath to the Church Committee about the CIA's covert operations in Chile.)

Amazingly, one of Hunt's associates in the Mullen operation was Robert Oliver, the father of Hunt's victim, Spencer Oliver. Bennett had placed the senior Oliver in day-to-day charge of the firm's most important account, the Hughes Tool Company. At one point there were discussions about Spencer Oliver also becoming a member of Mullen—a prospect which had apparently made Howard Hunt unhappy. (Spencer at that time enjoyed a prestigious job with a different international organization that was covertly funded by the CIA.) In that context it is remarkable that Spencer Oliver's phone was selected for tapping by Hunt and Liddy—and that this tap was the only one that functioned following the first Watergate break-in.

The liaison between the Hughes interests and the CIA was Robert A. Maheu, who had been employed by Hughes since the Kennedy administration. As Charles Colson noted, "The guy who handles all of the CIA-Hughes work is a guy by the name of Maheu. . . . Maheu had Larry O'Brien on a hundred-thousand-dollar-a-year retainer."

Not until after Nixon's resignation was it brought out that it was at Hughes's personal instructions that O'Brien had been hired by Maheu following the assassination of Robert Kennedy. And it was not until Jerry Ford became president that Congress learned that Maheu helped the CIA recruit Mafia leaders Sam Giancana, Santos Trafficante, and Johnny Roselli to try to assassinate Fidel Castro.

And the connections ran deeper. Howard Hunt, who headed the Watergate burglars, had been employed by the CIA during the Eisenhower administration, and had been assigned by CIA Director Allen Dulles to help Vice President Nixon develop plans to depose Castro. President Kennedy had kept Dulles on as CIA director, but after the Bay of Pigs fiasco, Kennedy (acting partly on the advice of his close friend Ben Bradlee) replaced Dulles with James McCone, whose tenure with the CIA dated back to the Truman years. President Johnson later replaced McCone with Richard Helms.

Against the advice of some of his conservative advisors, President Nixon had kept Helms on as CIA director. However, after press disclosures of the secret bombing of Cambodia, Nixon and Secretary of State Kissinger became certain that high-ranking government officials were leaking information to Nixon's political enemies in the press corps. Some of Nixon's closest confidants even suspected Helms of occasionally betraying the President. (Indeed, after serving time for his part in the Watergate scandal, John Ehrlichman published *The Company*, a novel in which a heroic President Richard Mockton is destroyed by a villainous CIA director. In the author's note, Ehrlichman claims that the characters in the book "are wholly fictional. But the forces . . . that motivate the characters are real.")

To help stop the leaks, Howard Hunt, who was considered to be a Nixon loyalist, was moved from the CIA to the White House in 1971. With Nixon facing a reelection campaign, Hunt's mission was to ferret out anyone in the government who was leaking sensitive information to the press. During the same period, Hughes Enterprises fired Robert Maheu and terminated Larry O'Brien's contract.

Also in 1971, with Nixon administration leakers under siege from Howard Hunt and the other plumbers, Woodward left his job with the Navy to become a reporter for a small Maryland newspaper. He later joined the *Post*. Within a matter of months, Hunt was arrested breaking into Watergate. Even though the story was within the regular beat of Carl Bernstein, a much more experienced reporter, Bradlee assigned Woodward to the story as well. By the time Woodward and Bernstein reported the discovery of the White House tapes, the two journalists had become nationally prominent.

The Friday-the-thirteenth revelations of the White House tapes had an eerie effect on Capitol Hill. At one time or another many members of Congress had visited the Oval Office and made confidential political deals with the President. It came as a special shock to learn that the President had bugged their conversations, and that the conversations might be brought out into the sunshine. Thus, as confrontation with the President grew more imminent, most members of Congress grew more reticent. They knew the power of the person who held those secret tapes.

However, in Washington's political jungle there are always a few rare birds who defy the rules of survival. During the Ninety-third Congress there were two politicians who were then members of an endangered species. One was Father John McLaughlin, a conservative Republican. The other was Father Robert Drinan, whom most Republicans regarded as a left-wing radical. Each of them was both Jesuit priest and politician—a hybrid species that was eventually exterminated by edict of Pope John Paul.

In 1970 McLaughlin challenged John Pastore, the Democratic Senator from Rhode Island, and lost. He then went to work in the White House as a public relations expert. As a White House spokesman he defended Nixon for having given the country "outstanding moral leadership." At the time of Watergate, McLaughlin gave his political blessings to such conservative groups as Rabbi Bernard Korff's National Citizens Committee for Fairness to the

Presidency and Reverend Sun Myung Moon's National Prayer and Fast Committee.

Democratic Father Robert Drinan had won an election to the Congress from Massachusetts. Often, after crossing himself, Drinan would stand in the well of the House chamber and denounce Nixon as a "fascist war criminal." The more McLaughlin defended Nixon from his White House pulpit, the more outraged Drinan became. Finally, on July 31, 1973, dressed in black suit and white clerical collar, Drinan introduced a resolution with only one sentence of text: "Resolved, that Richard M. Nixon, President of the United States, is impeached of high crimes and misdemeanors."

Charles Morgan was delighted. After seven months of lobbying, he had finally persuaded one member of Congress to move against the President! But Tip O'Neill was furious. He had been hoping that the first formal resolution would be based on an evidentiary record co-sponsored by a bipartisan coalition. In fact, at that very time, Congressman Pete McCloskey of California, an ex-Marine war hero, was working behind the scenes to put together the beginnings of such a coalition. In his autobiography, O'Neill recalled the realities of the situation:

> Morally, Drinan had a good case. . . . But politically he damn near blew it. For if Drinan's resolution had come up for a vote at the time he introduced it, it would have been overwhelmingly defeated—by something like 400 to 20. After that, with most of the members already on record as having voted once against impeachment, it would have been extremely difficult to get them to change later on. . . .
>
> I went to Drinan and tried to talk him out of it. "The timing is wrong," I said. "It's premature. Let's wait a few months until the evidence is in and we can get the votes we need.

After Drinan defiantly introduced his resolution, O'Neill asked me to draft a press release "to make it clear that just as Father Drinan was not speaking for the Pope so too his personal crusade against Nixon did not have the blessings of the Democratic leadership." The press release, issued over Rodino's signature, was the first public statement in which Peter used the word *impeachment.* Its conclusion read:

At this time no formal action on the Drinan resolution is scheduled. Removal from office of the president, or any other federal official, is an extraordinary remedy. Extraordinary remedies are applied only under extraordinary circumstances. As legal historians have noted, impeachment is a "sword of Goliath" which ought not to be brandished lightly. As a result, only the most careful, the most sensitive, and the most thoughtful deliberation will precede any action taken by the Judiciary Committee.

When the media correctly interpreted the release to mean that Rodino would sit on the Drinan resolution, the feisty priest became irate, denouncing Rodino and me as "fascists—like Nixon!" One day he threatened us with, "I'm going up to Boston this weekend, and if you don't move on impeachment, I'm going to blow the whistle on you. I'll call it what it is—a coverup!" The next morning at a break-fast meeting with O'Neill I summed up the situation: "Father Drinan is more of a thorn in Rodino's side than all of the Republicans on the Judiciary Committee put together." O'Neill's reply was: "Don't worry about Bob—I'll take care of him."

As Majority Leader, Tip O'Neill had ties to the Vatican as well as to the Massachusetts archdiocese. In addition, Tip had a major say in how Democratic Party campaign funds were distributed to candidates, especially in Massachusetts, and Drinan always had trouble raising funds because he was considered to be so radical. Therefore, I was not surprised when Drinan came over to Peter and me at the Monocle Restaurant a few days later, and with a broad smile gave us his blessing: "Mr. Chairman, you and your counsel are doing a wonderful job. I'm proud to be on your team." We shook hands all around.

At our next breakfast meeting with O'Neill, I thanked him heartily for "tranquilizing" Father Drinan, as his influence with Drinan and the other recalcitrant committee Democrats made my life much easier. O'Neill replied with a twinkle, "It was easy. He got a message from above!"

5

AGNEW CLEARS THE DECK

On August 6, the country was rocked by the second major revelation in less than a month—Vice President Spiro Agnew was about to be indicted. The major media reported that, according to unidentified "reliable sources," when the Vice President was governor of Maryland, he got kickbacks from contractors. Some accounts related that bagmen were still bringing bundles of payola to Agnew's White House office. Agnew held a press conference and called the charges "damned lies." Nixon refused to comment.

Aftershocks reverberated for the rest of the summer. With public confidence in the administration plummeting, at least two of the Judiciary Committee's senior Democrats, Jack Brooks of Texas and John Conyers of Michigan, began to talk about impeaching both Nixon and Agnew—which would make Speaker of the House Carl Albert of Oklahoma, a Democrat, the next president.

Don Edwards of California, Robert Kastenmeier of Wisconsin, and other liberals regarded Albert as too conservative to be their president—he had supported the war in Vietnam. Instead, they savored the prospect of Nixon remaining in office twisting in the wind until the end of his term. As they saw it, that would pave the way for a staunch liberal such as Ted Kennedy to win the presidency easily.

Any discussion of a prosecution of Agnew raised political questions as baffling as the riddles of Watergate: Did Nixon personally want Agnew to be convicted and out of the vice-presidency? Or did Nixon want to keep his tarnished Vice President in office to discourage Congress from impeaching him? Was there an anti-Nixon cabal within the executive branch that was conspiring to use the Agnew scandal to accelerate Nixon's downfall? The answers lay hidden in the careers of both Agnew and Nixon.

When Agnew first ran for governor of Maryland in the 1960s, a faction of Democrats nominated George Mahoney—whose slogan "Your home is your castle" was a battle cry against equal housing rights. With the support of civil rights groups, blacks, and anti-Mahoney Democrats, a more moderate Agnew won the election.

In 1968, Agnew went to the Republican national convention pledged to support liberal Nelson Rockefeller over Nixon. When Nixon won the nomination, he bridged the gap with the party's liberal wing by selecting Agnew as his running mate. After winning the 1968 election, Nixon and Agnew began to recycle their political images.

In the arena of foreign affairs, Nixon gave Henry Kissinger, a Rockefeller protege, a key role—and won the support of liberals for fostering detente with the Soviet Union and China. To broaden his political base at home, especially among southern conservatives, Nixon appointed Democrat John Connally, former Governor of Texas, as Secretary of the Treasury.

Agnew shifted to the right, shedding his former mantle of Rockefeller liberalism and lambasting the Democrats as "nabobs of nihilism" and "left-wing radicals." Appealing to what the *National Review* had called "the constituency of the discontented," he rapidly won the support of hard-core Republican conservatives.

The results were impressive. In 1972, with the Democratic party torn between its own liberal and conservative wings, the Nixon-Agnew ticket trashed the Democrats as advocates of "abortion, acid, and amnesty." Nixon won reelection over McGovern by a landslide that rivaled Franklin Roosevelt's victory over Alf Landon in 1936.

But on the night of his greatest victory, as reported by his closest aides, Nixon became despondent. The Twenty-second Amendment to the Constitution limited him to two terms in office. Ironically, as Eisenhower's vice president, Nixon himself had lobbied for adoption of the amendment. Now Nixon was the lame duck—with Spiro Agnew waiting eagerly in the wings.

As an antidote to his despondency, Nixon reportedly toyed with a plan to repeal the Twenty-second Amendment. The fantasy included dumping Agnew in favor of a bipartisan ticket that would include Connally as vice presidential candidate in 1976. My first hint of the plan came from an offhand remark from none other than John Dean during Congress's 1972 Christmas recess.

We met one day for lunch at the Rayburn Building cafeteria.

Dean had just returned from a vacation with his new wife Maureen. In contrast to the way the public was to see him on television only a few months later, he had lost his law library pallor, had acquired a golden tan, and was ebullient. He asked casually what I thought of Nixon's chances of persuading Congress to repeal the two-term limit. Since this was the first I had heard of it, John had to assure me that he was not out of his mind. My half-joking response was: "Sometimes I wonder if your boss is demented." (If Dean then had any foreboding of his coming clash with the President, he did not let on. But later, after he had pleaded guilty to a felony and had been placed in the Justice Department's witness protection program, he confided in me, "Some of the Justice Department officials are afraid that Nixon is demented—and has asked his friend Bebe Rebozo to have one of his boys bump me off.")

By January 1973—while Dean was still his counsel—Nixon had abandoned his designs for a third term. But he had also made it clear to key Republicans that he favored Connally as his political heir apparent. Agnew became disaffected with Nixon, and after Charles Morgan and the ACLU started passing out "Impeach Nixon" buttons, at least two members of Agnew's staff became titillated by the political possibilities. One was Agnew's speechwriter, Victor Gold, who had previously been an aide to Barry Goldwater. Years earlier Gold had been Morgan's roommate at the University of Alabama. For the conservative Gold, "Impeach Nixon!" tantalizingly suggested "Make Agnew President!"

Agnew's chief Senate aide at the time was Sam Garrison, a young lawyer from Roanoke, Virginia who, like Dean, had previously been one of my counterparts on the staff of the Judiciary Committee's Republican minority. (Garrison eventually returned to the Judiciary Committee's staff, becoming the Republicans' chief impeachment inquiry counsel.) Working behind the scenes, Gold and Garrison tried to convince some congressional Republicans that it would be better if Nixon were impeached soon. As they saw it, a quick decision would give Agnew three full years as president to reunify and strengthen the party sufficiently to retain control of the White House in 1976. But, as Garrison related to me many years later, "Our shameless anti-Nixon strategy got back to the White House like a shot!"

It was not surprising that when Nixon learned of these activities, he ordered Chief of Staff Haldeman to throw Agnew to the wolves. As he had done often before with others on the administration's enemies list, Haldeman prodded the federal prosecutors serving under then-Attorney General Kleindienst to initiate criminal investigations against Agnew.

When Kleindienst himself was forced to resign in May 1973, the criminal dossiers on Agnew fell under the control of Elliot Richardson. When Richardson moved into the Attorney General's office, he was no longer a figurehead. He had presidential ambitions, making him a potential rival of both Agnew and Connally.

By then there was enough evidence in the Justice Department's files to indict Agnew for bribery—and Nixon for conspiring to obstruct justice in the Watergate case. But had he tried to bring down both Agnew and Nixon, Richardson would have been regarded by fellow Republicans as the culprit who lost the White House to the Democrats. Richardson decided to indict Agnew—and shield Nixon.

In August I received a call from Martin Danziger, a former law school classmate of mine who had become one of Richardson's top aides. Danziger give Rodino and I advance notice that Richardson had settled on the legal opinion that the Constitution prohibits the indictment of the president, but not the vice president. Danziger added, "In other words, Archie Cox is prohibited by the Constitution from asking a grand jury to indict the President. But if we have charges against Agnew, the Constitution does not bar us from seeking an indictment."

I was shocked at how politically motivated this decision seemed. Based on all of my research, my view was that the Attorney General had blithely hacked to pieces a root of our Constitution that dated back to the Magna Carta. By accepting this opinion, Richardson had placed the President above the law. As Charles Morgan put it, "Honest El, the hair-splitter, had found reams of reasons to rationally subordinate his beliefs to Nixon's."

As the summer progressed and the Agnew case played itself out in the press, my skepticism about Richardson grew. It was a brazen violation of legal ethics for Justice Department officials to leak evidence of felonies to the press before presenting it to a court. Yet every other day, it seemed, another "high-ranking Justice Department official" was being cited as "a reliable source" of stories about Agnew's alleged crimes.

Finally, on September 18, the *Washington Post* ran this banner headline: *AGNEW WILL RESIGN.* On the same day I had a visit from Jerry Landauer, a prominent *Wall Street Journal* reporter. Landauer claimed that the *Post* story was incorrect, and had been planted by one of Agnew's enemies.

Landauer told me in confidence that Agnew and his lawyers were preparing an elaborate legal defense in opposition to Richardson's stance. They would assert that the Vice President could not be prosecuted unless he was first impeached by Congress. As part of their plan, Agnew was about to petition the House to hold impeachment hearings on him—purportedly to give him a chance to clear his name. He would be relying on the nineteenth-century case of Vice President John Calhoun. That night I took my file of impeachment materials home and reviewed the Calhoun precedent.

In 1826, then-Vice President John Calhoun was charged in the press with having received a $15,000 bribe while he had been Secretary of War. In a letter to the House of Representatives, Calhoun stated:

> 'Conscious of my entire innocence in this . . . and resolved,
> as far as human effort can extend, to leave an untarnished rep-
> utation to posterity, I challenge the freest investigation of the
> House, as the only means effectually to repel this premeditated
> attack to prostrate me, by destroying forever my character.

In the absence of any pending criminal proceedings against Calhoun, a House committee had looked into the matter and found no reliable evidence of wrongdoing. In my view, though, this was hardly precedent enough for the House now to impede on an ongoing criminal proceeding.

On September 25, Agnew telephoned Carl Albert and told him he would be arriving at the Speaker's office within a half-hour for an emergency meeting. With the sirens of a police escort wailing, Agnew's flag-bedecked Cadillac sped to Capitol Hill. Meanwhile, Albert alerted Tip O'Neill and Minority Leader Jerry Ford. By the time Albert and O'Neill got to the Speaker's office, the Vice President was already there.

Agnew produced a petition which asserted that as a sitting vice president he could not be tried in the courts, and that he had a right to an impeachment investigation to clear his name. As Tip O'Neill scribbled notes, Agnew said:

I am being framed by young zealots in the White House and the Department of Justice. They are offering immunity to racketeers who I never saw or even heard of to come in and build a case against me. . . . They will do anything to destroy me. Destroy us all. I don't know whether it is out of jealousy or insanity. . . .

As Vice President of the United States, and presiding officer of the Senate, I request that my matter be turned over to the House Judiciary Committee for a complete and open investigation, with hearings on television, so I can prove my innocence to the people of the United States. . . .

After only a few minutes, Agnew and Ford departed—leaving reporters clamoring to interview Albert. The Speaker had to order the Capitol police to clear his office. O'Neill hurriedly summoned Rodino and me. When I arrived, I could tell from the looks on O'Neill's and Albert's faces that Landauer's prediction had come true. As soon as I walked in, Albert asked what I thought about the Vice President's petition. O'Neill snorted, "For Chrissake Carl, let him read it first!" I read the petition. It cited the case of Vice President Calhoun as a precedent.

My preparation had proved fortunate, and I replied that the Agnew petition had no constitutional basis—that it was a political ploy intended only to delay his prosecution. I even noted that in a more recent case (1873), a similar petition from Vice President Schuyler Colfax was rejected by the House.

O'Neill, who was standing alongside me, nodded his assent and said, "This matter is before the courts. Now Agnew says the Constitution protects the president and the vice president from prosecution. That's what he says. I think we ought to leave that up to the courts."

Turning his broad countenance on me, Tip asked, "Whaddya think we should do?" I agreed that the courts should decide the issue, and added, "The Constitution doesn't even protect the *president* from criminal prosecution." I recommended that the leadership ignore Agnew's petition, and keep it at the Speaker's desk and not refer it to any committee.

But House Parliamentarian Lou Deschler, who had joined the meeting, brought up a strong counter-argument. He contended that the Speaker should refer Agnew's petition to the Judiciary Committee—"After all, it is a petition from the Vice President of the United States." Caught on the horns of this dilemma, and reluctant to make a prompt decision, Albert asked all of us to sleep on it and return to his office the next morning.

But that night, something in the back of my mind kept jogging me awake, and I got out of bed before dawn to have another look at the Vice President's letter. Before long, I was on the phone to Rodino. An obscure sentence tucked away in the letter noted that Agnew would deliver his relevant records to the Clerk of the House, which, under House rules, meant that the records could not be subpoenaed by a prosecutor unless the House voted to release them! If Agnew brought the records in, he would force a vote on his petition on the House floor.

After rousing Peter, I called Clerk Pat Jennings and told him to meet us as soon as possible at the House restaurant. When he arrived we explained the problem to him, and advised him to reject Agnew's records. Jennings responded, "I can't do that. Every citizen has a constitutional right to petition the Congress. Even if the Vice President wants to submit a crate of documents with his petition, I have to accept them."

We argued with as much heat as we could muster, but Jennings was unmoved. Time was growing short as Rodino and I rushed to the Speaker's office to advise Albert of the situation. Carl immediately phoned Jennings and ordered him not to accept any records from Agnew. It was obvious from Albert's side of the conversation that Jennings was standing his ground, replying that he had no authority to refuse the Vice President's records. Albert retorted, "Pat, I'm the Speaker and I'm giving you the—Yes, I'll put it in writing if you insist, goddamit!" He slammed down the telephone.

We looked at each other uneasily, not knowing what to say. Then the phone rang. Albert picked it up, listened intently, and then laughed out loud. Pat Jennings had solved the problem gracefully— the Clerk's office would be closed for the day!

Having won some time, we returned to the question of a response to Agnew's letter. Tip O'Neill came into the office and Albert read the draft of a statement that was a compromise between Deschler's position and mine: He would refer the Agnew petition to the House Judiciary Committee with the understanding that Rodino would take no action on it.

Tip was not happy with this. Turning first to Deschler, he said, "If we refer this to the Judiciary Committee we'll be doing just what the Republicans want. They'll try to turn the committee into a damned three-ring circus to keep Agnew from being tried in the courts, divert attention from Watergate, and help keep Nixon in office."

Then addressing political plain talk to Albert, Tip said: "Carl, if you let Agnew get off the hook—and the Republicans get away with this—the boys in the Democratic caucus will skin you alive!"

To further buttress the rejection of Agnew's petition, Tip mentioned that my book on impeachment was ready for printing—and that the precedents discussed in it would shatter the arguments advanced by Agnew. Until that time, Rodino had kept the galleys on hold. But now, under pressure from O'Neill, Peter agreed to publish the impeachment book.

Convinced, Albert quickly redrafted his statement so that it came out Tip's way. Later that day, the Speaker announced that he had summarily rejected the Vice President's petition.

On September 29 Agnew made a speech in Los Angeles to the National Federation of Republican Women accusing the Justice Department of trying to destroy him politically "to compensate for their ineptness in the prosecution of the Watergate case . . . and their failure to get any of the information out about the true dimensions of the Watergate matter." With his characteristic bombast, he concluded with a flourish: "I am a big trophy. I will not resign if indicted. I intend to stay and fight!" The audience gave him a mighty ovation.

On October 10 the Government Printing Office delivered to me the first copies of my impeachment book. As Sam Garrison had requested, I sent a personal copy to the Vice President, with bookmarks at the pages relating to Calhoun and Colfax.

In his memoirs, O'Neill recalled the impact of the book: "[Rodino] had bought a little time by putting out a 718-page book of historical documents on impeachment that was prepared by Jerry Zeifman, the chief counsel of the Judiciary Committee. When that book came out, it was like a godsend. . . . I don't think anybody on Capitol Hill actually read the book. But it was the kind of concrete symbol that people were looking for."

At the time, a *Newsweek* reporter described the book as "what every member of Congress needs to know about impeachment, but has been afraid to ask." New York journalist Jimmy Breslin called it "a loaded gun for use in a duel."

The next day, Agnew entered into a plea bargain with the U.S. Attorney in Maryland. He resigned his office, paid a small fine, and stayed out of jail.

At our next breakfast meeting, Tip told Peter and me, "By copping a plea and resigning, Spiro has done the country a great service. He has cleared the deck for the impeachment of Nixon!"

PART TWO

IMPEACHMENT

My story is not a pleasant one: It is neither sweet nor harmonious. It has the taste of nonsense and chaos, of madness and dreams—like the lives of men and women who stop deceiving themselves.
                                        —Hermann Hesse

6

THE FORD CONFIRMATION AND THE FIRING OF COX

On October 12, 1973, President Nixon nominated House Minority Leader Gerald Ford to be his new Vice President. The highly respected Ford had the support of Carl Albert and Tip O'Neill as well as the Republicans. When his confirmation was referred to the Judiciary Committee for consideration, it seemed certain that there would be no trouble.

The committee had just started work on Ford's confirmation when all hell broke loose in the capital. On October 20, vexed by Cox's subpoena for his White House tapes, the President had ordered Attorney General Richardson to fire Cox. Richardson resigned rather than do this. William Ruckelshaus, now acting Attorney General, also refused to fire Cox, and was sacked by Nixon. Solicitor General Robert Bork was next in line. Unflinchingly, Bork fired Cox. The media called it the Saturday Night Massacre.

On the preceding Friday night, I had received a call from *Newsweek* reporter Henry Hubbard, whose wife was Henry Kissinger's personal secretary. Hubbard had told me that Nixon would fire Cox within twenty-four hours. To warn Cox and his staff, I had called Cox's assistant, Philip Lacovara. The warning was to no avail. On Saturday night Lacovara called me and shouted, "The FBI has just entered our office and they are armed. This may be the end of the republic. You've gotta do something!"

Both Bernie Hellring and I tried unsuccessfully to reach Rodino to urge him to contact the FBI and insist that no files be removed from Cox's offices. Unknown to me, Lois D'Andre did not want me to talk to Peter. Having established ties to Ted Kennedy's staff, she

59

wanted Rodino to confer with the senator before returning my call. Kennedy wanted us to move cautiously, and so did Peter.

But events forced Rodino's hand. Nixon's own deeds aroused a new outcry for impeachment. Eighty-four members of Congress introduced impeachment resolutions. On October 24, Speaker Albert referred the resolutions to the Judicial Committee and directed us to act on them.

Sitting side-by-side in the House chamber, O'Neill advised Rodino to expedite Ford's confirmation and then impeach Nixon as soon as possible. This was not what Peter wanted to hear. Lois D'Andre wanted him to go slowly, as did his friends in the Justice Department. His own committee members were divided. Being pulled in several directions, and being wary of quick action of any sort, Rodino flared. Although he had never before clashed with O'Neill, Peter hissed, "Get the hell off my back!"

O'Neill, at least a foot taller and a hundred pounds heavier than Rodino, rose from his chair and placed a large hand on Rodino's shoulder. "Look!" he growled. "You've got one guy on your back. But I've got two hundred and forty guys on *mine!*" Grudgingly, Peter agreed to move on impeachment.

That night, Rodino and I held an emergency meeting of the committee staff in my office to discuss how to handle the dual burdens of confirmation and impeachment. Satisfied that our staff would hold up, we adjourned well after midnight and I dragged myself home for a few hours sleep. When I awoke, the morning news seemed unreal. Nixon had declared a military alert, putting U.S. air, ground, and naval forces worldwide in a state of combat readiness because of a supposed crisis in the Middle East.

At breakfast in the House dining room, O'Neill, Jack Brooks, and John Conyers feared the alert was a counteroffensive against the House Democrats in the media war that Watergate had become. The frightening thought arose that Nixon might be irrational; if so, Congress had to act promptly to challenge this abuse of the presidency's considerable powers. Because of the extraordinary events of that time, I decided to keep a diary of the impeachment inquiry. My first entry was November 12, 1973.

November 12 At breakfast this morning Rodino encouraged me very much and assured me that I was very needed and that I might well end up as the Special Counsel to the impeachment inquiry.

Later in the day Rodino told me about a conversation he had with Jack Anderson. According to Anderson there is a scheme afoot in the Department of Justice to engage in criminal investigations of Rodino, John Murphy, Fred Rooney, and Shirley Chisholm. Needless to say, this gives me much food for thought about our future and the future of the country. There is a question as to whether the United States will be the kind of country in which I want to live if Richard Nixon is not removed from the White House.

When I left Rodino tonight I expressed this view to him—as I have often. He spoke in favor of an "objective inquiry" and also expressed misgivings about the ability of Congress to cope with impeachment.

The Judiciary Committee was split on impeachment, and not just along party lines. A number of Democratic members of the committee, whom the media nicknamed "the fire-eaters," were encouraging Rodino to defy O'Neill. The fire-eaters were opposing Ford's confirmation and were publicly the most vociferous critics of Nixon. But at closed-door meetings of the Democratic caucus, they favored prolonging the impeachment proceedings for their own political gains.

The fire-eaters included Don Edwards of California, who was my closest personal friend on the committee. Others were Bob Kastenmeier, Robert Drinan, Jerry Waldie of California, and Liz Holtzman.

In contrast to the fire-eaters, Jack Brooks was O'Neill's staunchest supporter on the committee. Brooks's public and private personas differed sharply. Privately he was a man of intense sensitivity who feared being bruised by close contact with other politicians. Publicly, he was the archetypical Texas lawman. The press saw him this way: "Brooks was a cigar-chomping, fast-talking Texan, who liked to use whatever power he had and liked cracking heads. He was gregarious and his humor and language were salty. . . . Jack Brooks would have voted to impeach Nixon if the vote were taken . . . the day after Nixon was first inaugurated. It wouldn't look good to have done it on the same day, Brooks might have said; let the son of a bitch have one good day."

November 13 I picked Rodino up and drove him to the Capitol this morning for a caucus with the Judiciary Committee Democrats.

Don Edwards was the principal spokesman for the fire-eaters. Since

Nixon has announced that he will turn over the tapes, Don said "the steam was out of the impeachment movement." He expressed the thought that we would probably not be able to impeach Nixon—and it would be very good for the Democratic members who were running in the next election to be able to run against Nixon. I feel that there is too much sentiment of that sort among the fire-eaters, who seem willing to watch Nixon twist in the wind.

Privately, I said to Don: "The fundamental question is: What kind of a country are we going to have if Nixon is not removed from office?" I feel strongly about this. Nixon has put Congress to a test.

The enjoyable part of the meeting was my conversations on the side with Jack Brooks. He joked about the burdens of impeachment and is raring to go ahead with it. He said, "You and Pete better start eating plenty of raw meat for breakfast—or the Republicans will screw us."

To assure the privacy of the caucus, we often met in a hideaway office behind the House dining room. During the Prohibition Era, the beautifully furnished room—known as the "Board Room"—was used by Speaker Nicholas Longworth for drinking parties with other House members. (The hideaway's name originally came from "Board of Education"—a nod to what Longworth learned from his guests after plying them with whiskey.)

Like Longworth, Rodino mostly played the role of a good listener. Jack Brooks tended to play the role of our reticent chairman's executive officer. I tried to be the good navigator—to take political and legal bearings and occasionally recomend changes in speed and direction.

November 14 There was a rancorous meeting of the Democratic members this morning in the Board Room. It went on and off all day long. Essentially the theme was the same—the fire-eaters oppose Ford's confirmation.

Drinan and Holtzman were brazenly political and talked about not even allowing the confirmation to be put to a vote. When I tried gently to suggest that the Twenty-fifth Amendment might give the committee a constitutional duty to at least vote on the question of Ford's qualifications, Holtzman scoffed.

Rodino took a strong position—stronger than I've ever seen him take. He agreed with me. He told Drinan: "Father, you can take all the political positions you want. As for me I will not be guided by you, but by my conscience."

The shallowness of the fire-eaters—especially Holtzman—is shocking. In the middle of the meeting Jack Brooks reminded us that at the desk where Peter was sitting, Sam Rayburn had once sat. On the very spot where Bob Kastenmeier was sitting, Harry Truman had once sat—and had received a call from Eleanor Roosevelt telling him that President Roosevelt had just died. Harry had asked Eleanor, "Is there any way in which I can be of help to you?" Eleanor said, "The more important question is: How can I help you?"

In other words, to be decent one must have a generosity of spirit. To have political integrity one must have a sense of history. I don't think this made the slightest impression on most of the members. Holtzman couldn't care less.

Tomorrow morning we begin the hearings on the Ford confirmation. Although there seems to be some unanswered questions about Ford, he seems so far to be basically clean. In the afternoon, the House is going to vote on a special funding resolution to give the Judiciary Committee a million dollars to use for the impeachment inquiry.

November 15 Before the Ford hearings began this morning, Rodino and I had breakfast with Tip O'Neill. We told him about the flack we were getting from Drinan and Holtzman. O'Neill seemed sympathetic and quite surprised.

After breakfast Rodino and I went back to the Rayburn Building to meet with Jerry Ford in advance of the hearing. Ford was accompanied by a former Republican member of the Judiciary Committee, Bill Cramer of Florida—I think the closest a human being has ever come to being a full-fledged shark! I felt like a hypocrite telling Cramer that we missed him on the committee. The truth is that Manny Celler and everyone I knew well on the committee and staff had regarded Cramer as rancid. He was always an arch-enemy of civil rights and of Manny Celler, who considered him vicious.

With the media present, the hearings began promptly at 10 A.M. I think they went well. Most of the members—as we predicted—were not such firebrands when having to face the TV cameras.

I somehow didn't like the looks of Jerry Ford this morning. There seemed to be something very cold about his eyes. Perhaps I was more put off by the sight of his advisors—Cramer, Benton Becker, and William Bittman—sitting in back of him. Those three looked so sinister that they were almost like the caricatures of villains in a Chaplin movie. Bittman's role as one of Ford's attorneys seems particularly questionable. [Bittman was also the attorney for Watergate defendant Howard Hunt, and Nixon had acquiesced in the payment of hush money for Howard Hunt to Bittman.]

Some time around 1 P.M. we had to recess the Ford hearings to go over to the House floor on the funding resolution. . . . The million-dollar funding resolution was conceived out of the desire of the Democrats to go home to their constituents and explain that they were doing something about Watergate. Actually, we don't need the money right now. We have about $200,000 to get by for the next six weeks.

But as media-conscious and partisan as are the Democrats, the Republicans are worse. After all, Nixon created the mess.

Tonight I continue to feel jaded. When I count heads on the Judiciary Committee on both sides of the aisles, the men of good will and decency are the exception and not the rule. Hutchinson [the Judiciary Committee's ranking Republican] is a pro-Nixon conservative, yet he is decent, with integrity, and a man of good will.

For me, the people of good will also include Democrats Ray Thornton of Arkansas and Barbara Jordan of Texas. This afternoon on the House floor Barbara needled me a bit and then apologized and told me that she was only kidding—and then put her arm around me. I told her, "I'd vote for you—for anything." Charlie Rangel overheard this and said, "Maybe there are some things she doesn't want." I said, "I'm sure she knows I'd vote for her for anything she wants."

I enjoyed Jack Brooks during the debate on the House floor: all piss and vinegar, but at least with balls. If he doesn't always have good will, at least he has integrity and balls.

Larry Woodworth and his auditors met with the members tonight at 8 o'clock to go over the audits of seven years of Ford's income taxes—all of which are remarkably clean. I still dislike Elizabeth Holtzman intensely. She is now down to the point of questioning $25 items on Ford's tax schedules.

At about 9 o'clock Rodino and Lois and I went to dinner. I told them that I was keeping a diary and that I hoped eventually to write a book. He told me that he thought I should.

As the hearings progressed I began to change my perceptions of Jerry Ford and became more sympathetic to the views of the fire-eaters. There were a few aspects of Ford's background that I began to find disturbing.

In response to a question as to whether a president should ever lie to Congress or the public, Ford stated that it might be necessary, in extraordinary circumstances, for the president to "blur" the truth or authorize a "temporary lie."

From our staff investigations I had learned for the first time that Ford was one of the fourteen members of Congress who were informed of the more than 3,000 bombing raids conducted clandestinely over Cambodia in 1970 and 1971. Under questioning by Drinan at our hearings, Ford denied anything wrong with his complicity in keeping from the public the information that we had bombed a neutral country without the consent of Congress. As Liz Holtzman was later to write of Ford in her dissent to our committee report on his nomination: "Unfortunately, he cannot claim high marks for candor. Knowing full well that Mr. Nixon had lied to the American people about the secret bombing in Cambodia, Mr. Ford nonetheless gave his personal assurance on the floor of the House in 1970 that Mr. Nixon had never deceived the Congress or the public."

Still another disturbing feature of Ford's record brought out by our staff investigation was his voting record on civil rights. Conyers, Rangel, and Clarence Mitchell of the NAACP emphasized at our hearings that, as minority leader, Ford had attempted to derail every major civil rights law authored by Celler. Jordan characterized Ford's civil rights voting record as "trying to stall a train as long as possible and jumping on when the train is moving and there is nothing left to do."

Ford's attitude on this issue was best summed up by Conyers in his dissent to Ford's confirmation: "The nominee, Mr. Ford, was closely assisted [at our hearings] by William C. Cramer, a former Congressman and arch-foe of civil rights legislation. Mr. Cramer has been at the center of several controversies involving illegal political activity in Florida. The record of the committee's hearing shows that the nominee stated that he 'would have no hesitancy to recommend his [Cramer's] appointment to any job in the administration.' I am not prejudging either Mr. Cramer or the nominee. However I do wish the record to clearly show that I have strong reservations with respect to the kind of people the nominee may bring into public office if he is confirmed."

November 16 Our Ford hearings resumed today.

I am chilled by the way Ford looks and by the three people in back of him—Cramer and company. Most of all I am very disturbed by his saying it is okay for a president to lie to the American people.

Who knows? Maybe the hotheads are not so wrong. For, the years I have known him, Ford has always seemed benign. Today at the hearings there was the smell of fascism all about him.

Among facts that were not widely publicized in the media we learned that several years earlier Ford had consultations with a psychiatrist who had also treated Nixon. We also learned that although Ford was a conservative Republican, his wife, Betty, who had been a member of the Martha Graham Dance Company, was a "closet liberal" and supported ERA, feminism, and abortion rights—and became an alcoholic.

In those years, the public disclosure by a congressional committee of such personal material was considered inappropriate—even by most of the fire-eaters. What they hoped to find was some form of financial corruption. Since the staff investigation of Ford's finances and tax records indicated that Ford was clean, several of the fire-eaters excoriated the staff. Holtzman recommended that the Democrats hire outside investigators from New York to help find dirt on Ford—a recommendation that was rejected by all of the other Democrats. However, a majority of the Democrats insisted that we hold an executive session to hear closed-door testimony from two witnesses. The first was Robert Winter-Berger, who had written a book called *Washington Pay Off* and had signed an affidavit claiming that a number of members of Congress, including Ford, were known by the FBI to be on the take and were being blackmailed by J. Edgar Hoover. Eventually, the committee found "no credible evidence" to sustain such allegations.

The other witness whose testimony was heard in executive session was Dr. Arnold Hutschnecker, the psychiatrist whom Ford had consulted briefly regarding his marital problems. His testimony did not reflect adversely on Ford.

November 17 Before the executive session began I had Winter-Berger alone in my office for a while. He seemed to me like hundreds and hundreds of impecunious people I meet. I was both surprised and sympathetic to his concern about being reimbursed as quickly as possible for the airfare to and from New York and his expenses. I finally put Winter-Berger in the chairman's holding room and entertained Dr. Hutschnecker in my office.

Incidentally, at dinner a few nights ago Dick Cates and I discussed the need in the trial of a criminal case against Nixon to prosecute the "whole man." In every area of Watergate there seems to be the reflection of Nixon as a little person—the little sneak, the little liar, the little cheat.

Jerry Ford is not a little person. He is probably not as psychopathic as Nixon. But who knows? Perhaps that will make him more dangerous. Maybe Drinan and Holtzman are right: maybe Ford would foster fascism in a more open and friendly way—without the petty type of self-destructive corruption that caused Watergate.

By November 20, every head count in the House and Senate predicted that Ford would soon be confirmed. The Senate Committee on Rules and Administration unanimously approved his nomination.

November 21 The Ford hearings began again at 11 A.M. Although it is the day before Thanksgiving the hearing lasted for most of the day—with testimony from Ford. I avoided the hearings and tried to continue working with Dick on putting together the impeachment inquiry.

November 22 It is Thanksgiving day—the tenth anniversary of the Kennedy assassination. I am in a hammock in the Blue Ridge mountains. It is a beautiful day. But I am exhausted—battle fatigue.

Of the various issues relating to Ford's ties to Nixon, one of the most sensitive was the matter of Ford's attempt a few years earlier to impeach Justice William O. Douglas. As was subsequently set forth in Jerry Waldie's dissent, Ford commenced the Douglas impeachment for the Nixon administration a short time after the Democratic-controlled Senate had rejected Judge Clement Haynsworth, Nixon's nominee to the Supreme Court. Our staff investigation uncovered the fact that Ford had called Attorney General Mitchell and asked that "the full resources of the Department of Justice" be placed at his disposal to impeach Douglas. Mitchell had willingly complied and sent his assistant Will Wilson to Ford's office with information from the FBI's dossier on Douglas.

As a result, Waldie and other opponents of Ford's confirmation charged Ford with having "used the Department of Justice for political purposes in secretly seeking and obtaining confidential information to politically attack a United States Supreme Court Justice."

November 23 Although I was still exhausted I tried to spend an hour in the office straightening things up and then got waylaid by Jerry Waldie. He started to gripe about why the staff wasn't working. I told him why! We had been working night and day for a month, and I had given them the day and the rest of the weekend off with the chairman's approval. He calmed down a bit.

Waldie wanted us to subpoena Ford's administrative assistant Bob Hartman to testify about the role of the Justice Department in the Douglas impeachment matter. I called Rodino—who criticized me for having failed to talk Waldie out of this. I ended up more angry with Rodino than Waldie.

I decided to go to Ford's office to talk with both Hartman and Ford. Ford readily agreed to open all of his office files. He promptly turned over all of the copies of the so-called "unidentified memoranda" that Wilson had provided to Ford. He said jokingly, "You probably know more about me by now than I know about myself." Person-to-person, Jerry Ford seems like a very decent, open person with a minimum of hostility, hardly any malice, and little duplicity.

I went back to see Waldie and gave him the memoranda. He was very appreciative, but he also seemed a bit disappointed. He could no longer get press coverage for demanding that we supoena Hartman.

November 25 It is Sunday and I am back in Front Royal in my hammock again—trying to rest. In the last few days I have come to see the Ford thing in a somewhat different perspective. I am now more sympathetic to Waldie—even to Drinan and Holtzman, although the latter two are especially outrageous in their self-righteousness and in their lack of decency and courtesy in dealing with the staff.

November 26 I felt tired just going to the office. I really want to get out of Washington—and do something creative. I'm fed up and could use a month's vacation.

Anyway, we held the last confirmation hearing today with an additional three-and-one-half hours of cross-examination of Ford—much of which was done by Waldie regarding the Douglas impeachment. In all, the total hearings consumed about thirty-seven hours—of which about nineteen hours consisted of questions addressed directly to Ford by members of the committee. The truth is that no one has really laid a glove on Ford in terms of demonstrating any form of basic corruption or criminality.

Tonight while I was in Rodino's office Bella Abzug raised holy hell with him on the phone. I had spoken to her earlier. She was furious because Rodino didn't let her testify today against Ford in prime time. Rodino spent about forty-five minutes arguing with her. She wants him to table the Ford confirmation—not even allow it to come to a vote in the committee. He tried to tell her off—but couldn't quite. I had never seen him so angry with anyone. When he put down the phone, he said: "She is a goddamn pain in the ass!" It was an unusual outburst for him: he rarely used any form of profanity.

November 27 We met Don Edwards at breakfast. He complimented the staff for its work on the Ford investigation. At last!

In the afternoon, the Senate voted to confirm Ford 92 to 3. Three Democrats voted against Ford: Eagleton of Missouri, Hathaway of Maine, and Gaylord Nelson of Wisconsin.

I met Rodino again at about 8:30 P.M. in the office. I talked to him about a letter from Holtzman. Now that we have concluded the hearings on schedule, and it is absolutely certain that Ford has the votes to be confirmed, that bitch wants us to reopen the hearings and have John Dean and other Watergate witnesses testify about Ford.

November 28 I had scheduled a staff meeting in the morning to complete a proposed draft of the committee report on the Ford confirmation. In the middle of the meeting Rodino called. He is afraid that if he votes to confirm Ford, the blacks and liberals in his district will be distressed. I spent a long time listening to him expound on the possibility of voting to report the confirmation to the full House—and then switching his vote on the House floor to "no."

Later in the day we talked further about it. He said he had spoken to Ford privately and had told him that he would help get the confirmation out of committee and onto the floor, but that he might have to vote against him during the recorded votes on the floor. He said that Ford was very understanding and thanked him for his handling of the whole situation in the committee.

Rodino seemed to be particularly irritable today. We don't seem to be getting along as well as usual.

The next morning, the committee voted 29 to 8 (one voting "present") to recommend that the House confirm the nomination of Gerald Ford to be Vice President.

November 30 The committee voted to confirm Ford. Seiberling voted "present." Rodino voted with the majority.

The meeting went well. The members behaved themselves fairly well except for Holtzman, who was sanctimonious and tried to prevent the issue from even being brought to a vote. She brought a formal motion to table the confirmation, then insisted stridently that the committee debate her motion. Even though Rodino advised her gently that under House rules motions to table are not debatable, she started shouting. Rodino had to gavel her down.

Rodino handled the meeting extremely wall. If anything, he was perhaps a bit too relaxed.

As usual, Jack Brooks's speech was a lot of fun and very good. "I don't think Vice President is good enough for him," Brooks said. "I hope we can promote him as quickly as possible."

November 30 I had another hectic day. I had to take a few hours off in the morning to deal with personnel. Some of the committee staff secretaries are crying about pay raise problems and are complaining about Lois being so domineering.

Rodino is still trying to decide how to vote on the Ford confirmation when it comes up on the floor. I hope he votes "no." We discussed a possible speech. I developed a theme with him that went like this: "Ford is a decent, courteous, honorable man—especially in his relations with his colleagues in this Congress. But as a political leader he is nonresponsive to the great social needs of our time—the needs of the poor, of women, and of minority groups. As benign as his neglect of these needs might well be it is a neglect that the American people cannot and should not be willing to tolerate."

I filed the committee report on the Ford confirmation today. While conferring with the Parliamentarian I learned that after the floor vote there will be a swearing-in ceremony in the House chamber and that Nixon will attend. Tonight I have a premonition that someone might take a shot at Nixon.

December 6 Rodino and I went to the House floor for the debate on the Ford confirmation and the swearing-in ceremony. The only enjoyment I had during the debate was joking with Jack Brooks and Gillis Long.

Tonight I am trying to rest. As I sit in bed recording this tape, the following radio newscast is on the air. "Gerald Ford was confirmed as the Vice President of the United States by the House of Representatives this afternoon by a vote of 387 to 35. He replaces Spiro Agnew. Ford was sworn into office about 90 minutes later during a joint meeting of the Congress as his wife and the President stood beside him. There was never any question about the Ford confirmation, only how soon it would come and how extensive the opposition. . . . In the House, the "no" votes totaled 35, all from California, New York, and Massachusetts. Ten of the 16 black members of the House opposed Gerald Ford."

Rodino voted against Ford. After the vote Frank Polk asked me whether this was a matter of conscience or politics. A lot of other people have already asked me that.

Several years later, one of Rodino's detractors was to write:

When Ford's name was finally placed in nomination, Rodino remarked that never before had any man undergone such an investigation and emerged so well. So what did Rodino do? He voted against confirmation.

Later Rodino was to explain that his vote on the floor in no way reflected on Ford's integrity or qualifications. Rodino, who represents a largely black constituency, said he voted "no" because he had a fundamental difference in perception with Ford on the government's role "in serving the needs of all of our citizens."

"But," Rodino added, "Jerry wrote me a beautiful letter afterwards."

7

IMPEACHMENT BEGINS AND THE DEMOCRATS QUARREL

By the time Ford was confirmed, the AFL-CIO had followed the ACLU's lead—officers of 111 international unions, representing more than 14 million members, had come to Capitol Hill to lobby for impeachment. They not only denounced Nixon for Watergate, but also decried the chilling "spectacle of the apparatus the President had set up to pervert the Department of Justice, the FBI, and the IRS." The public record was already replete with evidence to impeach Nixon for obstruction of justice and abuse of the powers of his office.

All the President's Men became a best-selling book and a box-office hit. Under the aegis of the *Washington Post's* publisher, Katherine Graham, "Deep Throat" had acquired respectability as a "reliable source." On Pennsylvania Avenue, "Honk for Impeachment" became Washington's best-selling bumper sticker. Other bumper stickers urged Congress to "Impeach the Coxsacker."

That Nixon's impeachment had become viable was clear to Tip O'Neill. As majority leader, he was Congress's best-informed vote counter. O'Neill engaged William Hamilton, a pioneer in political polling, to take soundings in each of the 435 congressional districts. According to Hamilton's figures, among Democrat supporters, only 7 percent would vote for any candidate who opposed impeachment.

O'Neill was getting plenty of personal readings of the mood of the House Democrats. As he put it:

> On the Monday after Congress returned from its Thanksgiving recess, I spent the entire morning hearing what I call

"confessions" as the members came to me with their problems and their reports from home. I must have had sixty or seventy guys come up to condemn the Judiciary Committee for dragging its feet. They had spent the holiday talking to their constituents, and by now most people believed that the evidence was there against the President. Jim Stanton from Cleveland came to me and said: "The whole country knows this guy is guilty. When are we going to get moving? My constituents aren't just disgusted with Nixon. They're starting to get on me too. They don't think we're doing anything about it." It wasn't just Jim Stanton. By December we were all taking heat from our constituents. When they went back to their districts the members were starting to look stupid because they didn't know what was going on in the Judiciary Committee.

Our impeachment inquiry had officially begun on October 23. Jerry Waldie was chosen by the Democratic leadership to give the keynote speech. After a morning prayer, Waldie was recognized by Speaker Albert to introduce the first impeachment resolution of the day. Waldie charged that: "The President's incredible and bizarre actions last week have culminated a long pattern of pure and unmistakable obstruction of justice. His arrogance and lawlessness can no longer be tolerated."

O'Neill had assumed that Waldie would support the get-moving attitude of the leadership. But as O'Neill and I saw it, Waldie also had his own agenda. He wanted to ride the crest of the anti-conservative impeachment wave and replace Ronald Reagan as governor of California. Embroiled in a bitter Democratic primary fight with his fellow firebrand, Jerry Brown, Waldie needed to play the impeachment issue for as much media coverage as he could get.

Waldie and the other fire-eaters were keeping the committee in turmoil. They wrangled mostly about two questions: whether we should hire a "big name" lawyer to head the impeachment inquiry staff; and which committee members Rodino should appoint to have overall supervision of the staff's investigation.

November 12 I see Jerry Waldie as an opportunistic, loner kind of type. Not a team player. [Soon after Waldie came to Washington, he had a direct confrontation with then-Speaker John McCormack, and he sought a vote of no-confidence against the Speaker. In a newsletter to his constituents, Waldie wrote, "I no longer will remain a quiet, cooperative cog in a machine pretending that all is not as bad as it may seem-because, in fact, it is worse than it seems."] The essence of democracy, I believe, is in respect for the team's collective wisdom.

Like Waldie, some of the other Democrats on the committee are irresponsible and pursue their own hidden agendas. It is amazing the number of devils who join a fight on the side of the angels.

November 13 I spoke with Gene Hardy [vice president and chief lobbyist of the National Association of Manufacturers] today on the phone. He called me to try to place an investigator with the committee. Gene told me, "I am afraid to ask myself the ultimate question as to whether Nixon should be impeached. I can only go so far as to ask whether he can continue to govern."

Later this morning I received a request from Margaret Heckler. [Republican representative from Wellesley, Massachusetts] to meet with her privately in her office. . . . When I arrived she offered me coffee and told me, "I think Nixon ought to resign. He's ruining the Republican party." She also added that she didn't think she could "face up to the responsibility of having to cast a roll call vote on the House floor to impeach a Republican president." She asked me to brief her on what was going on in the Judiciary Committee, because she had to go back to her district and face a group of students, and wanted to be knowledgeable.

November 14 I called Dick Cates early this morning at his farm in Wisconsin. He told me that he had been up for several hours cutting firewood. . . . I hired him as assistant general counsel. He agreed to start work early Monday morning, if I would find a place for him to sleep on Sunday night.

Later, Dick called me back and asked if he should bring a sleeping bag or some sheets. I told him that would not be necessary. I also said; "Hey, before you got here I ought to confess that I'm a babe in the woods about trial preparations." He replied: "That's okay, 'cause I'm a babe in the woods about the inner workings of Congress." I think he and I will get along just fine.

November 16 At the end of the day Lois was very disturbed about a news story in the *Newark Star Ledger* the effect that Rodino had offered the Special Counsel job to Fred Lacey [the Nixon-appointed U.S. Attorney who had prosecuted Hugh Addonizio and was then tabbed by Nixon to be a federal judge]. I was distressed by this too.

As Howard Fields later observed, "It would be political suicide . . . for Rodino to hire as his Special Counsel someone who was from his own district and whose appointment would prompt stories dredging up Lacey's connections with Addonizio and all the old suspicions that Rodino was somehow connected with the Mafia or at least with persons of questionable character."

I called Bernie Hellring in Newark and spoke to him at length about the Lacey problem. Bernie is urging me to be the lead impeachment counsel—with a couple of assistants like Dick Cates, who is arriving tomorrow.

November 17 On the way back from my cottage in Virginia I met Dick Cates at National Airport, and checked him in at the Coronet Hotel on Capitol Hill. We discussed the case against Nixon until late tonight. I think Dick sees Nixon pretty much as I do, but perhaps in a more lawyer-like way. Dick made me realize that it is not Congress's case, my case, or his case—it has to be tried as the "people's" case.

I was impressed by Dick's picture of himself as trial artist. He used a lot of musical terms, such as orchestration, tone, and style, in describing how he thought we should try the case against Nixon in Congress.

Howard Fields later described Cates this way: "Cates had built a reputation in Wisconsin as a sharp trial lawyer. . . . Cates did not look like a high-powered lawyer. Tall, with sandy, stringy hair and the cauliflower ears and crooked nose and nasal twang of a prizefighter, Cates was more at home in denims than he was in a suit."

November 18 I spent most of the day working with Dick reviewing all of the files and material on Watergate that my small impeachment staff had already assembled, including all of the nine volumes already published by the Ervin Committee as well as copies of all impeachment resolutions introduced to date and all of the other research materials we had collected.

During my discussion with Dick I was annoyed when Lois walked into my office unannounced—and after only three minutes with Dick, asked him to excuse her for taking me aside. She then whispered to me: "I don't like him. He's arrogant." Lois is getting to be a chronic irritant. I suspect she will scream at Rodino to stop him from appointing Dick Cates as our special counsel.

Tonight Dick and I had dinner. We discussed Nixon and the trial of the case. Dick helps me understand the need to prosecute the "whole man." In the whole picture of the White House and Watergate there is a reflection of the President as a liar and a cheat.

November 20 Tonight while the Ford hearings were going on Rodino and I left the hearing room and interviewed John Doar, who apparently has already become Lois's first choice. I was favorably impressed, but there is also something a bit dour about Doar, a kind of Republican streak. He reminds me of some Maine types of Republicans. He seems to be a first-rate fellow.

At first the interview was little more than a conversation between Rodino and Doar about the "extraordinary burdens" and "awesome responsibility" that Rodino has been bearing for some months now. After a while Rodino went back to the hearing and I stayed with Doar to ask him detailed questions about his background and the possibility of conflicts of interest.

After meeting Doar I began to feel that he might well be a better choice than Dick Cates. Doar is tougher and has had more Washington experience.

November 21 Today I prefer Dick Cates. Dick has more of everyman in him. But who knows? I continue to wonder about my own role in this.

One of the things that Dick and I have been anxious to do all week has been to meet with the staff of the Watergate Committee. I had called Sam Dash on Monday—it became a big production and finally a meeting was scheduled for this afternoon at 3:30. When Dick and I and Frank Polk went over to Dash's office, we were kept waiting for a half hour. Finally Dash came and told us how busy he was. He asked us to reschedule the meeting for next week.

My few contacts with Dash have not been very rewarding. At our first meeting he kept Frank and me waiting for well over an hour—and then we got nothing from our conversation with him. My second contact was on the morning after impeachment was first referred to the Judiciary Committee. It was an extraordinary day. When I arrived at my office a three-page list of telephone calls was waiting on my desk. One was from Dash. Assuming that he was at last ready to open up his files on Watergate to us, I returned his call immediately. His secretary apologized that he was too busy to come to phone, but that she had a message for me. Dash wished to ask a favor—could I put his niece on the committee payroll as a House employee? His secretary explained that the press had criticized Dash for having his niece on his own payroll.

November 23 Rodino called me from Newark with some crazy idea about having informal discussions with experts without having committee hearings. I urged him to appoint a special impeachment counsel and a subcommittee to supervise the staff investigation as quickly as possible. [Under House rules, unless at least a few committee members actually presided at a hearing, we could not take depositions of potential witnesses.] He expressed concern as to how we could have a hand-picked subcommittee and bypass John Conyers—whom he dislikes and fears. I said, "Well, I think you just have to bite the bullet and do it."

Although Rodino seems to have risen to the occasion greatly, he still has pockets of weakness.

November 26 Rodino seemed to be treating me curtly today. I asked him whether he was annoyed with me. He said, "No, I'm just worried and tired." We met again tonight in his office and discussed the special counsel problem. He is still leaning heavily toward Lacey. While I was there he spoke for about a half hour with Sargent Shriver, who is promoting Ted Kennedy for President in 1976.

Rose Mary Woods testified today that she pushed the wrong button or something and created an eighteen-minute gap in one of the subpoenaed White House tapes. Bella Abzug raised holy hell with Rodino again. The stock market dropped enormously.

I feel numb tonight. Impeachment means a colossal chunk of staff work—a staggering burden.

November 27 On the way to breakfast Rodino told me about his conversation with Jane Engelhard. [She was the widow of multimillionaire Charles Engelhard—a prominent Democrat who had established a precious metals industry in South Africa and whose U.S. headquarters were in Rodino's district.] She told Rodino that she had learned from a top official of the *New York Times* that the Justice Department is "out to get Rodino" for being such a "flaming liberal."

Dick Cates is convinced that there is already more than enough evidence to convict Nixon on the obstruction of justice charge alone. [I had come to that conclusion myself several months before after a confidential discussion with Judge Ed Weinfeld—who was an Eisenhower Republican and was my first choice for the special counsel's job.] I am anxious to get moving on impeachment. I wish Rodino would hurry up and hire a special counsel already.

This morning we interviewed Dean Kirby of Ohio State University. He seemed like a nice fellow. I didn't quite cotton to him, though. Also,

I don't think he has the requisite trial experience. I greatly prefer Judge Weinfeld, John Doar, or Dick Cates.

In the afternoon, Dick, Frank, and I finally met with the staff of the Watergate Committee, including Sam Dash, Rufus Edmiston, and the minority counsel, Fred Thompson. I like Edmiston and Thompson. Dash exudes an air of insecure superiority that is rather amusing. He strikes me as a person of mediocre ability and little or no imagination.

Dick called it "a fruitful meeting," but I don't think so. I can't recall anything of value that we learned from it. But after the meeting Edmiston and I had an interesting private conversation about Nixon. Rufus said, "The impeachment case against Nixon seems simple. Nixon is a liar, a cheat, and a fraud—and he disregards the law. That ought to be enough to remove the son of a bitch."

Rufus, his boss Senator Ervin, and I apparently all feel very much the same way about the whole Nixon crowd at the Justice Department. Like Rehnquist [who served as their legal counsel before being made Supreme Court justice], most of them regard the Bill of Rights, and the Fourth Amendment in particular, as a threat to our national security. I see Rehnquist and his friends in the Justice Department as moral midgets—committed to making the trains run on time. My god! What a horrible picture.

Rose Mary Woods testified again about the tape gap. I think the noose drew a little tighter.

November 29 Frank Polk tells me that Sam Garrison may be hired as the minority counterpart for Dick Cates. That would be great. I trust Sam. I suspect he shares my views of Nixon.

Frank Thompson [a senior member of New Jersey's congressional delegation] called me this morning inquiring as to where we stood with Lacey. Thompson has no confidence in either Lacey or Rodino. He made no bones about his personal animosity toward Rodino and said he was ready to "screw" Rodino because Rodino had tried to screw him out of his seat in Congress.

This afternoon I had an extraordinary experience. Rodino had asked me to call Clark Clifford and give him the list of the names of lawyers under consideration for the job of special counsel. I called him and he asked me to come to his office at 4 o'clock. He has a palatial office with a beautiful view looking down over the White House. When I arrived he apologized for asking me to come there, and explained that he will not speak freely on the phone or in government offices because of the possibility of illegal wiretaps and bugging devices. Amazing!

Then Clifford proceeded to pontificate a bit. He gave me a twenty-minute lecture on Nixon. I was annoyed that he felt the need to lecture me on why Nixon should be impeached. He went through the whole bit—from Helen Gahagan Douglas to Jerry Voorhis—the picture of Nixon as a "ruthless character assassin" with a political philosophy that is "totalitarian" and "antithetical to our way of life." The one thing that Clifford contributed to my thinking about Nixon was his heavy emphasis on Nixon's personal finances. For example, he talked with some knowledge about Nixon's lots in Key Biscayne.

We then proceeded to discuss how strongly we both really felt about Nixon, Mitchell, Rehnquist, and most of the other Nixon loyalists. "They are the real things," I told Clifford, "the American counterparts of the communist commissars."

I also told him that for me the aura of unreality about impeaching a president had disappeared months ago. Then we discussed plans for him to review a list of candidates for the job of special counsel.

Clifford advised me not to be impressed at all with big names. He said, "Most big names are simply people who have good public relations staffs." He looked at names like Ed Levy on the list, and said "I'm not impressed at all with deans of law schools or university presidents. About Archibald Cox: "Archie Cox was a good Solicitor General but he is a babe in the woods when it comes to Washington politics. He was the last person that the White House would talk to about political matters because of his ineptitude."

When I returned to Rodino's office, Bernie Hellring was there. He had only a few minutes, and he gave me a confidential report on Judge Weinfeld from another judge in the same federal court in New York. The reading given to Bernie about Weinfeld was "senile" and "a terrible idea." Bernie said he knew I would be unhappy to hear that. I said, "I don't believe it. Ed Weinfeld seems to be a prophet without honor in his own court."

I walked Bernie to his taxi, and on the way he again urged me to take personal charge of the impeachment investigation with Dick Cates as my assistant.

November 30 I had a two-hour lunch with Henry Hubbard of *Newsweek*. We discussed Nixon's personality. Henry tells me most of the people who cover Nixon at the White House believe that he is "off his rocker."

Joe Rothstein [a political consultant hired by Rodino to help him win reelection] discussed the Lacey question with me. I think that my initial reaction is correct: Lacey is a Nixon appointee who prosecuted Hughie Addonizio. Appointing him as our special counsel would be perceived as tainted by "New Jersey politics." In addition, if Lacey and Rodino were to move toward impeachment, Nixon would try to knock off both of them with one corrupt informer who could be offered immunity or a pardon.

I learned that Sam Dash has told the press of our "confidential" meeting of Wednesday. He said that we had not asked for any documents, which is not true.

December 1 I slept late, and woke up ruminating on a conversation I had several weeks ago with Henry Ruth of Cox's office. He thinks that a sitting president ought not to be subject to criminal prosecution because it would interfere with the functioning of his office. Cox had the same view, and they both perceived immunizing the President as within the "prosecutorial discretion" the Attorney General had given Cox.

To me, this view reflects a common form of moral corruption. I believe in the "Becket" principle. Like Thomas a Becket, Archbishop of Canterbury—who had a special responsibility to compel his patron and friend Henry II to comply with canon law forbidding divorce—the Attorney General has a special responsibility to keep the President who appointed him within the bounds of the law.

December 2 Rodino called early this morning to tell me that he has a new "big name"—William Gossett, a Republican, former president of the American Bar Association, and now a corporate lawyer from Detroit.

December 3 I spent the early morning in the dentist's office. When I got back, I called Clifford to add Gossett to his list. Laughingly, he said, "University presidents are specialists at climbing academic ladders, corporate presidents specialize in climbing the corporate ladders, and any man who could rise to become president of the ABA has got to have something wrong with him." Nevertheless, Clifford agreed to get us a reading on Gossett. He also said he had a slight reservation about John Doar as "too close to the Kennedy crowd through Burke Marshall." He promised to get back to me by Thursday with other ratings.

I also told Clifford of Bernie Hellring's recommendation that we not have a special counsel and that the investigation be conducted as a committee project. His reply: "I have never been in a town square where there was a monument to a committee." (I *have* seen such a monument, in England—to the barons who put a sword to the king's throat and forced him to sign the Magna Carta.)

December 4 Rodino, Cates, and I had dinner last night at the Monocle. I had a pleasant chance meeting with Father Drinan, who was having dinner with his staff. He beckoned me to their table. When he referred to me as his "boss," his staff applauded. He was cordial and friendly. For the first time, I began to like him as a person. I told him, "I promise you, Father: now that the sword of Goliath is being removed from the temple, we will keep the blade very sharp."

When we were alone with Dick Cates Rodino listened carefully while Dick said, "I pay taxes to my country, have gone to war for my country, and have sent my son to war for my country. There are a lot of wrong things that I can accept in my country, but I cannot accept a President who is a liar and wants us to believe things that defy reason and logic. If I give up my reason—which I simply cannot do anyway—I am no longer free." He went on: "Once the case is properly presented Nixon can and should be convicted by any jury anywhere in the United States."

Dick then told us that he wants to start questioning witnesses such as Dean, Haldeman, Ehrlichman, and Mitchell next week. Rodino wants him to hold off. I knew that Rodino would be nervous about that.

Since Lois dislikes Dick so much, I was pleased that Dick and Peter seemed to get along so well. Dick massaged Peter's ego, referring to him as "Mr. Congressman" rather than "Peter."

Tonight, I am convinced that Nixon will be impeached. He has to be impeached. It now seems simple. He will be viewed as a liar because he is liar, and viewed as a criminal because he is a criminal.

I also now see the entire drama in a new way. It is not a matter of Nixon wanting to remain President—clinging desperately to his desk in the Oval Office and shuddering about how he will be treated in the history books. What is motivating him now are the same forces that motivate every other guilty criminal. His real objective is exactly the same as Agnew's—to stay out of jail.

December 4 In the afternoon Sam Garrison walked into my office. He is starting work as Dick Cates's Republican staff counterpart. In between telephone calls I greeted him as warmly as possible—and called Dick over to meet him. I am very pleased to have Sam aboard. I think we will impeach Nixon together.

The rest of my afternoon was almost intolerable. Capitol Hill has become a jungle in which most of the tigers are made out of paper—but where the administrative problems can kill you, like vicious, swarming mosquitoes that can eat you alive. I went home thinking that

I would really prefer a job at half the salary on the impeachment inquiry staff working on a single project that I can get my teeth into and master.

December 5 Today was an excruciating day. Charlie Rangel called me. He is outraged at the prospect of a select subcommittee supervising the investigation of Nixon. I also had an argument with Chuck Morgan. He wants us to move the impeachment resolution onto the House floor for debate and a vote—with no prior impeachment inquiry. And perhaps the worst part of the day was the 28-minute bawling out I got from Bella Abzug for not putting her name in the committee report as opposing Ford. She is not even on the committee!

December 6 Rodino and I had a breakfast meeting with some of the junior Democrats: Waldie, Seiberling, Holtzman, Owens, Mezvinsky, and of course Charlie Rangel. Rangel had written a letter to the *New York Times* yesterday because of an article suggesting that Rodino would create a subcommittee of senior members.

At breakfast Rodino told us a story that he heard the night before from Bob Lehman, Democrat from Florida. Lehman had visited the White House and reported that Nixon had commented that as President he "alone had control over the button for which their was no fail safe" and that he alone could "initiate the annihilation of over 75 million Russians." This strange comment had made him feel like vomiting.

As soon as Rodino finished the story, Rangel jumped to the subject of the meeting—how the staff investigation was going to be supervised and by which members. Rangel and the other junior members approach the problem entirely from a political point of view. There was no discussion of how best to conduct a vigorous and effective investigation of the President or of the responsibility of committee members to supervise such an investigation. Most of the junior members are afraid they will be upstaged in the media if the staff investigation is supervised by a small subcommittee selected on the basis of seniority and ability. Holtzman in particular is concerned only with enhancing her own image by demonstrating her intelligence—which, it seems to me, is quite limited.

Tonight in my car on the way home from the Capitol, Rodino and I discussed our vexing day. We were both shocked by how shallow and irresponsible many of the committee Democrats seem to be. I have to keep reminding myself of the musical comedy *1776*. This is what the system is all about: flesh and blood, weakness and frailty. Hopefully, its checks and balances will work, and wisdom and sound judgment will prevail.

By this time, more than two months had passed since the impeachment resolutions had been referred to the committee and we began our search for a special counsel. As a result of the persistent wrangling among the Democrats as to which committee members were going to supervise the investigation, I and the impeachment inquiry staff were limited to studying documents obtained from other committees. We had not even been permitted to do any original investigations by taking statements from any of the witnesses on Dick Cates's list.

The press was getting on Rodino for his indecision. Adding to the heat, some of the more militant impeachment proponents in the House were considering introducing a privileged resolution—a parliamentary device to debate and vote on impeachment without waiting for recommendations from the Judiciary Committee.

December 7 Today is Jerry Ford's first full day as Vice President. It is also Pearl Harbor Day—and the Judiciary Committee battleship is still in dry dock.

The first call I got this morning was from Randolph Phillips. He kept me on the phone for almost an hour looking for advice and discussing the possibility of bringing a privileged motion on the floor to bypass the committee. He says he could get his friend Wilbur Mills to bring such a motion. I advised him simply to get Mills to introduce an impeachment resolution. I explained that just the introduction of such a resolution by Wilbur Mills would be very helpful and would be a major shot across Nixon's bow.

Today we had held the first scheduled meeting of the inquiry staff that I have been assembling. The top staff people included Dick Cates, Frank Polk, and Sam Garrison.

We discussed procedural alternatives for giving committee members bipartisan control over our investigations. We agreed unanimously that the best approach would be to have a small blue-ribbon investigative subcommittee of carefully selected responsible members.

Until our staff meeting yesterday Rodino was in favor of postponing the actual creation of an investigative subcommittee. But Frank Polk and Sam Garrison pointed out that, in effect, the staff was proceeding without any direction from either Rodino or Hutchinson. Frank felt this was irresponsible. Garrison—and to my surprise Dick Cates—also agreed. Now I think they're right. As a result I spoke to Rodino, told him about the staff's recommendations and urged him to create an investigative subcommittee and appoint John Doar as special counsel as soon as possible. [By that time, it was clear to me that Doar was probably the only candidate supported by Lois who was acceptable to me. Also, Doar had a good reputation on civil rights, which was important in Rodino's district.]

Tonight I believe the next few weeks will be crucial. A lot will depend on how Jerry Ford sits on the nation's stomach and on the extent to which the Republicans now begin to separate themselves from Nixon.

Rodino seems to grow stronger and stronger each day and seems more inured to criticism by the media. In fact, he seemed less concerned about criticism in today's paper describing him as "weak and indecisive" than is Don Edwards—who like the other fire-eaters has been encouraging Rodino to delay the impeachment. What worries me most tonight is that in spite of Peter's growing strength he doesn't yet seem strong enough to take the bull by the horns and proceed with an effective and vigorous investigation of Nixon's offenses.

December 10 I spent the weekend in New York. Rodino wanted me to substitute for him as a speaker at the Harvard Club before a group that Joe Rothstein and Herb Tenzer had organized of wealthy contributors to Rodino's congressional campaign fund. When I got back to Washington tonight Rodino told of a surprising visit he had from Senator John Stennis, who came personally to Rodino's office unannounced. He said he wanted very much to talk to him, that he felt that somehow fate had selected Rodino "as the very right person to handle the impeachment matter."

Stennis said that Nixon had deceived him and lied to the public and Congress. Stennis assured Rodino that he had not agreed to listen to the White House tapes as claimed by Nixon. He would never agree to substitute himself for the court by providing the court with his transcription as publicly alleged by Nixon. According to Rodino, Stennis has in so many words said, "The President is a liar and should be impeached."

December 11 We had a full-committee meeting today that was closed to the public and press. To get around the new House rules against such meetings, we called it a "briefing session" and agreed to take no official action. At the meeting there now seems to be a clear consensus in favor of a vigorous select subcommittee to start an immediate investigation.

The House Republicans are now agreeing with Jack Brooks in

pressing for expeditious action. Their party line now is that we "should impeach the President or get off his back." Even Vice President Ford is now commenting to reporters that if the committee does not resolve the question soon "you can say it is partisan."

It seems clear to me that Ford would like to become President as soon as possible, and that some Republicans—including McClory, Fish, Railsback, Cohen of Maine, and maybe even Trent Lott of Mississippi— would like to have Nixon off their backs and make Jerry Ford President in a hurry. In fact, a Harris poll came out yesterday showing that Ford is now the preferred Republican candidate for 1976, ahead of Reagan, Connally, and Rockefeller.

December 12 Bernie Hellring came down from Newark and our plan was to nail down the special counsel question. Rodino was indecisive all day and the discussion went on well into the evening.

The evening was extraordinarily frustrating. Hellring reiterated his belief that it would be better not to have a special counsel, and to have me direct the investigation. I told him I thought it was too late for that, and that I preferred a special counsel, either Doar or Dick Cates. We accomplished nothing all evening.

December 13 We had meetings of the committee Democratic caucus all morning, and again in the afternoon. Between the two meetings Jack Brooks and I had lunch with Bernie Segal [another former president of the American Bar Association] to discuss a number of candidates for the special counsel job. We got no help from him—he was only interested in talking about Bernie Segal.

On the way back from lunch Jack and I had a heart—to-heart talk. We are both distressed that Rodino has agreed to allow the Wilbur Mills—Russell Long Joint Committee do the investigation of Nixon's income tax. Ever since the day in October when Nixon called a worldwide combat readiness alert, Brooks and I have been pressing Rodino to have the Judiciary Committee request copies of Nixon's tax returns and financial statements. This week Brooks wrote another letter to Rodino urging him to assert our jurisdiction over Nixon's finances as part of our overall impeachment inquiry. Rodino continues to refuse to do that. Brooks says, "Our chairman is chicken."

After our two caucuses and my discussion with Brooks I am exasperated with Rodino and most of the Democrats. Holtzman is impossible. She is insisting that the Committee break up into seven separate task forces—to give each member a piece of the media action to help get Democrats elected to Congress next year.

I sometimes think that Holtzman and Waldie are the same kind of political animal as Nixon. Drinan is a separate case; for him, impeachment is a moral crusade.

Jack Brooks, Barbara Jordan, and I had some private conversations today. They—and I think John Conyers—are the only committee Democrats who really understand that the best way to proceed is with a proper investigation without showboating before the media.

At these caucus meetings Rodino's weakness as a leader become quite discernible to everyone, including Rodino. I have always said that his greatest strength is also his greatest weakness—his willingness to confer and consult with everyone for so long that issues are decided by themselves.

This evening I spoke with Peter more strongly than I ever have before. I told him it would be irresponsible for him to succumb to the "seven-ring circus" approach of Holtzman and the other junior members—and if he was thinking of doing so he had a responsibility to tell anyone who was considering coming on as special counsel that he was coming aboard a showboat for the Democrats to use to run against Nixon in the next election.

Tonight I am ready to resign. Not really—but I think to myself how wonderful it would be to leave Washington and become my own man.

December 14 Today was a better day. Rodino seems to have taken my criticism to heart. This morning he was very respectful to me and assured me he would resolve the special counsel problem promptly.

The most amusing experience I had was to interview Harvard professor Robert Keeton. I learned that even though he taught a course in trial advocacy, Keeton himself has not tried a single case in twenty-two years. I found him to be overflowingly full of himself. I had the impression that he thinks we are not quite good enough for him—and I don't think he is quite good enough for us.

After Keeton, Rodino asked me to interview a guy named Lombard—the son of a judge. Seiberling had recommended him to us. He is a handsome "Great Gatsby" kind of guy. We had an amusing conversation. "Why should I want to do this?" he asked. "After all, if I try to impeach the President and fail, I could get ruined." I said that I hoped he would want to do this case for its own sake—that it was not the kind of opportunity to turn one's back on. I said, "It's like the opportunity for love. If one does not accept it out of fear, then one is dead." His reply was, "Hell, I've turned down a lot of opportunities like that."

I had dinner and spent most of the evening with Dick Cates. Before that we talked to Kastenmeier, who had called us to his office. At first we thought he wanted to discuss how best to resolve the conflicts between Brooks and the fire-eaters, but what he really wanted was help in preparing himself for an appearance on the *Today Show*. Basically Kastenmeier, like Holtzman and Waldie, wants to ride a showboat—or maybe I should say a slowboat—until the next election.

December 15 Rodino called me from Newark. He says he has spoken to his "Italian Americans" about the possibility of appointing Lacey as our Special Counsel. Apparently, they will not forgive him if he hires the guy who put Hughie Addonizio in jail, so Lacey is out of the running. But Rodino has not yet told him; he is hoping that Lacey will decline anyway.

I called Sargent Shriver to get a reading from him on Doar. He told me that he had not yet called "the people he wanted to speak with." I assumed he meant Ted Kennedy. But he had another name to recommend: Cyrus Vance.

I also talked with Bernie Hellring. Neither he nor I can imagine a barnacled politico like Vance as our impeachment counsel. Bernie let his hair down. He is very much against John Doar—but did tell me from what sources he had negative information about Doar. Bernie favors Keeton.

Later Shriver called me back. He had been speaking to Archie Cox, who very much prefers Keeton over Doar. I was both annoyed and amused by Shriver's quoting Cox that "Keeton would have the cooperation of the Harvard faculty." [Keeton was then a big name at Harvard.] If anything, Cox's support for Keeton makes my support for Doar stronger.

So here we are now on Saturday night with three candidates left on Rodino's list: Doar, Jenner, and Keeton.

December 16 Rodino called me at my cottage and told me that he has finally decided on Doar. He is relieved that Lacey has bowed out, and so now Rodino does not have to turn him down. Rodino asked me to call Keeton and to get rid of him "gracefully." I told him I was sure he had made a good choice—and that I am now feeling very optimistic. He seemed in a good mood too. He told me he had seen the Becket film on the late show (I had mentioned it to him several times) and now understood exactly what I mean by the "Becket principle"—the playing of one's role to the fullest—and that he was ready to live by it. I reminded him jokingly that "of course Becket got beheaded for playing his role." He said, "Yes, I know that—but that's okay." I was very pleased.

December 17 There was a big snowstorm. Washington is completely closed down. It is very quiet here on the Blue Ridge, snowing again—and there is time to think. I feel optimistic. I find comfort in the snow. It is a reminder that we are all subject to forces that we cannot control.

The Judiciary Committee may well be in the eye of the most bizarre political storm of our century. Yet the aura of unreality about the impeachment of Nixon seems to have disappeared. More and more I see the process as a chore. "Place one foot in front of the other and keep moving forward," as Dick Cates says.

In a book that I keep here in Virginia there are some wonderful lines by Yeats: "You ask what makes me sigh, old friend,/What makes me shudder so?/I shudder and I sigh to think that even Cicero/And many-minded Homer were mad as the mist and snow." It is comforting to think that we are all flesh and blood, that we all have foibles and fears—are all "mad as the mist and snow."

But Nixon's madness seems buried and locked in. It seems to be the insanity of guilt and complicity, of cover-up and deceit.

8

DOAR TAKES OVER

W hen John Doar was chosen to head the impeachment investigation, he had not practiced law since leaving the Justice Department in 1968. He had gone to New York to become the director of an integrated housing project in Bedford-Stuyvesant, and later became president of the New York City Board of Education.

Although a few members of the Judiciary Committee were concerned that his legal skills might have become rusty, he had a public reputation for integrity as well as strong bipartisan support. He had originally come to the Justice Department during the Eisenhower administration with the backing of then-Congressman Melvin Laird, Republican of Wisconsin, who was well-respected throughout the House. Laird, as Nixon's Secretary of Defense, supported Doar's appointment as special counsel. Liberals tended to support him because he had been a key aide to Burke Marshall in the Kennedy Justice Department, and had become Assistant Attorney General for Civil Rights under President Johnson.

December 18 After a Democratic caucus, Rodino, Cates, and I went back to Rodino's office and met with John Doar. It was a bit of an odd situation. Rodino had not yet really offered Doar the job, but Lois had already told Doar that he would be hired. For a while we talked mostly about yesterday's snow and life in Washington in general.

I am impressed with Doar. He has dignity and a granite-like integrity. I am a bit concerned that he might take too long and be too much of a plodder. But I think Dick Cates will keep him going, as Dick puts it, "one foot in front of the other."

At one point Doar referred to himself as "chief counsel." Rodino

89

told him that his title was "special counsel"—and that I was chief counsel. Later Doar said he would be pleased to go up to Newark to confer with Rodino during the coming recess. Rodino said that wouldn't be necessary and told him to confer with me—that he had confidence in me, and that, were it not for all of my other responsibilities as chief counsel he would have had me head the impeachment inquiry staff directly. I was pleased by Doar's response: "That's fine. I think it is very important that we have a team." Doar is a good follow.

After our meeting with Rodino I was alone with Doar for a few minutes. I reminded him of the fact that the first night we had met I told him that I was in favor of impeaching the President. Doar told me tonight, "I am in favor of pressing the case to its maximum."

Doar will be officially coming on board our staff on Thursday. I wonder how it will end up. I'm afraid that Doar will be a bit too thorough—a bit too meticulous, although I think he is very impressive. He reminds me of a seventeenth-century landscape by Poussin—there is an austere conservative streak in him. Dick Cates has a kind of Cezanne pine-and-rock sturdiness—and strikes me as more of an artist. Doar seems the kind of person whom I probably will never become close to. With Dick I feel that we are like shipmates manning the guns together on a Navy destroyer.

Dick says: "This is a peaceful revolution." Strange feeling to view oneself as a lineal descendant of revolutionaries who deposed a corrupt and wicked king.

December 20 Yesterday afternoon Bob McClory had taken out a special order, and the Republicans filled the *Congressional Record* with speeches advocating open impeachment hearings and a vote on the impeachment question by no later than April.

Today there are clear signals that the Republicans are getting ready to impeach Nixon and make Jerry Ford President. Barry Goldwater has called Nixon a "liar." Also, implying that Nixon is dangerous and perhaps deranged, Goldwater is now telling reporters such things as this: "I've never known a man to be so much a loner in any field. . . . The President, I think, thinks of himself as the supreme politician in this country. And being a loner he sits by himself and tells himself what he's going to do. Now we went through this gesture period of having congressmen and senators down to see him but it seems to have ended. . . . And as a result he's not getting advice. That's his problem, he's not getting it. And when he gets it he doesn't listen to it. . . . My God, we've never had so many serious problems in the history of this nation."

I think it is also noteworthy that Senator Goldwater has a son—Barry, Jr.—who is a House member and who just happens to be a close personal friend of John Dean. It is interesting to speculate as to whether that friendship doesn't enhance Dean's credibility in the eyes of Barry, Sr.

Another signal to the Republicans to revolt came from Mel Laird, who has been Nixon's Secretary of Defense. He announced today that he is resigning on February 1. Laird is urging the Congress to vote on what he calls "the question of indictment" by March 15. I see his choice of the word *indictment* rather than *impeachment* as a reminder to Republicans that Nixon has committed a felony.

With Goldwater and Laird now separating themselves from Nixon, and Jerry Ford ready to take over the presidency, there is, it would seem to me, no way in which the organization Republicans can unite themselves without getting rid of Nixon.

In response to Laird's urging a vote by March 15, Rodino has announced that the Judiciary Committee will finish our impeachment inquiry by April 1 at the latest. He also called an informal meeting today of the senior members of the Judiciary Committee—eight Democrats and seven Republicans. There was a very good atmosphere. Wiggins and Conyers were actually agreeing that the Ervin Committee ought to turn over its files and leave impeachment to us. Most of the Republican members seemed temperate and reasonable, except for McClory, who continued to carp a little bit.

Rodino made a speech to the effect that we will all be judged by the endproduct and that the Democrats must now "do the right thing." I am convinced that Rodino wants to do the right thing; in fact, things are coming together to make him do the right thing. It is good politics to do the right thing.

It reminds me of what Congressman Hays of Arkansas has humorously described as Political Axiom Number 1: "When in doubt, do right."

December 20 Today was Doar's first day. It has been an extremely trying day for me.

I had breakfast with Rodino and later we went back to the office. The press conference was scheduled for 10:30 A.M. Rodino sat at the microphones between Doar and myself. Hutchinson reluctantly sat a bit sideways on the other side of Doar. The conference went well. Nevertheless, I became very disturbed.

Last night Rodino had prepared a press release announcing Doar's appointment. The last four paragraphs of the release defined Doar's role as it related to mine: "Until Doar's appointment today, the inquiry staff worked directly under the supervision of Committee General Counsel Jerome M. Zeifman. Zeifman will retain overall responsibility both for the impeachment inquiry and regular staff activities. . . .

"'Both Zeifman and Doar will work closely with me,' said Rodino. 'I want to stress that my intention is to proceed in an orderly, lawful, dignified way to carry out my responsibility to determine what actions, if any, [the committee] may wish to take with respect to the impeachment resolutions now pending before me.'"

This morning the release was sent to the House press gallery, but at the last minute it was retracted by Lois and then recirculated with the last four paragraphs omitted. I later checked this out with Lois. According to her, the only reason for this was because of a typographical error in the very last words of the release, which read "before me" rather than "before us." But in the terribly political world in which I live I will never know for sure whether or not some policy consideration caused the release to be killed by Rodino at the very last minute. My guess is that the release was killed by Lois, without Rodino's knowledge. The subjective problems created for me by the last-minute retraction of the press release were exacerbated by events following the press conference. As soon as the reporters left, I said to Doar, "And now what can I do to help?" Doar replied, "The first thing I want to do is talk to Lois alone." Surprised by his curtness, I suggested that we talk to Lois together—and then have lunch together to talk about the investigation that had been already begun under my supervision.

Doar and Lois and I then sat alone together in Room 2141. Doar turned to Lois, and without consulting me, they began formulating policies for putting lawyers and investigators on the committee's payroll and handling public relations and press inquiries for the committee.

Afterward we had a short lunch in the cafeteria. Then I took Doar to meet the top staff members—starting with Dick Cates and Bill Dixon—who have been accumulating confidential files on Watergate and possible charges against Nixon. Since the committee's rules preclude persons who are not members of Congress or on the official committee staff to have access to such files, Lois left us reluctantly.

When he talked to Dick Cates and Bill Dixon I was struck by Doar's curtness. Dick had carefully prepared a written memorandum as well as some reading material for Doar in anticipation of his arrival. The material included an excellent legal analysis known as the Dobrovir

Brief, which analyzed evidence of twenty-eight violations by Nixon of federal criminal statutes. Dick and Bill both suggested that Doar begin by reading the brief. Doar whitened and said, "No! I refuse to do that." He then explained, "If the press wants to write a story about my first day on the job I don't want anyone to be able to tell them that the first thing I began with was that brief!"

Cates and Doar are very different types of people. Doar is rigid and unshakable—and somewhat constipated. It will be interesting to see if he can work well with Dick and Bill, both of whom are top-notch investigators.

I was confused and angered by Doar all afternoon—and concerned about his latching on to Lois in a way that is intended to bypass me in his dealings with Rodino and the committee.

In the evening Doar came back to my office to talk to me. I couldn't quite understand what he was saying except that it seemed clear that he was not about to buy Cates and Dixon's understanding of the case against Nixon. Doar seems to want to leave these kinds of criminal charges to the Special Prosecutor and to the Watergate Committee. He talked to me as though he believed that we ought not to be going into those things. I said, "Suppose Nixon has engaged in a conspiracy to obstruct justice, or suppose he has received bribes? The Constitution says he can be impeached for bribery. Don't we have an obligation to develop that case?" He remained stonefaced and didn't reply. When I said that I thought we had an obligation to investigate whether Nixon had committed criminal tax fraud, he said, "No! To do that we would be substituting ourselves for the Internal Revenue Service. That would be inappropriate for a congressional committee."

Doar then went into Rodino's office without me, closing the door behind him. A few minutes later Rodino called me in and Doar apologized, saying that he did not mean to exclude me. In front of Rodino he then recapitulated his concern about going into charges for obstruction of justice, bribery, or tax fraud.

It ended up with Rodino trying to gloss over the differences between Doar and me. He suggested that what Doar had probably meant to say was that we ought not to start from scratch but should take up where other investigations have left off and expand them.

After our conversation with Rodino, Doar and I left the Rayburn Building together. I offered to drop Doar off at an address near my house. In the car I tried to be friendly. He remained silent.

There is something aloof about Doar that is not to my liking. I tried to crack that aloofness in my way, but did not succeed. Maybe it is more a matter of shallowness than aloofness.

I have very mixed feelings about Doar right now. I think he has a lot to learn about Congress. He obviously still has the bureaucratic Justice Department view of Congress—the sort of attitude that promotes concerns about Congress substituting its judgment for that of bureaucrats in the Department of Justice or the IRS.

December 22 Yesterday was the last full day before the Christmas recess. The House was in session until after midnight. While on the House floor Rodino and I had a conversation with John Rhodes [new Minority Leader]. He has been telling the press that he thinks the chances are "pretty good" that the Judiciary Committee and the House will vote to impeach Nixon—and if this happens, he thinks the President should consider resigning. Rhodes seems anxious to avoid embarrassing Rodino—and has also been trying to assure the press that the Judiciary Committee is not likely to stall the impeachment proceedings. Like Goldwater, Rhodes is from Arizona and a conservative. My impression is that he is more anxious than Rodino to get Nixon out of office—but wants the Democrats, and not the Republicans, to take the lead in making the case.

Because of the all-day session it was not until late last night that I was able to talk to Lois—and to air my concerns about Thursday's events. I don't know the extent to which my relationship with Lois will survive. I don't believe that I can really put it to Rodino on the subject of Lois. I don't think that he is strong enough to stop her from trying to dominate him.

I am also not certain as to whether Lois is a good or bad influence. For the most part I think that her social and political values are very good and are similar to my own. I suppose that in the long run it adds up that she is a good influence. At any rate, I am tired of adjusting, tired of adapting, tired of defining and redefining roles. I'll be glad when I can retire and become my own man.

December 24 It is now Christmas Eve. I am trying to rest. The swollen veins in my left leg are aching. I keep postponing surgery. I am in a strange mood, saying half-jokingly, "This may be the world's last Christmas." It is indeed a gloomy Christmas, with the god-awful cloud hanging over the government. Washington is in the grip of a terrible disease. I think Rodino feels this way too. He called me a little while ago from New Jersey—not about anything in particular, but just to wish me "Merry Christmas!"

After Doar became an official member of the Judiciary Committee's staff, he had an agenda that he kept mostly to himself. It was not until after Nixon's resignation that New York journalist Jimmy Breslin was to inform the public that "Doar had made two major decisions about how the case should be conducted. He decided not to do any investigating of his own, but to simply pick up the materials gathered by the Ervin Committee and the Special Prosecutor's office and work from there. He thought that an investigation, interrogating witnesses on television, would give the public the idea that everybody was doing the same thing over and over and the entire idea of impeachment might lose its effect."

In a best-selling book entitled *How the Good Guys Finally Won*, Breslin gave Doar's hidden decision a favorable spin. Breslin ignored the fact that the Ervin Committee's authority had been expressly limited by Ted Kennedy's amendment to preclude the committee from investigating presidential misconduct, and the Special Prosecutor had decided to exercise "prosecutorial discretion" to intentionally avoid investigating Nixon.

In the winter of 1973, Doar confided only in his key staff aides and in Burke Marshall—who had been Doar's Justice Department boss during the Kennedy administration. Since the Kennedy Justice Department had conducted illegal wiretaps as well as black-bag burglaries and a variety of political surveillance programs, Doar decided it would be impolitic for him now to investigate the Nixon administration's continuation of such government-sponsored crimes.

It was not until 1975—after Watergate was no longer a burning issue—that Doar's own secret surveillance activities first became public. A commission headed by Vice President Nelson Rockefeller was established by President Ford to investigate the CIA. Although the media took little notice, the commission's report revealed that, as Assistant Attorney General for Civil Rights in 1967, Doar had recommended the establishment of "a single intelligence unit to analyze the FBI information we receive about persons who make the urban ghetto their base of operations." In approving Doar's recommendations, Attorney General Ramsey Clark had cautioned Doar and other assistant attorneys general that "the planning and creation of the unit must be kept in strictest confidence."

As the Rockefeller Commission Report of 1975 further noted:

WITHOUT HONOR

The FBI was to constitute only one source of information for the proposed unit. As additional sources Doar suggested federal poverty programs, Labor Department programs, and neighborhood legal services. Doar recognized the "sensitivity" of using such additional sources, but nevertheless thought these sources would have access to relevant facts. Other sources of dissident information suggested by Doar included the Intelligence Unit of the Internal Revenue Service and perhaps the Post Office Department. . . .

Several years later, during the Carter administration, Rodino recommended that Doar be appointed as Attorney General or head of the FBI. Shortly after that, a conservative critic of both Rodino and Doar accused each of them of being in league with Arthur Schlesinger, who had authored *The Imperial Presidency,* a critique of the Nixon administration. With extensive documentation, conservative author Victor Lasky wrote:

In Congress many years before coming to public notice, Rodino had never expected to be courted by the likes of Schlesinger, one of the nation's more publicized intellectuals. And in all probability Schlesinger had never expected to be courting the likes of Rodino, a product of the Essex County Democratic Organization. But the stakes were high.

One of [Schlesinger's] pals from Camelot days now actually running the impeachment inquiry was none other than John Doar, formerly head of the Civil Rights Division in Robert Kennedy's Justice Department. This of course was the same Doar who, when informed of the FBI's campaign to denigrate Martin Luther King, had done nothing to stop it. And it was the same Doar who had urged Attorney General Clark in 1967 to seek intelligence information from government workers in the nation's black communities. Doar's memorandum, written September 27, 1967, following the Detroit riots, led to the creation of a computerized intelligence file that eventually grew to contain some 18,000 names, mainly of black militants. This was the kind of activity which Doar and others on the impeachment panel [had] sought to characterize as "abuses of power" under Nixon.

[During the Nixon administration] as president of the New

York City Board of Education Doar did a switch. He catered to the black militants, refusing for example to dismiss extremist teachers who made anti-Semitic remarks in class. Arnold Forster and Benjamin R. Epstein of the Anti-Defamation League pointed out that "when William O. Marley, chairman of the Brownsville Model Cities Committee, in a long anti-Semitic diatribe, repeatedly attacked Jews as dominant in the school system . . . there was no challenge from President Doar."

When Frank Thompson had brought our impeachment funding resolution to the House floor, Rodino had pledged that we would use the $1 million for "an investigation of Watergate that will leave no stones unturned." Extending his remarks in the *Congressional Record,* he added: "Let us now proceed—with such care and decency and thoroughness and honor—that the vast majority of the American people, and their children after them, will say: 'That was the right course. There was no other way.'"

I was beginning to have my doubts.

9

THE NON-INVESTIGATION BEGINS

Dick Cates had told Rodino and me, "We have enough evidence to convict the President of conspiring to obstruct justice. My God, if this wasn't the President of the United States, and I couldn't secure a conviction, they could take my license. It is horrendously solid." When Doar became our Special Counsel, Cates handed him a stack of documents and told him the same thing, adding, "You don't have a firecracker here, you have a hell of a howitzer."

Yet at the beginning of the Christmas recess, Doar requested that Cates be fired because, as he advised Rodino and me, he considered Cates to be a reckless advocate of impeachment. Peter was indecisive. Bernie Hellring and I opposed Doar's request; Lois D'Andre urged Rodino to follow Doar's advice. In the end, Cates stayed.

That recess, Peter decided to spend some time resting in Florida, and he asked me not to contact him unless it was an emergency—in which case I was to call Bernie Hellring first. He also suggested that I confer with Bernie as freely as I did with him.

Before he left, Rodino instructed Doar to recruit a staff for the impeachment inquiry. He had made it clear that before anyone was hired, my approval was necessary. Peter also authorized me to sign his name on any payroll vouchers.

I worked in my office daily between Christmas and New Year's, but I made no diary entries. I was not too busy—I was simply reluctant to record conclusions that I feared I might be reaching too quickly. It seemed to me that Doar was unwilling to do the job which he was hired to do—of conducting a thorough investigation of possible misconduct by the President.

Particularly troubling was that Doar used Burke Marshall as a behind-the-scenes advisor. Doar had previously told Rodino and me that he wanted the freedom to consult with Marshall about problems that might arise during the inquiry, but I had advised against this. Committee rules as well as House rules prohibited disclosure of confidential evidentiary files to persons who were not members of the committee or its staff. In addition, I reminded Rodino about Clark Clifford's warning to me about Marshall's connection with Ted Kennedy, whom the public saw as an enemy of Nixon—a connection that could destroy the credibility of the inquiry. Somewhat reluctantly, Rodino had granted Doar's request on the condition that Doar be very discreet about communications with Marshall.

After Rodino left for Florida, Doar began to quarrel with me frequently about personnel matters and hiring policies. He was recruiting appellate lawyers from large Wall Street and Washington law firms who had no investigative experience. Many of them came from firms whose clients had interests in Watergate-related matters. Doar wanted me to sign payroll vouchers summarily, without inquiring into the background or qualifications of the impeachment staff.

Doar also wanted to hire some individuals to whom he had personal ties. One of these was his longtime companion, Renata Adler, who was a writer. He wanted to hire her as a speechwriter and public relations consultant for Rodino. Others included his daughter, his former law school roommate, his brother's law clerk, and children of friends. None of these people had appropriate investigative experience. I was particularly concerned about one applicant because of her close ties to Burke Marshall. This was Hillary Rodham, who had been Marshall's protege at Yale and who had been recommended by Peter Edelman, a former top aide to Robert Kennedy.

Incredibly, Doar rejected my suggestion that we hire lawyers who were experienced enough to take depositions and cross-examine officials of the Justice Department and the CIA. His response was, "I do not believe in cross-examination. I win cases on the basis of my witnesses and the other guy's documents." Doar also insisted that it would not be necessary to interrogate Justice Department lawyers under oath since they could be relied on to tell the truth to Congress.

Doar refused even to interview two tax lawyers whom I had

highly recommended to investigate Nixon's finances and income tax returns. One was Charles Rump, a state prosecutor from California who had many years of experience investigating tax fraud. In discarding their resumes, Doar maintained that it would be improper for us to investigate charges of tax fraud against the President.

Frustrated that Doar seemed to be jeopardizing the inquiry by rejecting the most basic operating procedures, I called Bernie Hellring. Bernie and I agreed that Doar seemed to be intentionally delaying the proceedings. Instead of calling Rodino in Florida, however, Hellring recommended that I simply announce to Doar that I could not act on his staff appointments without adequate information. The signing of any official appointment vouchers would have to be postponed until Rodino's return.

Because of my disagreements with Doar, my relationship with Lois became severely strained. Doar had wanted me to put Lois on the committee payroll as his administrative assistant and to give her an office adjoining his. I was already concerned that by acting as Rodino's personal surrogate Lois was undermining the morale of the staff lawyers and secretaries, and I was becoming fearful that the press would begin to report Lois's key role as Rodino's eminence grise.

I decided that it would be irresponsible for me to share my concerns only with Hellring. He was not associated with the Judiciary Committee in any official way. Just as Doar was officially restricted by House and committee rules from divulging evidence in our confidential files to Marshall, I could not share evidence with Hellring.

Therefore, on the morning of January 2 I walked into Jack Brooks's private office and closed the door behind me. I told Brooks that I wanted to share some conclusions I had come to: "One, Doar is inept as a lawyer. Two, Doar refuses to investigate any illegal roles that the FBI, CIA, or Justice Department may have played in Watergate. Three, Doar is unwilling to investigate the possibility that Nixon has committed tax fraud. I have also come to another, tentative, conclusion about Doar. Although I don't yet have all the facts, I have a very strong feeling that Doar wants either to avoid impeaching Nixon or to delay it for as long aspossible. I feel that Doar is improperly relying on Burke Marshall for advice on the evidence against Nixon. I have a strong feeling that Marshall's political strategy is to keep Nixon twisting in the wind until the end of his term to increase the chances of electing Teddy Kennedy President in 1976.

Admittedly," I added, "I don't know if I can trust my feelings."

Brooks bit down on his cigar and said, "Goddammit! You remind me of me! I went to Sam Rayburn once when I was a freshman congressman and said the same thing—that I didn't have all the facts, but that I had strong, strong feelings. Jerry, let me give you the same advice that Sam Rayburn gave me: 'Trust your feelings. If you can't trust your feelings you'll never survive around here. Trust your feelings or you're dead.'"

That night, I resumed my diary.

January 2, 1974 Many things have happened. The situation with Doar has reached a climax. Last week I conferred daily and at great length with Bernie Hellring. I have checked out every move with respect to Doar. Bernie [who had recommended we hire Bert Jenner or Robert Keeton rather than Doar] says, "I was afraid this would happen. Doar is a son of a bitch. Doar is an incompetent lawyer. Doar is not very smart." Bernie says, "You and Peter are going to have to stop Doar from becoming a Frankenstein. As chief counsel you will have to teach Doar what a congressional impeachment investigation is all about."

All last week Doar insisted, "I'm going to do things my own way." I told him, "The House of Representatives is made up of 435 members. They delegated the responsibility to conduct an impeachment inquiry to the 38 members of the Judiciary Committee—which has a chairman who can be overruled by a majority vote of the committee and is also subject to the rules of the House—most of which go back at least two centuries to Jefferson's manual. The impeachment of the President is not going to be done your way, my way, Peter Rodino's way, or Tip O'Neill's or Jack Brooks's way. It is going to be done the congressional way. No one person's judgment can he relied on. The judgments of Congress are collective judgments. That is what the Congress is about! That is what democracy is all about."

Stonefaced, Doar replied, "That is not what this case is about! I will do this case in my own way." At one point in our discussions he also said: "You have had no actual experience in the prosecution of criminal cases. I have. I was an Assistant Attorney General."

I told Doar that this was not a criminal prosecution, but rather a civil proceeding based on a congressional investigation. I added that I had previously headed a congressional investigation of the Nixon Department of Justice that focused on Assistant Attorney General

David Norman's failure to enforce civil rights laws in Mississippi. I considered Norman to be dishonorable, and reminded Doar that a federal judge had characterized Norman's failure as "Pilate-like."

I thought Doar would be sympathetic to my criticism of his successor as Assistant Attorney General. But Doar became angry: "Don't try to impugn David Norman's integrity!" I replied, "Every member of our subcommittee on civil rights—including such Nixon supporters as Chuck Wiggins—has officially signed on to a congressional finding that Norman had abdicated his responsibilities as Assistant Attorney General by refusing to enforce the Voting Rights Act." Doar demurred strongly, claiming that Norman had been intimidated by Ehrlichman into doing what he had.

Reflecting on this tonight, I see David Norman as immoral. Norman permitted himself to be emasculated by the White House, and Nixon rewarded him with the high honor of wearing a black robe and sitting on a bench in Superior Court. My deepest fear is that John Doar and David Norman are both products of the same mold.

Thank God that I have talked to Bernie at length and have dissociated myself from any decision that Doar has made in Rodino's absence. Thank God for Bernie, who helped me understand the need for that. Also, thank God for Jack Brooks. I see Brooks as the most patriotic politician on the committee. His partisanship is so deep and fierce that he believes that the best politics for the Democrats is to do now what is best for the United States—to impeach Nixon and make Ford President. Brooks says he knows Burke Marshall and also thinks that Marshall wants to help Nixon stay in the White House.

Brooks described Doar's delaying tactics as a flawed seduction strategy: "Doar would wine 'em, dine 'em, take 'em to night clubs, buy 'em drinks, and dance all night. Then when Doar gets 'em home, they're too tired to fuck." He also told me an interesting story. When he was a Marine in World War II, he served under a craven officer who ran away from the Japanese, leaving Brooks in charge. I left with the impression that if Rodino doesn't take control, Brooks will.

January 3 Janet Howard [a personal friend of Lois's whom Lois had recruited to serve as a secretary on Doar's staff], who until now has been loyal to Lois, talked to me today in confidence. She is very distressed. She dislikes Doar—thinks he's a "martinet." Jane also thinks Lois is going too far in acting as Rodino's surrogate and throwing her weight around.

A few weeks ago Rodino invited her to dine with him in the member's dining room. Carl Albert was there dining alone with an exotic young woman. Referring to the Speaker's companion, Rodino said, "That's Carl Albert's girl. She has the nicest clothes, the best of everything, but I don't see what he sees in her."

. Rodino had also told Janet laughingly that one of the reasons why Albert had wanted to have Ford confirmed so quickly was because—as next in line to be President—Albert was being guarded around the clock by the Secret Service. It was interfering with his sex life. Janet said it made her feel sick.

Tonight I wonder if maybe Rodino is relying on what Bernie Hellring calls "the Calabrian fisherman's strategy—keeping many lines in the water." As I see it tonight, Rodino has at least two lines in the water. Dick Cates is one line; John Doar is another. If we do right, we will catch the Nixon impeachment fish on the Cates line. To catch a larger political fish—the presidency for Teddy Kennedy—it seems Rodino hopes to use the Doar line.

January 4 Today Doar wants to hire one Joe Woods, his close friend and former law school roommate—a corporate lawyer who specializes in railroad reorganizations—to be "Senior Associate Special Counsel." Woods wants to sign on for only 120 days. Also, Doar asked me whether the conflict of interest statute applies to lawyers hired by Congress. I said, "I don't know, John. I never had that problem before. But even if it doesn't apply, we should be stricter than statutory requirements."

January 5 I chopped some firewood earlier this morning to let off steam about Doar. But I'm still angry and am now sitting by the fireplace with my tape recorder trying to sort things out.

Doar's got a formula—cases are won with the other guy's documents and your witnesses. When he was Assistant Attorney General for Civil Rights, he must have had the same formula, and here is how it probably worked: Black man brought to police station—cops call him "nigger," beat him on the head till dead. No documents, no cross-examination of police. Apply the Doar formula—no documents, no case. And he was Assistant Attorney General for Civil Rights!

Dick Cates could do it. He would do it right—would get the facts.

Remember the lesson in law school: "The most effective engine invented by man to arrive at the truth is cross-examination." That's what Professor Wigmore used to say. I talked to Doar about that. "Why not cross-examine Haldeman? Why not Ehrlichman? Why not Howard Hunt? Why not Mitchell? How about the President? Why not at least ask him some questions? We could even do it politely. Why not just ask him about his income?" Doar said, "We shouldn't go into his personal finances—we can't do a tax fraud case." I said, "Why not? How about the evidence that Nixon has received bribes? Shouldn't we let Bill Dixon continue to investigate that?" Doar said, "No! Dixon is not a good lawyer. He's a fool."

Doar doesn't even want to question John Dean. It seems to me rather that Doar is the fool.

This morning here in Virginia I see clearly what "doing it right" means! Doing it right means we get the facts. We ask the right questions. Who ordered Hunt and Liddy to break into Watergate? What were they after? We should get the facts by taking depositions and by cross-examination. Damn it, Doar—get the facts!

January 6 Francis called me first thing in the morning. [Francis O'Brien, Rodino's administrative assistant, had been recruited by Lois D'Andre. Several years later, he became a political consultant, working on the national campaigns of Geraldine Ferraro and Michael Dukakis.] He told me that Rodino is back. He also gave me the news that Lois left Washington. He said it as though he were announcing that Caesar had crossed back over the Rubicon. I thought perhaps the Lois problem was over.

Later Bernie called and explained that he had met with Rodino in Newark last night and they had talked again at length this morning. Bernie now has a strong suspicion that Francis is "in cahoots" with Doar, Marshall, and Ted Kennedy—and along with Lois and Doar is not only bad-mouthing me to Rodino, but is bad-mouthing Tip O'Neill and Jack Brooks.

Another interesting thing. Rodino has learned that the Republicans have decided to hire Bert Jenner as their minority counsel as a counterpart to Doar. Ironically, Jenner was one of the people whom Bernie had sounded for the Special Prosecutor's job before we hired Doar. Jenner had told Bernie then that he was not interested. Later, Bernie had conferred with Jenner about Doar—and Jenner had given Doar a very low grade. Bernie thinks that Jenner is probably tied to the White House. I said, "I hope not. Jenner is from Chicago and has the support of McClory and Railsback, both of whom are Illinois Republicans like Jenner. I believe that most Illinois Republicans are ready to impeach Nixon." Bernie also agrees that maybe Jenner will "do right."

Bernie is a fascinating guy. Maybe some of his Mafia clients, through Bernie, have a kind of control over Rodino. The Mafia might well have an interest in keeping democracy alive. Organized crime did not do well under Mussolini or Hitler, and apparently does not thrive under Castro or the Soviets. I don't think there are as many well-paid criminal defense lawyers in all of Russia as there are in New Jersey.

Tomorrow the Advisory Group meets. On Wednesday I am scheduled to check in at GW Hospital for surgery on my leg, which has knots of swollen veins.

January 7 Today things went just the opposite of the way Bernie anticipated. Rodino had Francis summon me to a meeting in Peter's office. Rodino sat me down in front of Francis and proceeded to reprimand me. He did it "Mafia style"—starting with a kiss. He began by telling me that he was fond of me, admired me, respected me, etc. Then he reprimanded me for resisting Doar's effort to put Lois on the committee payroll and for failing to cooperate with Doar. He told me my sensitivity was a great asset to him but that it was also my greatest weakness.

Rodino also told me that I really owed my job to Lois. Had it not been for Lois, he said, I would not be Chief Counsel—that he had chosen me over his closer friend Jim Cline primarily because of Lois. He told me how much he trusted Lois, and that there was no reason why I should be upset by her working as Doar's assistant. He ended by insisting that there was simply a communication problem, that I was too sensitive.

It was quite a performance. (I think tonight that it was probably mostly for Francis's benefit so he could report it back to Lois.) I quietly stuck to my guns and told Rodino in front of Francis that I still felt that I had protected the Judiciary Committee's interest all the time that Rodino was in Florida and had consulted with Bernie continuously in accordance with his instructions. I also said that it was Doar more than Lois whom I mistrusted, since it had become clear to me that Doar was unwilling to investigate Nixon.

Rodino then called Doar into his office and gave him the mildest of suggestions concerning the need to cooperate with me. I suspect that Rodino is really torn between his desire to acquiesce to the demands of Lois and his desire to keep his manhood intact. But even if all of this was only an act on Rodino's part, it marks a turning point in my relationship with him.

I recall my friend Ed Willis [former congressman from Louisiana for whom I worked]. Once at a hearing Ed also put on an act of chewing me out. While I was cross-examining a witness—the president of a coal company—he leaned over and whispered to me, "Jerry, don't worry. Everything is okay, but I'm about to chew your ass out. I'll explain the reason later." He then made a public display of reprimanding me for badgering the witness. After the hearing, Willis explained that he had done it for the benefit of a constituent who had walked into the hearing room with a lobbyist for the coal industry.

After Rodino finished reprimanding me in front of Francis, we went off together to the meeting of the Advisory Group. At the meeting I found myself surprisingly calm. Rodino sat sheepishly in the chairman's big leather chair. Although he had treated me shabbily, I think he knows that he has abused himself more than me.

The Advisory Group meeting was a bit of a joke. Doar did not discuss any plans for the investigation itself. He distributed a three-page memorandum to the members containing an outline of administrative matters relating to the size of the staff and its budget as well as the need to develop security procedures.

In contrast to Doar, Dan Cohen of our regular staff gave the members something of value: a 900-page book he had prepared entitled *Impeachment: Selected Materials on Procedure.* After the closed-door meeting, Francis brought the press in, and although Doar had nothing to do with Dan's book, he had the press photograph him handing a copy to Rodino. [The photograph appeared the next day on the front page of the *New York Times.* The caption indicated the book was a lengthy report that Doar had prepared.]

The members of the group were very pleased by the swarm of reporters and TV cameras that flooded the hearing room when the closed doors were finally opened.

After the meeting I was alone with Peter for a short time in his cubbyhole office next to the hearing room. He was especially friendly. We talked again about the situation with Francis and Doar, but avoided the subject of Lois. In private he seemed to be agreeing with me. He was pleased that I was pressing Doar—a role which he is reluctant to assume directly.

January 8 Rodino went back to Newark today. I spent the day clearing up some routine administrative matters in my office in preparation for my going to the hospital tomorrow for surgery on my leg.

I worked late in the evening with Dan Cohen and then he and I had dinner at the Hawk and Dove with Dick Cates. Dick began to explain his theory about the "White House horrors."

We discussed the possibility that Howard Hunt's wife had been murdered—a mind-boggling thought. [Mrs. Hunt had been killed in an unusual air crash while carrying a large amount of cash in her suitcase.] According to Dick, Hunt was a key guy in Watergate, and Dorothy Hunt was perhaps even more important in the cover-up since she was demanding the hush money from the White House on his behalf. [Some years later I was to learn that Dorothy Hunt had been in psychiatric treatment, and that her psychiatrist had subsequently disappeared under mysterious circumstances.]

Dick also indicated that he is less unhappy with Doar. I have not told Dick that I had a major clash with Doar and Lois and Francis over their efforts to persuade Rodino to fire Dick.

January 9 I checked into George Washington University Hospital. Rested in preparation for surgery tomorrow. I was pleased with the professionalism with which the surgeon and anesthesiologist involved me in a collective decision to use spinal anesthesia. Democracy in microcosm.

January 10 The operation was successful. After the anesthesia had worn off, Rodino called to see how I was doing. Also, Bob Kastenmeier dropped in to see me. His wife was operated on by the same surgeon this morning and is in a room near mine. He is very brooding—expressed concern about Doar's role.

January 11 Stayed in bed all day. Have had a lot of time to think. Have been thinking about resigning from the Judiciary Committee—but, of course I won't.

The strongest member of the committee is Jack Brooks. A reporter had once described him as "the only member of Congress that President Johnson is afraid of." I recall the conversation I had with him shortly after Rodino had chosen me to be chief counsel. Brooks had called me to his office and said he wanted to get to know me better and to let me know that he expected me to regard myself as accountable to the entire committee and not be "just Pete Rodino's water boy."

"Ziffman," he snarled, deliberately mispronouncing my name, "I just want you to know, you better be straight with me, 'cause if you're not I'll fuck you like you never been fucked before." I replied, "Let me tell you something. There is no way you can fuck me. There is nothing I want or need from you or Peter Rodino or the whole Judiciary Committee. As for being straight with you, you can count on that because that's my style."

Brooks smiled and offered me a cigar from a box on his desk. Then he said, "Wait a minute, that's not my best box." He went to the safe in his office and returned with a box of Havanas. From that moment on, we were friends.

I have also been doing some reading, mostly Yeats. I enjoy "Marching Song"—about an Irish soldier hung by the English:

> *There, standing on the cart, He sang it from his heart . . .*
> *"A girl I had, but she followed another,*
> *Money I had, and it went in the night,*
> *Strong drink I had, and it brought me to sorrow,*
> *But a good strong cause, and blows are delight."*

January 12 Dick Cates visited me in the hospital. We talked further about John Dean, and agreed that Dean was brought into Nixon's inner sanctum and given the title of "counsel" as a way of enabling Nixon to assert that his conversations with Dean were confidential attorney-client communications and so exempt from disclosure to a court.

January 13 I was discharged from the hospital today, but will have to recuperate at home for a few more days before I can go back to work.

An hour or two after getting home I went for a walk and met Charlie Joelson [former congressman from Paterson, New Jersey, who had become a judge]. For several years Joelson refused even to speak to Rodino. He confided in me that he did not think Peter could rise to the occasion. Like Joelson I fear that Rodino will not be able to cut the mustard. If there is hope for Rodino it will be through the prodding of Bernie, O'Neill, Brooks, Cates, and me.

January 14 To my surprise Lois, Doar, and Francis all called me this morning. Lois called first. She told me she is resigning from the committee staff as of January 31 and is going back to Newark and law school. Later Doar called. He and I had a better conversation than we ever had before. He asked my opinion of Jaworski's refusal to turn over evidence to us. We also discussed a statement by Attorney General Saxbe—who is saying that we have no right to investigate the President. I suggested that we start preparing subpoenas for service on the President as soon as possible.

January 15 Nixon has appointed James St. Clair, a trial lawyer with Hale and Dorr in Boston, to represent him in the impeachment proceedings. St. Clair is also the criminal defense lawyer for Nixon's former aide Charles Colson. A new strategy seems to be emerging from the White House. It is the traditional strategy of the guilty criminal defendant—delay. In this regard Jaworski, Saxbe, and now St. Clair are trying to slow down our investigation.

I suspect that there will be significant support among the Kennedy Democrats for going along with this strategy. In that context, Bernie's comment that "Francis is in cahoots with Kennedy" comes back to me.

Bernie and I both believe that John Kennedy corrupted the Justice Department by appointing his brother Bobby, who had also been his campaign manager, as Attorney General. I wonder about the Doar-Kennedy connection. God save us from lawyers who sell out to politicians. I hope that Doar is not one of them.

January 16 Still recuperating. I went out for a walk this morning and bumped into Merle Baumgart. He is still unemployed, and is still angry at Rodino and Lois because Rodino fired him last year on the urging of Lois. [Merle had been Rodino's administrative assistant—and Lois's boss—until he was replaced by Francis O'Brien in 1973. In 1975, he was killed when his car was forced off a road and over a cliff under suspicious circumstances.] Merle and I had a gloomy conversation. He said, "Rodino's seat in Congress is more important to him and to Lois than bringing Nixon to justice."

January 17 Still recuperating at home and taking longer walks to exercise my leg, which now feels great. No more pain at all. I am again in a mood to leave Washington. My few days of walking along the streets, talking with shopkeepers, has reminded me that there is a real world of people away from Capitol Hill who buy and sell things other than political influence.

Rodino called me today. Asked how I was feeling, and then proceeded to tell me what a strain he is under. He says he needs me back at work by the end of the recess. The members are pressing him to subpoena the Nixon tapes. He says he has instructed Doar to consult with me more frequently, especially about the committee's subpoena authority.

I had an interesting chat with Frank Polk on the phone about Wiggins. Wiggins is critical of Bert Jenner for suggesting to the press that a president could be impeached for the acts of his subordinates. Frank and I are convinced that Wiggins, whom we both respect, will defend Nixon to the bitter end.

January 17 Wilbur Mills made a statement that Nixon ought to resign. I feel optimistic. Nixon cannot possibly survive in office. Yet if he gets out by resignation the dangerous disease that created him may well persist. The greatest danger is the weakness of our national will as reflected in the weakness of Congress.

Other people besides myself were making noises about the delay in the impeachment proceedings. Vice President Ford made a speech at that time to a national convention of farmers. Ford lashed out at those Democrats who he said were "bent on stretching out the ordeal of Watergate for their own purpose" and accused a "relatively small group of political activists" of scheming to "cripple the President by dragging out the preliminaries to impeachment for as long as they can and to use the whole affair for maximum political advantage . . . their aim is total victory for themselves and total defeat not only of President Nixon but of the Republican policies for which he stands."

January 19 Bill Dixon came to see me at home. Bill wants to resign from the impeachment inquiry staff and to return to the committee's regular staff. He is one of the most able congressional investigators I have known. [Subsequently, Dixon enjoyed a successful career as Chief Counsel to the House Banking Committee, Insurance Commissioner of Wisconsin, Alternate Director of U.S. World Bank, and manager of Senator Gary Hart's presidential campaign.] Before becoming a lawyer, Bill had been employed as a private investigator. Prior to Doar's appointment as Special Counsel, I had assigned Bill the task of investigating the possibility of bribery charges being brought against Nixon.

Bill is distressed by Doar's refusal to allow any investigation of the bribery questions, such as the ITT scandal and the milk fund case. Bill feels that there is already evidence that will lead to clear cases of criminal misconduct by Nixon.

Bill says "Doar is a horse's ass. Doesn't understand people or politics and will probably fuck up the whole impeachment inquiry." Yet Bill is also convinced that Nixon will not survive. As Bill puts it, "It will not be because of Doar but simply because of all the other pots that are boiling."

I asked Bill to postpone his final decision until after Congress reconvenes. Hopefully Tip O'Neill and Jack Brooks will be able to persuade Rodino to light a fire under Doar.

Bill and I also talked a bit about Edwards and Kastenmeier and their abdication of responsibility to press for an investigation. As I told Bill, I respect Edwards as a fine person, yet he is not able to go into combat. At best he would be a conscientious ambulance driver. As for Kastemeier, Manny Celler used to make fun of him: "Kastenmeier is a brooder. He stalks the halls of Congress, like a political Hamlet holding the skull of Yorick."

After listening to Bill, I have been thinking that Rodino and Doar may well keep Nixon in office. Rodino will avoid investigating Nixon out of fear of the Department of Justice and the weakness born of excessive flexibility. Doar will avoid investigating Nixon out of the weakness that comes from excessive rigidity.

Tonight I hope and pray that Nixon will resign in the very near future and that the country will be spared the agony of an impeachment trial. But if he does resign, the question will persist as to whether the symptom has been removed without curing the disease.

January 20 I have been studying Edmund Burke's impeachment of Warren Hastings in the House of Lords. I got Burke's entire four-day speech from the Library of Congress and have been reading it. Beautiful stuff.

Burke was the strongest supporter of the rights of the American colonies, as well as the just causes of the Irish and Indian colonials. The 1778 trial transcripts of Burke's impeachment of Hastings for abusing his powers in governing India were sold by book dealers in Philadelphia and inspired the framers of the impeachment clause of our Constitution.

January 21 Today was my first day back at work since the surgery. I felt a certain kind of serenity going back to work. I resolved that from now on I will be own man—with no personal loyalties either to Rodino or anyone else.

In the morning Bill Dixon came to see me. To my surprise he insists on resigning from Doar's staff immediately. Bill was a bit shaken and quoted Doar as having said to him, "Someday I am sure you will make a good lawyer." I will try my best to utilize Bill's talents and skills in whatever role I and the regular committee staff have with respect to the impeachment.

I had lunch today with Frank Polk. Frank shares my view of Doar. We had a very candid conversation. I told him of my fears of Doar's rigidity and contempt for the political processes of Congress. Frank understood perfectly. He and I seem to see things exactly alike. If anything I think his convictions concerning the test of the integrity and will of Congress that is now unfolding are deeper than my own.

We discussed our views as to which of the members of the Judiciary Committee might be most motivated by the public interest. Frank feels particularly confident about William Cohen. [Republican Cohen, who later became Senator from Maine, was then a freshman member of the Judiciary Committee.] Frank also feels confident about Henry Smith [Republican from New York].

I told Frank that it was difficult for me to assess the Democrats since my own conviction was that Richard Nixon ought to be impeached. I mentioned Barbara Jordan. Frank wasn't sure that Barbara would vote "no" if the evidence so indicated. Yet Frank and I both agreed that the evidence on the public record so far certainly warranted impeachment.

Frank hopes that Nixon will not resign. He feels that Congress must rise to the occasion, and more important is "our right to know the facts."

We agreed that the question for the Republicans now is whether they are willing to do things to create a delay and thereby align themselves with those Democrats who prefer to keep President Nixon twisting in the wind. A related question for both parties is whether Doar will face up to his responsibilities to investigate Nixon or continue to foster delay. Frank and I agreed to try to give Doar the benefit of the doubt.

Jack Anderson's radio program and column today accused Doar of floundering, setting up an elaborate file system with nothing in the files, conducting no real investigation. The Anderson story is very accurate. Nevertheless, I believe it is really meant as intimidation to get better access.

At 6:30 this evening I met with Rodino, Doar, and Francis to discuss the upcoming meeting of the Advisory Group and the question of our subpoena authority. I was surprised at how Doar remains stuck in the mud, not coming up with anything constructive. He hasn't even drafted a subpoena resolution yet!

Doar is going to have his staff provide all committee members a press clipping service—distributing daily copies of articles on impeachment from five leading newspapers. I told him that ordinarily such services were provided to the members on request by the Library of Congress, and need not be paid for out of our budget.

Francis informed me that each of the thousands of letters concerning impeachment that the committee has received from the public will be replied to. He tells me that he is contracting with a private computer service to make a tape with all the names and addresses of citizens who have written letters to the committee either in support of or opposition to Nixon's impeachment. He thinks the tape alone ought to be worth about $150,000 as a mailing list. He insists that only one copy of the tape would be made, which would be available only to Rodino and kept in Rodino's safe. Broken down into two categories—enemies and friends of Richard Nixon—the names have a special kind of political sensitivity as well as a commercial value. I suspect that the mailing list—which is really committee property, and not Rodino's—will be misused for political fundraising purposes.

January 23 This morning I picked up Rodino and we drove to the Capitol for breakfast. After that we went to a meeting of Doar's entire impeachment staff, which now includes more than 100 employees, of which about half are lawyers. They occupy three floors of the former Congressional Hotel. Their offices are off-limits to the public and the press and protected by armed guards.

After meeting with the whole staff we had a meeting with what Doar called "the senior people on the staff," which included Dick Cates, Sam Garrison, Bernie Nussbaum, Robert Sack, and Joe Woods. We had an overly long discussion about our subpoena authority. When it became obvious that no one on Doar's staff had even begun drafting a subpoena resolution, I put together a drafting team. We met an hour later in the House Legislative Counsel's office with Doug Bellis. The team consisted of Sam Garrison, Frank Polk, Bernie Nussbaum, Joe Woods, Dan Cohen, and me.

Despite their lack of congressional experience, I think that Bernie Nussbaum and Joe Woods are very good lawyers and feel relieved that Bernie in particular is working on this. Of all the lawyers hired by Doar, he is the only one who seems to be a heavyweight—and to have real litigation experience.

In the afternoon, Rodino called me away from the drafting session to appear as his representative to receive a petition from a few thousand right-to-lifers who were denouncing the Supreme Court on the anniversary of the *Roe v. Wade* decision. They are petitioning the Judiciary Committee to hold hearings on a constitutional amendment to outlaw abortion.

To get Rodino off the hook, I quickly arranged an exchange of correspondence between him and Don Edwards, who chairs the subcommittee on constitutional rights. On paper Rodino "wholeheartedly supports the petition for hearings by the Edwards subcommittee." Privately Rodino encouraged Edwards to refuse. Edwards graciously took the heat, explaining that a majority of the committee members were in favor of freedom of choice and opposed to amending the constitution.

January 24 Rodino, Doar, and I met with Carl Albert and Lou Deschler this afternoon to discuss reporting out a resolution giving us authority to serve a subpoena on the President. Deschler has worked out a procedure whereby the committee can report the resolution as privileged, thereby avoiding the need to have it considered by the Rules Committee.

In a draft of the resolution prepared by Deschler's staff, the subpoena authority related only to the "official conduct" of the President. Doar pointed out that this might create trouble with respect to such questions as the President's income taxes and other similar matters. Good for Doar, for a change!

The Speaker talked about the subpoena authority. He emphasized the need to stay out of courts, explaining to Doar that "the authority of the House is plenary. If the President does not comply with our subpoena he can get cited by the House for contempt, which in itself could be an impeachable offense."

I am impressed by Carl Albert; I believe him to be a man of considerable integrity. Despite his public stance of apparent disfavor with the notion of actually impeaching the President, I believe the Speaker favors impeachment.

Tonight Doar, Rodino, Francis, and I met to discuss the Advisory Group meeting scheduled for tomorrow. The session was mostly a tedious rehash of matters that Peter has failed to resolve.

Doar again argued that we ought to have no witnesses cross-examined! I find his continued opposition to cross-examination very disturbing, but I tried to disagree with him as tactfully as I could. I said there would be objections from members of congress of both parties if witnesses on whose credibility the ultimate vote would depend were not subject to cross-examination.

Doar also said that we cannot develop any conspiracy to obstruct justice charges against Nixon. He continues to insist that as a matter of law a president cannot be a "co-conspirator." I consider that to be a lot of crap.

Rodino and Doar have decided to hold hearings on the legal definition of "impeachable offense." Francis thinks this is a great idea, and so does Lois. This is simply *not* the way to proceed, for it casts doubt on what the law is, creates delay, and will divide the committee into warring factions arguing needlessly in public over matters which each member has a constitutional right to decide for himself.

Then Rodino told us about a meeting he had today with Wilbur

Mills [chairman of the Joint Committee on Internal Revenue Taxation], who has been investigating Nixon's income tax liabilities. Mills told Rodino that the Joint Committee had determined that Nixon owed over $400,000.00 in back income taxes, and there was a finding of tax fraud and the filing of false documents. However, the Joint Committee intentionally avoided a determination of whether the President himself knew about the fraud and false documents, deferring such questions to us. Even more interesting was that Mills told Peter that the "son of a prominent economist" can provide the Judiciary Committee with incriminating evidence concerning secret funds Nixon has in Swiss bank accounts, but will come forward with the evidence only if he is subpoenaed.

This was just what our investigation needed, but Rodino and Doar were at best slightly intrigued. There was no discussion of whether to issue a subpoena and take the deposition of the economist's son under oath. Perhaps I should have spoken up about this, but I could tell it would have gotten me nowhere with either Rodino or Doar, and would have simply poured salt in the wounds.

January 25 On our way to breakfast Rodino and I discussed Ed Morgan's statement in today's *Wall Street Journal*. Morgan is predicting that tanks will be rolling up Pennsylvania Avenue and federal troops entering the Oval Office. Morgan says that Nixon is finished—not just because of the fraudulent deeds connected with his income tax return, but because there are so many other things as well. [Morgan had been an Assistant Secretary of the Treasury who had resigned out of disenchantment with Nixon. He later pleaded guilty to a charge of conspiracy to impair, impede, defeat, and obstruct the proper and lawful government functions of the IRS.] Later, I was glad that we had this conversation.

At 8:15 we met with Doar. To my amazement, Doar introduced a fellow named Don Kopeck to us as our newly hired press officer. When Rodino asked him a few questions about his background, he revealed that he was formerly with the Immigration and Naturalization Service in their border patrol. I was astounded that Doar and Francis would be so inept as to hire a former INS official without first informing Rodino. [Rodino had formerly been chairman of the Subcommittee on Immigration and had many friends as well as enemies in the INS.]

Later in the day I mentioned this to Jim Cline (counsel to the immigration subcommittee) and suggested that he quietly get a rundown on Kopeck. This evening Jim told me that Kopeck is a close friend of

Bryce Harlow, Nixon's most effective lobbyist. Jim told me that he called Doar to make sure that he had the name correct and mentioned to Doar that Kopeck was a friend of Bryce Harlow. Doar said, "Does that make any difference?" Kopeck is definitely not to be trusted to protect either the interests of the committee or the interests of Rodino.

The Advisory Group met this morning at 9 A.M. behind closed doors. It was a weird meeting. Doar reported on his dealings with Jaworski and on the number of lawyers who have been hired. He briefly discussed the subpoena authority. Then, with grim seriousness, he discussed at length a complaint he had received from an irate citizen who claims to have sent a letter to the committee, and which some staff member had allegedly returned stamped "bullshit."

Jack Brooks broke into laughter. He said it reminded him of a gift he had sent to Texas Judge Homer Thornberry when Thornberry retired from the bench: "I sent Homer a rubber stamp and told him to use it in answering his correspondence. The stamp said 'fuck you.'"

Doar then informed the members that so far he planned no work on Nixon's personal finances. Before anyone could comment, he quickly changed the subject and recommended that the first order of business ought to be for the committee to hold televised hearings at which constitutional experts could testify as to what the Constitution's impeachment clause means by "treason, bribery, and high crimes and misdemeanors."

I had been worried about this. So I was pleased that some of the members immediately realized the delay, confusion, and divisiveness that such hearings would create. The members who were most outspoken against such hearings were mostly Republicans, including Bob McClory, Charlie Sandman, and Tom Railsback. Of the Democrats, Brooks got the picture immediately: "I don't want to have any hearings in which six Harvard professors are going to come and say one thing and another six fucking professors are going to come with another point of view."

Wiggins, who has clearly become Nixon's strongest defender on the committee, seemed pleased by the idea of such hearings, and suggested that the President's counsel ought to be afforded the opportunity to submit a brief. But there was enough opposition to the hearings to persuade Rodino to hold the decision in abeyance.

Although I thought the Advisory Group meeting was one of the worst I have ever attended, at the press conference afterward Rodino did extraordinarily well talking about our constitutional power to issue subpoenas. Henry Hubbard of *Newsweek* thought that Rodino was "superb." Henry said, "Rodino was off on such a high constitutional road that he could got a nosebleed from breathing such rarefied air." He thought that the important thing was that it now "looked like" we were moving forward.

After the press conference, Peter came down to my office and closed the door behind him. He seemed very worried. He sat down in my chair and asked me what I thought about how things were going.

Quite spontaneously, I found myself giving him a lecture which went something like this: "I am concerned about what can happen to you. Congress is now dealing with one of the most volatile issues in our history. As you and I and everyone else who understands Congress knows, it is important to continuously fathom what we all refer to as the 'mood of the House.' Right now, who knows what the mood of this place is from one day to the next? The crisis is so volatile that within a week or a day or an hour something could happen that will blow the lid off this place. Maybe Ed Morgan's statement to the *Wall Street Journal* is correct—the tanks may start rolling down Pennsylvania Avenue and troops may enter the Oval Office.

"So here is what can happen to you personally. The Speaker could suddenly call you to his office, sit you down and say 'Peter, we have to move fast, the son of a bitch has gone to far.' If the Speaker were to ask you how soon you could get an impeachment resolution out of committee, you would probably call Doar and he would say that it would take months. Where will that leave you?

"The very worst thing that could happen to you would be that the mood of the House and country would shift so strongly against Doar's transparent strategy of delay that the Speaker would allow a privileged motion on the floor to impeach the President. The issue would be taken immediately from the Judiciary Committee and brought to the House floor for a debate and vote. Under the House rules and the precedents, the actual articles of impeachment wouldn't even have to be drafted until after the vote.

"If the President is impeached by the House on the basis of a resolution that has not been reported by Judiciary, you could be finished—in an immediate sense politically, and in a larger sense historically.

"I am not predicting that it will happen that way—but I want you to know that a few of the members are beginning to talk about offering a privileged resolution on the floor, which would discharge the committee."

As soon as I stopped speaking, Peter telephoned Doar. Without telling Doar he was in my office, he gave him a modified version of my advice. He ended with, "John, you have to be ready to bring articles of impeachment to the House floor—just in case."

When he hung up, Rodino told me that Doar did not know of Ed Morgan's statement, but that he would read it and then interview Morgan promptly. [Morgan was never questioned by Doar or his staff.]

Tonight as I was leaving for the weekend I bumped into Bella Abzug by the elevator in the Longworth Building. She greeted me warmly, "I heard you had an operation. I'm glad to see you back. But tell me— when are you going to do something about impeachment?"

I held her hand and said, "Bella, somebody else owns my body and my soul, but my heart belongs to you. I'm with you, I'm for you."

She giggled and said, "You always tell me that, but I still want to know when are you going to do something about impeachment?"

I said "Bella, I think it's very important that you keep asking that question, but I think you should ask Peter Rodino."

Tonight I feel a bit better about Bella. At times she is a self-righteous loudmouth. But she is often on the side of the angels.

10

POLITICAL CHARADES: RODHAM, NUSSBAUM, AND THE "IRREGULARS"

B y January 1974, Jack Brooks, Bernie Hellring, Bill Dixon, and I had come to oppose most of Doar's questionable policies. However, it was not until 1976, more than two years after the impeachment inquiry staff was disbanded, that an article was published confirming our suspicions that Doar was intentionally orchestrating a charade. The article—"Searching for the Real Nixon Scandal"—was written by Renata Adler, who had been one of Doar's closest confidantes for several years prior to Watergate. Although I had objected to allowing Doar to put her on our payroll, Rodino eventually agreed.

The biographical material accompanying her article identified Adler as an official member of the impeachment inquiry staff. She reported that on January 2, 1974—the very day I first confided my fears about Doar's hidden agenda to Jack Brooks—Doar had exchanged confidences with her.

According to Adler, Doar had decided that he had to impose restrictions of absolute confidentiality on all of the members of the impeachment inquiry staff, and that he also had to proceed under the assumption that he could trust almost no one. When Adler inquired how he was going to assure complete confidentiality in so large a staff, Doar replied, "You work them very hard and you don't tell them anything."

Adler's article also indicated that Doar had lied to Rodino and me during his job interviews and later to the committee. He had repeat-

119

edly assured us that from the outset he had taken no position as to whether Nixon should be impeached. He had also assured us that his inquiry staff of approximately forty lawyers had no view one way or the other about the matter. Doar said, "Every staff member was questioned whether or not they had taken a position, and if they had . . . they were not considered for the job."

Yet Adler reported unequivocally that "Doar had, in fact, been the second non-radical person I knew, and the first Republican, to advocate impeachment—months before he became special counsel, long before the inquiry began." Maintaining that it would be unthinkable for Doar not to have been an advocate for impeachment from the time that he accepted employment by the committee, Adler reported that Doar could not disclose that determination to the committee members or his own staff for fear that it would create a public impression of unfairness.

As for the inquiry itself, Adler noted that at least one effect of the restrictions imposed on the entire staff was that the impeachment brief and other documents eventually prepared by the staff were "predictably deficient." According to Adler:

> [The deficiencies] turned out to be unimportant. What was important was that the staff keep silent. What they were working on, or thought they were working on, was another matter. . . . While what they were doing was essential, the only thing essential about it was that they were seen to be doing *something* in secret, day and night for months. . . . [They] produced, naturally enough, no investigation and in the end, no case.
>
> The fact was that most of the work, almost all the time by almost all the staff, was a charade. A valuable charade, in that a machine was seen to churn while . . . the courts and a smaller group of Doar's could do their work.

Adler further reported that the most important work was done by a very small group, one of whom was Adler herself, and five of whom she described only as "ad hoc irregulars." In not identifying any of the irregulars, Adler did not disclose that the dominant strategist of the group was Yale professor Burke Marshall, Doar's former boss in the Kennedy Justice Department.

Nor did Adler disclose that one of Doar's key official aides was Hillary Rodham, who acted as a confidential liaison between Doar and Marshall. Rodham was also one of the very few staff aides to accompany Doar to confidential executive sessions of the Judiciary Committee. Another official staff member left unidentified by Adler was Bernard Nussbaum, a former Assistant U.S. Attorney in the Kennedy Justice Department, who was assigned to the most ethically questionable role of any of Doar's key aides. Nussbaum was directly in charge of investigating Nixon—an investigation that never took place.

Another conspicuous omission from Adler's article was any reference to the "Rules for the Impeachment Inquiry Staff," which were adopted by a unanimous vote of the Judiciary Committee on February 22, 1974. The first of the rules was that "the staff of the impeachment inquiry shall not discuss with anyone outside the staff either the substance or procedure of their work or that of the committee."

With Rodino's permission, that rule, as well as House rules prohibiting disclosure by staff members of so-called executive session materials, were disregarded by Doar—who as reported by Adler conferred regularly on important committee business with Marshall and the other members of his team of irregulars. And as further suggested by Adler, the rule was honored only in the breech by Rodham, Nussbaum, and Adler herself, as they also conferred with Marshall and the irregulars on the important work of the committee.

In August 1974, a few days after Nixon's resignation, a young lawyer who had suffered from what Adler described as the "ordeal" of Doar's "valuable charade" confided to me that he considered the work of the impeachment inquiry staff to be flawed. The young lawyer was John Labovitz, who over the next twenty years became a prominent partner of Steptoe and Johnson, one of Washington's most prestigious law firms. He was particularly concerned about the unethical activities and erroneous legal opinions of Hillary Rodham.

August 12 Another interesting thing today was a conversation I had with John Labovitz, who came to my office and apologized for having participated to some extent to conceal from me the work that was being done. Some months ago he and Hillary lied intentionally to me and told me that there were no drafts of proposed rules of procedure for the impeachment inquiry. They were only willing to take from us but not to give us the benefit of their thoughts. I was touched by John's apology for this. I was also touched by his desire to express his agreement with me on several other points. One was the question of the insane Doar notion that a president cannot be involved in a conspiracy. Labovitz said that comes from "Yale." I said, "You mean Burke Marshall, don't you?" Labovitz said "Yes." . . . Labovitz's apology was significant to me not because it was any great revelation, but because of his contrition.

By then Jack Brooks, Bill Dixon, myself, and several other members of the committee and its regular staff had been long aware of the ethical shortcomings and erroneous legal opinions of not only Doar, but of at least two of his key aides, Nussbaum and Rodham. What I referred to as Doar's "insane notion" was but one of a variety of flawed procedural rules that had been politically fabricated by Burke Marshall.

From his first day on our payroll, it was Doar's contention that, as leader of the executive branch, the President was constitutionally shielded from impeachment for acts of his subordinates which he did not personally direct. After Nussbaum and Rodham were hired, they both quickly became advocates of Doar's bizarre interpretation.

Months before Labovitz came to me, both Bernie Hellring and I had advised Rodino that Doar's theory was not only bad law but was identical to what we called the "Nuremberg defense." Lawyers for most of the Nazi war criminals had argued that their clients had never personally directed the execution of any Jews and were not reponsible for the criminal acts of their subordinates. It was a chilling comparison.

Even more chilling was the view which Doar articulated privately to me as well as Rodino that the Constitution's impeachment clause was obsolete in specifically including both treason and bribery. It was a view that Doar himself, as well as Nussbaum and Rodham, espoused in private but were unwilling to commit to in writing. Nevertheless, in her 1976 article Adler, who is not an attorney, espoused the Doar-Marshall view as her own.

In interpreting the constitutional definition of "treason, bribery, or other high crimes and misdemeanors" as impeachable offenses, Adler explains that Doar considered the terms *treason* and *bribery* as obsolete. His rationale was that under the circumstances of modern warfare, in which a president has to have discretion to enter into alliances with foreign powers previously thought to be enemies, "there seemed to be no sense in which treason, by any definition, could be committed by a modern president." Adler also explains that for Doar, "in addition, to the problems which followed from any Tax Fraud and Emoluments theory, bribery seemed just too difficult to prove."

For advocating the Nuremberg defense as well as a variety of other flawed legal opinions, I came to regard Doar, Nussbaum, and Rodham as somewhat less than honorable lawyers, unworthy of either public or private trust. As is documented extensively in my diary—as well as in the official impeachment files of the Judiciary Committee, which Rodino eventually placed under seal in the National Archives—to give Marshall and Doar absolute control over the impeachment inquiry, Nussbaum and Rodham espoused sucharcane procedures as obtaining gag orders from the courts to restrict members of the Judiciary Committee from disclosing the contents of documentary evidence; denying the President representation by counsel; prohibiting committee members from hearing any testimony from live witnesses or participating in any form of cross-examination; and denying committee members the power to draft or amend articles of impeachment—leaving such power solely to Doar and the impeachment inquiry staff.

Twenty years later, in her best-selling biography *Hillary Clinton: The Inside Story,* Judith Warner noted that, when Hillary joined the impeachment inquiry staff at the age of twenty-six, "the fact that she'd been chosen by civil rights giant Burke Marshall gave her added clout." Based on personal interviews with Rodham, her biographer conceded "that there was considerable tension between Rodham's group and the permanent staff of the House Judiciary Committee" which was attributed to the fact that "the lawyers on the House Judiciary Committee staff did not want the historic occasion of a lifetime taken away and handed over to a bunch of outsiders."

Rodham's authorized biography makes no mention of Adler's contention that most of the work of the inquiry staff was a charade or the fact that Rodham's role was primarily that of a covert emanuensis and conduit for Burke Marshall. As described by her biographer:

> Hillary Rodham's main assignment was establishing the legal procedures to be followed in the course of the inquiry and impeachment. It meant handling subpoenas, making sure the proper legal steps were anticipated and followed in line with

the Constitution. Her work ultimately led to suggesting drafting procedures to be followed by the committee in conducting
the formal presentation aspects of its work, what sort of rules
of evidence, definition of the role of Nixon chief defense attorney James St. Clair, what sort of objections would be deemed
appropriate or inappropriate, and the scope of cross-examination. It meant staying in the background . . . and being above all
discreet.

In 1974, I had discussions with Rodham on a number of occa-
sions. After she was hired, one of the first assignments that Doar
and Nussbaum gave her was to prepare confidential drafts of
impeachment procedures recommended by Marshall—who was in
touch with the inquiry staff on a daily basis by telephone.

After Rodham completed some early drafts, Doar and Nussbaum
instructed her and Labovitz to confer with me for clarification of
current rules and existing precedents—but not to disclose or discuss
with me any of the changes recommended by Marshall. When I
asked Rodham if she or anyone else on the inquiry staff had prepared any drafts of impeachment procedures, she said "No."

By that time, my personal staff assistant, Dan Cohen—who like
Rodham was a recent graduate of Yale Law School—had helped me
prepare and publish an official committee handbook codifying all of
the existing parliamentary procedures—many of which had been
in effect since the days of Thomas Jefferson. I gave Rodham and
Labovitz copies of the handbook and explained that "Speaker Albert
and Parliamentarian Deschler have both already emphasized to
Chairman Rodino and me that we should adhere strictly to the present rules. We feel strongly that it would be dangerous to try to
change the rules now. It would be like trying to change the traditional rules of baseball just before the opening of a World Series. It
would generate a national debate on the fairness of the new rules,
and polarize the Congress. It would also make it more difficult to
get enough votes to impeach the President."

A few days later, Rodham conferred with me again to inquire as
to whether I had opinions on two legal matters. The first was
whether the President should be allowed to be represented by counsel at any evidentiary hearings. My response was, "Yes, of course the
President should be represented by counsel. In fact, the committee
specifically considered the counsel question during our recent

impeachment inquiry regarding Justice Douglas, who was represented by Simon Rifkind, a former federal judge—who just a few months ago represented Vice President Agnew and advocated that we hold evidentiary impeachment hearings to clear Agnew's name."

The other matter was the legal definition of the term *high crimes and misdemeanors*. I reminded Rodham of the 800-page Committee Print on Impeachment Procedures that had been prepared by Dan Cohen before Doar had been hired. I also referred her to our committee files on the Douglas impeachment inquiry. Our files included extensive research establishing that the drafters of the Constitution had not intended impeachable offenses to be limited to statutory crimes. As recently as 1970, when Jerry Ford led the drive to impeach Justice Douglas, he had said, "An impeachable offense is whatever a majority of the House of Representatives considers it to be at any point in history."

It was not until months after my conference with Rodham that I learned that the supply of handbooks of traditional rules that had been reserved for future use had been unaccountably removed from the committee's storeroom. Even more distressing, Doar got Rodino's permission to place all of our Douglas impeachment files in his exclusive custody—and along with Rodham later ignored the Douglas precedent by advocating that James St. Clair be denied the right to cross-examine witnesses.

Over the next seven months, Doar, Nussbaum, and Rodham were to become unflinching advocates of a number of highly questionable strategies formulated by them in consultation with Burke Marshall and the former Justice Department lawyers whom Adler characterized as "ad hoc irregulars."

January 26 Late yesterday afternoon I had an interesting meeting with Frank Polk. His view is that if the Democrats are willing to make the case against Nixon for them, a significant number of Republicans are ready to vote to impeach the President. We also discussed the question of the Judiciary Committee's subpoena. Frank says John Rhodes is apparently under the impression that the agreement reached by Rodino and Hutchinson would require that both of them would have to authorize any subpoenas served on the President. According to Frank, Hutchinson simply does not want the responsibility and would be happier if the authority to issue supboenas is given both to Rodino alone and to Hutchinson alone—or if neither is willing to issue a subpoena on their own authority, to the full committee.

As Frank and I were talking, Neal Curry of Westinghouse TV phoned to tell me that he had just heard that the Judiciary Committee had appeared by counsel in a case pending in U.S. District Court. He asked me to confirm the story. I told him that it simply was not true. He said, "Your word is enough for me." A few minutes later he called me back. He had checked again and insisted that the story was true. I immediately called John Doar. It *was* true! Doar had sent Tom Bell [who shared an impeachment staff office with Rodham], a young lawyer from Doar's brother's law firm, to the district court to enter an appearance in a case brought by a Ralph Nader group alleging that the dairy industry had paid off Nixon with campaign contributions as a quid pro quo for political favors for milk producers. To gain access to confidential White House documents subpoenaed in the case, Bell had entered into a stipulation "on behalf of all of the members of the Committee on the Judiciary of the U.S. House of Representatives." The stipulation agreed to the imposition by the court of a gag order restricting the committee from making any of the documentary evidence known to the public. I asked Doar, "Does Chairman Rodino know about this?" He said, "No, but Francis O'Brien does."

I called back the TV reporter and told him that the story was "sort of true." I tried to make it seem like an innocuous administrative matter. I then called Francis. He denied that Doar had told him about the court appearance.

The implications of this are rather startling. No one has the authority to make a court appearance on behalf of the Judiciary Committee without the prior approval of the committee. In my view, Bell's action was unethical as well as inappropriate. Not only should the chairman and ranking Republican member of the committee have been informed, but Doar had breached his professional responsibility to both the committee and the court.

Even more profoundly, the political ramifications of the stipulation are staggering. The ultimate purpose of the impeachment inquiry is to make the public aware of evidence of any presidential misconduct. The stiputlation that Doar has unlawfully directed his brother's law clerk to enter into purports to subject any member of the Judiciary Committee to a contempt of court citation if he discloses evidence of presidential misconduct.

Another startling ramification is related to the fact that we are now trying to get a resolution through the committee and the whole House giving Rodino the authority to issue and serve subpoenas directly on the President. The Democratic leadership has taken a strong position that Congress's impeachment authority is independent of the power of courts to subpoena documents. In fact, just a few day ago, Rodino stated that "to engage in any controversy with a court would be a fatal mistake." For Doar now to attempt to submit the full Judiciary Committee to the jurisdiction of a federal court without the approval of the chairman or the ranking Republican member (let alone the whole committee) creates a danger that the upcoming debate in the comittee and the House on the subpoena authority will become muddled with a lot of controversy as to the failure of the chairman and ranking Republican member to control the activities of the staff.

Driving out to Front Royal tonight I became angrier and angrier about Doar's stupidity—and had the fear Doar is not just dumb. Maybe he and Burke Marshall orchestrated Bell's appearance in court to intentionally weaken Congress's powers to investigate the executive branch. If I were chairman of the Judiciary Committee, I would fire Doar.

January 28 Jack Brooks·called this morning and invited me to lunch to talk about the gag order. I suggested that we talk privately in his office. When I got there, we engaged in a few pleasantries. When he got to the subject of the gag order, he made it clear that he would not comply, and would inform the court in writing that he had not consented to the order.

We then discussed the possibility of Burke Marshall playing a role in this. He said he knew Marshall well, that he was "a good fellow and an honorable man," but that he, Brooks, was cynical enough to believe that Marshall was in fact capable of doing something "for Nixon." I suggested that if Marshall and company were playing a role in this, it was not in order to do something "for Nixon" but that perhaps Ted Kennedy had a political interest in keeping Nixon in office. I have never seen Brooks as solemn as during this conversation.

He discussed Rodino's weaknesses with me openly. He thought that Peter was not badly motivated, but was giving way to Doar out of weakness. He said he planned to discuss the whole matter of the gag order at a meeting tomorrow of all of the committee members.

Interestingly enough, the TV news tonight reports that Speaker Albert made a statement today that there will be a vote on impeachment in the House in this session regardless of what the Judiciary Committee does. Is the Speaker sounding a kind of signal? Did Brooks talk to him? Just what is going on? Brooks told me today, "It is fortunate that there are procedures for discharging committees that screw up." For some time now Brooks has been mentioning to me the possibility of a motion on the floor to take the impeachment inquiry out of the Judiciary Committee.

January 29 The briefing session this morning was the saddest committee meeting I have ever attended. Afterward, Frank Polk told me he felt like crying.

It started with Doar giving a monotonous presentation—a biography of himself and of Associate Special Counsel Joe Woods, who apparently was Doar's classmate and graduated first in his class. He also read to the members a tedious memorandum describing once again the organization of the staff and the security precautions.

For a while I was fearful that Brooks was so irate that he wasn't even going to show up. When he finally arrived about a half hour late he asked Rodino to recognize him to question Doar. He started with what he called "two simple questions" about the staff that Doar had hired. First, he asked whether Barbara Fletcher, a person whom Doar had hired for "Congressional liaison" had any prior congressional experience. Doar said "No." Brooks then asked whether Don Kopeck, who had been hired as "public information officer," had any press experience. Doar again said "No." Then Brooks raised the subject of Tom Bell's appearance before the court on Friday. He used typical "southern style"—gentle and mild-mannered. Brooks had obtained a copy of the gag order, and stated politely that he for one did not consider himself to be bound by the gag order of the court since he had not consented to it and the committee had not authorized it.

Brooks then got Rodino to agree that the court appearance ordered by Doar was unauthorized. Then Brooks gave Doar a mild reprimand, and Doar promptly apologized.

The fact that Brooks had done this was a signal to the other members of the committee that they too had powers that Doar had attempted to usurp. Drinan joined in with Brooks and protested, as did Charlie Rangel, and then around and around the committee—Wiggins, Froehlich, and just about everyone else protested. Kastenmeier was the only exception. He half-heartedly defended Doar, characterizing the action as "simply poor judgment, a good-faith mistake."

After the meeting, Doar made a point of telling me caustically that Brooks's criticism was "a lot of foolishness."

Afterward, Rodino called me about scheduling a meeting of the

Democratic caucus for tomorrow morning to go over a subpoena resolution prepared by Doar. He mentioned that he thought Doar had been unfairly treated. I said, "Yes, after Brooks got finished, there was really no need for the other members to jump on Doar."

Later this evening Brooks telephoned me at home and said, "I am going to have to teach Doar something—and I might even get him fired."

January 30 Rodino spent no time with me before the Democratic caucus this morning, nor did he consult with me the night before. As a result, he had no advantage whatsoever from my conversations with the other Democratic members.

The resolution Doar presented had been drafted by his people [apparently including Nussbaum and Rodham in consultation with Burke Marshall]. The drafting had initially begun as a team effort under my supervision in the House Legislative Counsel's office—and had included Nussbaum. But the team effort was abandoned by Nussbaum after the first afternoon.

At the caucus, Doar took my usual seat next to Rodino. I sat next to Barbara Jordan, who was sitting next to Jack Brooks. The other members seemed to be looking to Brooks more than Rodino for leadership. Brooks started in by saying that his dissatisfaction of yesterday was nothing in comparison to his dissatisfaction today. He made it clear that he considered the resolution drafted by Nussbaum and Doar's other lawyers to contain too much verbiage, to be too convoluted, and to be overloaded with matters that were traditionally extraneous to congressional subpoenas.

Brooks was aware that Carl Albert had previously called me and Doar to his office specifically to warn us not to draft a subpoena resolution intended for enforcement by the courts. Brooks was particularly shocked that the resolution actually cited court decisions and court rules, which made it clear that the resolution was intended to be the subject of litigation. He suggested that the resolution be redrafted to comport with the traditional subpoenas issued by congressional committees. Doar agreed to redraft the resolution to incorporate some of Brooks's suggestions.

Tonight, the President gave his State of the Union address in the House chamber. At the end of his speech he put away his notes and added what appeared to be an ad lib postscript, saying such things as "One year of Watergate is enough" and suggesting that he had already given the Special Prosecutor "all the material that he needs to conclude his investigation." Without using the word *impeachment,* he acknowledged that the Judiciary Committee had "a special responsibility in this area." He pledged to cooperate with our investigation.

After the address, I spoke with Dick Cates. For the first time since Doar came aboard, Dick really let his hair down and told me that Doar, Nussbaum, and Doar's people in general are insensitive to what Dick is trying to do to investigate Nixon—that Doar has not yet even looked at the facts and is "caught up with a lot of administrative bullshit." Dick said it was "like a group of doctors who had been called into an emergency room and insisted on taking a refresher course in diagnostic techniques before being willing to ask the patient for his medical history."

January 31 This morning at ten o'clock, the committee had a public meeting to consider the subpoena resolution. Again, Rodino had made no arrangements to meet with me beforehand. I got to the office early. When I went to the hearing room, I discovered that, on orders of Helen Starr of all people [she was a clerical assistant to Francis O'Brien], the seating arrangements on the committee rostrum were changed to replace me and Frank Polk with Doar and Jenner. When I countermanded her order and explained to her that, as a member of Rodino's office staff, Francis had no authority to speak for Rodino on committee matters, Starr seemed relieved.

Jack Brooks was his inimitable self. He complimented Doar for having improved the resolution. He said, "Today's draft is better. At least its written in Old English instead of Sanskrit." Rodino added proudly, "More than forty lawyers have worked on this subpoena resolution." Barbara Jordan chimed in with "Yes, Mr. Chairman, it looks it!"

Then Brooks asked Doar why it was necessary to include so much more language in the subpoena than is normally used for congressional subpoenas. Doar's reply was, "Congress's subpoena power is very important and it is essential that it be defined very precisely." Brooks retorted, "Let me tell you something about power, Mr. Doar. It is best defined by its exercise." Then Brooks turned aside to me and whispered, "Don't just talk about how you're gonna fuck 'em—fuck 'em!"

Despite our reservations about the litigation-breeding verbosity of the subpoena resolution written by Doar's in-group, the resolution included some language that both Brooks and Tip O'Neill had adamantly insisted on to Rodino. The language appeared in the very opening words of the resolution: "Resolved, that the Committee on the Judiciary, acting as a whole or by any subcommittee thereof, is autho-

rized and directed to investigate fully and completely whatever sufficient grounds exist for the House of Representatives to exercise its constitutional power to impeach Richard M. Nixon, President of the
United States. . . ."

Although the media had generally refrained from reporting that
Doar had chosen not to commence any original investigation of the
President, Doar had made his position intractably clear to me and
Bill Dixon. Through this language, we had hoped that Rodino and
Doar would take seriously the fact that the House of Representatives
was officially mandating that we investigate Nixon's conduct "fully
and completely." To our chagrin, the Marshall-Doar strategy of delay
and charade persisted. Although the subpoena resolution was
reported out of committee and adopted by the full House in
February, almost three months more passed before any subpoenas
were served on the President—and even then, Doar and Nussbaum
opposed sanctioning Nixon for refusing to comply with them.

Week after week, flawed legal opinions and dubious procedural
rules were being churned out by Nussbaum and Rodham under the
supervision of Marshall. Each of them served to foster delay. They
had to be shot down one by one by a coalition of Republicans and
Democrats led by Tip O'Neill and Minority Leader John Rhodes and
including Jack Brooks, Bob McClory, and Tom Railsback. Of these
flawed recommendations, three were particularly repugnant to
Brooks and me.

One was the notion that before Nixon could be investigated it
would be necessary for the committee to hold official hearings and
adopt precise rules defining the exact constitutional meaning of
"treason, bribery, and other high crimes and misdemeanors." Both
Brooks and Hutchinson considered that recommendation at best
frivolous pandering to the media and at worst a brazen effort to
polarize the committee and intentionally delay the inquiry.

A second was that before any investigation could be conducted,
the committee members would have to adopt strict rules of
secrecy—in effect, imposing gag orders on themselves. Even Rodino
privately had serious reservations about the wisdom of this. "After
all," he often told me, "Congress is a parliamentary body. That
means, as they say in Italian, *Parlare, Parlare, Parlare!*'"

The third and perhaps most invidious rule, one which was also
espoused by Rodino, was the surprising notion that the President

was not entitled to representation by counsel in the committee's impeachment proceedings. The staff lawyer who produced the flawed legal research that Rodino, Doar, and Nussbaum relied on most to advocate that rule was Rodham.

April 2 The odds now seem heavily weighted in favor of Nixon remaining in office for as long as possible. Too many liberal Democrats want to do nothing but talk and are not pressing Doar even to begin a real investigation. In a way, this recalls to my mind the McCarthy era, when all one had to do to qualify as a "liberal" was to oppose Joe McCarthy. Now the liberal Democrats have an easy out. All that is required to maintain membership in the fire-eaters club is to be appalled by the depravity and corruption of Richard Nixon. It is not necessary to make any effort to investigate or eliminate the cancer.

I felt very depressed by all of this today and decided to call Frank Polk. It was an interesting coincidence. Frank was also depressed, but for different reasons. This afternoon there was a caucus of the Republican members of the committee at which Frank was present. The Republican members are ganging up to attack Doar. Apparently Doar's memorandum on the counsel question is going to be circulated tomorrow and the Republican members have seen a tentative draft. According to Frank, whose judgment I trust, the draft is intellectually dishonest. The Republicans have been advised that, with the exception of Jenner, the entire minority staff of the impeachment inquiry disagrees with the memorandum.

Some of the research products, such as a chart prepared by Hillary Rodham outlining the historical precedents, have been locked up and not made available.

According to Frank, Doar is presenting the memorandum in such a way as to buttress his view of what the procedures should be in an impeachment inquiry rather than an objective analysis of the precedents. Having not yet seen the memorandum, I should reserve judgment—although I do have confidence in Frank Polk's intellectual honesty. . . . Frank and I agreed that we will jointly go to Doar tomorrow to warn him of what some of the Republican members have in mind.

Tonight I toyed with the idea of calling Rodino and also Bernie Hellring. I don't think that Frank and I will be able to change Doar's mind tomorrow about anything. . . . However, Frank feels a special responsibility to point out to Doar that he can in no way rely on

"Twinkle Toes" Jenner as a spokesman for the Republican members—who are separating themselves more and more from Jenner.

If Frank's view of Doar's memorandum is correct, then Doar is guilty of the same type of moral corruption that I have always found so abhorrent in the Nixon Department of Justice—bending the law to accomplish a political objective.

In the back of my mind also lingers Hellring's admonition that Doar and Francis are really working for Kennedy. Maybe there is a kind of mastermind in the form of Burke Marshall at work which would use the counsel question to polarize the committee and weaken the Republicans even more than they are now [by forcing them to defend Nixon and vote "no" on the question of impeachment]. In that regard I recall that even Jack Brooks—exasperated one day with Doar and Rodino—reflected for a moment and said, "Shit, I've got nothing personal to lose from this. If the SOB stays in office it makes it all that much easier for me to get myself reelected by running against him."

In his autobiography *Man of the House*, Tip O'Neill pointed out that delay in impeaching Nixon was a politically partisan tactic:

> At first [Rodino] was scared to death, and on more than one occasion I had to light a fire under his feet. . . . I would say, "This thing is going to hit us and you've got to be prepared for it. You also have to keep it from becoming political."
>
> It was extremely important to keep the impeachment hearings from deteriorating into partisan warfare. . . . Naturally, there were those in the House and in the press who believed that the impeachment hearings represented partisan politics as usual.
>
> Nothing could be further from the truth. [A tongue-in-cheek comment—O'Neill was always reluctant to criticize his fellow Democrats openly.] In fact, if the Democrats had really wanted to benefit from Watergate we would have moved much more slowly. After all, the longer Richard Nixon remained in office the more we would gain. Had the President stayed on through the 1974 congressional elections, we would have picked up even more seats than we did. And if Nixon had served out his full second term, the 1976 presidential election would have been a foregone conclusion.

April 4 Frank Polk and I met with Doar yesterday. Both of us tried our best to be as helpful as we could. Frank told Doar in precise and accurate terms the concern the Republicans have over the President's right to counsel. Frank pointed out that in the drafts [prepared by Rodham] much was made about the "lack of any precedent" for the President being represented by counsel. Frank felt this was intellectually dishonest. Doar seemed very quick to agree. He explained to us that [Rodham's] staff drafts were being too "tilted" and that he himself criticized the drafts for the same reason.

At that point renewed doubts arose in my mind as to Doar's honesty. I believe that his staff was tilting the draft to conform to his personal desires. I have serious reservations about Doar's integrity. I am sure he feels that he is always committed to doing right. Nevertheless, his failure to be straightforward and candid with the Democrats and to advise them of the true nature of the precedents is a big strike against him according to the rules under which Frank and I have always played the game.

April 5 The committee had a closed-door meeting today to discuss the recommendation of Doar's staff that the President be denied representation by counsel—which was still being supported by Rodino and the fire-eaters. As Frank Polk put it afterward, "The torpedo hit the ship, but it occurred offstage."

The minority staff had prepared a legal memorandum affirming that the President should be represented by counsel, with a right of cross-examination. Reciprocating only partially for Doar's past practice of not giving committee members advance notice, the Republicans waited until one hour before the meeting before telling Rodino. Peter immediately called me and said he thought that Sam Garrison had written the memorandum. He also reminded me of my endorsement of Garrison at the time he first came on staff.

I assured Rodino that based on my conversations with Frank Polk I was certain that Garrison had not done this on his own and that in fact the Republican caucus had directed the entire minority staff to prepare the memorandum. After his conversation with me, Rodino immediately called Ed Hutchinson. According to Frank, Rodino and Hutchinson then had shouting match.

At the meeting, all of the Republicans joined with Jack Brooks in opposition to Doar's proposal, and Brooks was easily able to muster enough votes to reject it. Afterward, this whole episode was narrated to the press in a distorted way by Rodino, Doar, Jenner, and Francis—all of whom depicted Garrison as a villain who was intentionally trying to politicize the proceedings because of personal animosity toward Jenner.

April 6 The closed-door wrangle on whether Nixon can be represented by St. Clair continued this morning. Republican Larry Hogan insisted that Garrison be allowed to defend himself against published allegations that he had defied Jenner. It became clear that Jenner had lied to the press as well as to Rodino and Doar. Jenner admitted that he had known about the Republican caucus. He assumed personal responsibility for the Republican's legal memorandum in opposition to Doar's recommendation, and had actually supervised the preparation of the minority memorandum. Although he had not done the légal research himself, he had directed Garrison to have it done, and had reviewed it. [Garrison himself had relied mostly on the legal research of two Republican lawyers, Bill Weld and John Davidson. Weld—now Republican governor of Massachusetts—and Davidson had been put on the inquiry staff with my approval before Doar and Jenner were hired. Later I advised Rodino that I had confidence in their professional integrity and agreed with their legal memorandum—and with Frank Polk's characterization of Rodham's legal research as intellectually dishonest.]

No decision was reached on Doar's recommendation. I think that utimately, with the help of moderate Republicans McClory and Railsback, Brooks and O'Neill will prevail over the fire-eaters. In fact, I understand from McClory that he hopes to persuade the Republicans to fire Jenner and replace him with Sam Garrison.

What disturbs me is the extent to which Rodino—who in the past has always attempted to avoid polarization—continues to allow ethically flawed legal opinions to exacerbate tensions between the Republicans and the Democrats, and between Brooks and O'Neill and the fire-eaters. As for me, I feel so strongly about this that I have told Rodino that I would resign in protest if the Judiciary Committee were to vote to deny Nixon representation by counsel.

I tried to explain privately to Rodino that Republican members such as McClory, Railsback, Smith, Cohen, and Fish are not simply puppets on St. Clair's string. They need to have St. Clair here to represent the President so that as Republicans they can feel free to vote "yes" on an impeachment resolution. As Republicans, their need for fairness to Nixon is even more compelling politically than the need of the Democrats.

To my chagrin, Rodino called Doar and Francis into his office and told me to repeat my explanation to them. After I explained it again to Rodino, Doar, and Francis, Rodino reproached me in front of them. He told me, "You have miscalculated the situation entirely."

Rodino was not only a member of the bar, but an astute politician. I found his insistence on denying the President representation to be distressing both ethically and politically.

Almost six months had passed since the House had appropriated $1 million for an impeachment inquiry and Rodino had pledged that we would "leave no stones unturned." By April 15, 1974—the target date that Rodino had publicly given for the completion of the inquiry—no witnesses had been questioned, no subpoenas had been issued, and no investigation had begun. Instead, the committee was kept in chaos by the questionable procedures formulated by Hillary Rodham on Burke Marshall's recommendations and advocated vigorously by Doar and Nussbaum.

The more Rodino and Doar disdained advice from Jack Brooks, the more Brooks's opposition stiffened. Brooks began carrying a small index card with a Biblical quotation from Jeremiah in his pocket which he would flash to Tip O'Neill and other members of the Democratic caucus. The card read, *Cursed be he who doeth the work of the Lord with a slack hand!*

11

SHAVING POINTS?

s spring of 1974 approached, the Judiciary Committee was in turmoil, and so was Rodino's private life. His normally supportive wife Anne was becoming exasperated by Peter's dependence on Lois D'Andre. Lois was now living in Newark and was on the payroll of Rodino's congressional office. Rodino was spending more time in his district office with Lois on his weekends in New Jersey than with Anne. Lois also continued to work behind the scenes by telephone on impeachment issues with Francis O'Brien, who was now manager of Peter's Washington office.

In April Rodino was hospitalized due to stress-related ailments. Without informing the House leaders, he arranged to be admitted secretly to Bethesda Naval Hospital. Anne, Bernie Hellring, and I wanted him to be treated by private doctors rather than Navy doctors, because we suspected that the President's Chief of Staff, General Alexander Haig, would be getting more complete medical reports on Rodino's condition than Peter himself would. But Rodino remained in treatment at Bethesda.

Keeping the hospitalization a secret from Tip O'Neill, Jack Brooks, and the senior Republicans on the committee—but not from the White House—until after Peter was discharged increased fears about Rodino's weakness and misguided dependence on Doar's delaying tactics. When Brooks would complain to him about Rodino and Doar, O'Neill would sometimes call me to his office to report, and to help "hold Peter's feet to the fire." As O'Neill later recalled:

> I can remember people coming in and saying, "Hey, when is that committee going to move?" After every weekend, they would come back and say, "Geez, what are we going to do

137

about this thing? It is reaching tremendous proportions. We're doing nothing." Every time Zeifman came to my office he'd say, "This thing is falling apart. There is no inclination to move, no head or tail." Zeifman had an ally in Jack Brooks. And, as the majority leader, it was my obligation [to press Rodino]. Peter used to get furious. . . . He'd always have an excuse.

O'Neill was also aware of other misgivings about Rodino. In October when Fred Lacey, Addonizio's Nixon-appointed prosecutor, had publicly expressed confidence in Rodino, Frank Thompson of New Jersey had told O'Neill that he suspected Rodino had made a deal to go easy on Nixon. Elizabeth Drew, a reporter for the *New Yorker*, later wrote that such suspicions were prevalent among Washington insiders.

One day O'Neill summoned me to his office and asked, "What the hell is going on with Peter? Sometimes it looks to me like he's shaving points." He was referring to occasional scandals in sports in which a team wins, but intentionally holds down the score so that certain bettors can beat the point spread.

I had to agree that it looked that way. We then discussed the Lacey matter as well as Rodino's political alliance with Ted Kennedy—and Rodino and Doar's apparent plan to avoid investigating Nixon and keep him in office for as long as possible. O'Neill, who often told his friends that he was "born a Democrat and baptized a Catholic," told me, "The Kennedys are not Democrats. They are Kennedys." He then assured me, "Jack Brooks has it right, and so do you. The best politics for us Democrats is *no* politics—impeach Nixon and make Jerry Ford President."

I discussed the question of point shaving gingerly with Jim Cline of my staff. Jim had been chief counsel to Rodino's subcommittee on immigration for many years, and had a closer personal relationship with Rodino than I. Jim shared my concern about Rodino's weaknesses. I confided that I was considering resigning.

February 20 Jim Cline advised me tonight to stop talking about resigning. He said "What would you do if you were the chairman of the House Judiciary Committee and someone on behalf of the President was able to make you some kind of an offer that would assure your reelection—with the quid pro quo being not that you would blow the impeachment but that you would just shave some points?"

I said I was confident that Rodino was not one to accept any kind of deal like that. Jim agreed. But who knows? Perhaps that is exactly what Rodino is doing—shaving points.

In April, when Rodino began recommending that we deny Nixon the right to be represented by counsel, the suspicions of O'Neill and others about point shaving increased. Were the Democrats to deny the President representation by counsel, Nixon would benefit politically. Every Republican in the House, as well as many Democrats, would have a good reason to vote "no" on impeachment. However, all of the fire-eaters on the Judiciary Committee initially supported the recommendation and accepted Rodham's legal research, which was endorsed by Doar, to be reliable. As usual, Brooks was the only Democrat who was outspoken in opposition.

One day at a luncheon meeting in the members' dining room, Brooks got into an argument with four of the leading fire-eaters: Edwards, Kastenmeier, Holtzman, and Waldie. Raising his voice loud enough to be heard by Republicans at other tables, Brooks said, "Your idea of keeping Nixon in office so that we can beat on him and the Republicans is shameful. The best politics is for us to do what's best for the country. Let's give the son of a bitch the right to counsel—and then impeach him and make Jerry Ford President as soon as possible. As for me, I just want to make sure that I can look my grandchildren in the eye."

At that time Brooks had a reputation as a moderately conservative Democrat, and most of the fire-eaters—all of whom were staunch liberals—regarded him with disdain. However, one of them—Don Edwards—was moved by Brooks's call to do the right thing. Edwards, who chaired the Subcommittee on Civil Rights, was the first of the committee's liberal Democrats to separate himself from Rodino and reject Doar's arguments that Nixon should be denied representation.

In doing this, Edwards ran somewhat counter to his political background. He was former president of Americans for Democratic Action (ADA), the Democratic party's liberal wing, and he was an activist member of the ACLU. Neither the ADA nor the ACLU were ready to challenge Rodino and Doar on the right to counsel issue.

But Edwards conferred closely with his administrative assistant, Ailsa Stickney, who had been in the WACs in World War II. Ailsa was then a single parent of four children, and was also an extraordinarily competent administrator with a rare clear-eyed vision of practical politics. For Ailsa, whatever was ethically or morally wrong was never good politics.

Edwards's decision to break with Rodino and Doar also grew out of his reaction to how Jerry Ford and the Republicans had tried to impeach Justice Douglas in part because of what they considered Douglas's permissive stance on pornography. (At private dinner parties, Douglas would sometimes relate this story about how he decided obscenity cases: "I review the alleged obscene material thoroughly. If it gives me an erection, I rule that it is obscene. And that's why my decisions have grown more liberal over the years.")

Edwards and Douglas had become close friends. When the Nixon administration forced the House Judiciary Committee to commence an impeachment inquiry in 1970, Edwards championed Douglas's right to representation by counsel, which was granted in full throughout the inquiry. Rodino had also supported Douglas's right to counsel.

April 5 I had lunch with Don Edwards. He and I discussed the question of Nixon's right to representation by St. Clair at evidentiary hearings in detail. He and I see it the same way. Edwards is strongly in favor of giving the President all the rights of representation that Douglas's attorney, Simon Rifkind, had requested and been granted by the Judiciary Committee. Edwards says that he will vote with the Republicans to give Nixon the right to representation by counsel and he will try to persuade Kastenmeier and Waldie to do the same.

April 8 There was another "briefing session" today. Since it was not a regular business meeting, no votes could be taken. Republicans Bob McClory and Charlie Sandman in particular took on Rodino. They were upset that no votes could be taken on the issue of St. Clair's representation of the President—which they are anxious to have resolved by a vote overriding Rodino and Doar. The meeting became rancorous.

At the end of today's House session Bob McClory and a group of Republicans took out a special order on the House floor. McClory attacked Rodino for denying the President the right to counsel. To Rodino and Doar's astonishment, Don Edwards rose and supported McClory.

Afterward, Waldie let Rodino know that he agreed with Edwards that it would be disastrous to deny the President the right to representation by counsel.

I spent a few minutes with Don and Ailsa in their office tonight discussing all of this with them. I am proud to have them as friends. If I had all of the votes I would give Ailsa a Congressional Medal of Honor.

April 8 At the Democratic caucus this morning, Rodino threw in the towel. He treated Edwards and me graciously and said that he now realized he had made a mistake. He instructed Doar to prepare a statement for him inviting St. Clair to participate in our proceedings as counsel for Nixon.

After that there was was a lot of discussion about the investigation of the President's income tax liability. The members asked Doar what efforts were being made to investigate the quarter of a million dollars of unreported income that had recently been discovered by Mills's joint committee. Doar admitted that he had not yet done any investigation and that he was reluctant to do so unless he was specifically directed to do so by the committee. His explanation was that as soon as he had an investigator working on that the media would find out about it.

This seemed to some members, as Ed Mezvinsky of Iowa put it, to be "hogwash." Brooks said, "In Texas we call it horsehit." Most of the Democrats expressed the view that Doar was at best too fearful of criticism by the media.

It has finally become clear to all of the Democrats that Doar has not yet developed any investigation of these matters, including the possibility of both tax fraud and bribery. Mezvinsky, who to his credit is our most starry-eyed freshman member, was stunned.

Although Doar and Nussbaum are assuring the members that all of this material will be developed, I will believe it when I see it. My impression remains that there is no investigatory material in Doar's guarded files that has not been obtained by investigations prior to ours.

Later tonight, Jim Cline, Doar, Francis, and I met with Rodino. The question again arose about the President's right to counsel. Although Rodino had instructed Doar to prepare a statement on the subject, Doar had not done so. He was more emotional than I have ever seen him in trying to dissuade Rodino from making such a statement. He disagreed with me very sharply, saying that he was concerned about "Rodino's personal dignity and self-respect and the self-respect of the members of the committee," and that making "those kinds of concessions to St. Clair" would detract from the dignity of the committee and would be a sign of weakness on Rodino's part.

I tried to keep my cool. I told Doar, "On the contrary, it would not be a sign of weakness. It would be a sign of strength—especially if Chairman Rodino would issue a subpoena on the President at the same time."

After the meeting broke up, Rodino asked me to stay. I made some suggestions as to what his statement granting the President right to counsel should include. He seemed pleased.

April 9 Since Doar's staff has already used up most of the million dollars we were appropriated six months ago, there was a closed-door hearing today of the House Committee on Administration to consider Rodino and Doar's request for an additional $979,000. When the hearing began, Chairman Hays announced that he would probably oppose the request because of his extremely low regard for Doar and the veracity of his staff. Hays then went into a tirade against Doar and some unnamed staffer with whom he had a personal encounter and had charged with not working very hard. When Hays finished the tirade he left the hearing, leaving the funding request up to a subcommittee chaired by Frank Thompson.

When the subcommittee recessed to go to the floor for a vote, Tom Gettys from South Carolina got me aside. He said he was very concerned about what he called "the arrogant master-race attitude of Doar and the inquiry staff." I suggested to Tom that he not make any statements about that at the hearing but that he should talk to Peter about it personally.

After the hearing, the subcommittee voted to give us our funds. By a party-line vote, they defeated an amendment to slash our budget by $200,000.

Tomorrow the Judiciary Committee is finally scheduled to have a public meeting to vote on issuing our first subpoena, but it was not until about 8 P.M. that Rodino and I got together. Doar's staff was supposed to have prepared a subpoena for review by Peter, me, and Dan Cohen, but Doar was nowhere to be found. I called Doar's assistant, Joe Woods, and discovered that Doar had not followed Rodino's instructions and no subpoena had been prepared. According to Woods, no one on Doar's staff had even thought about drafting the subpoena.

Dan and I were flabbergasted. We had to stay up all night writing the subpoena and preparing copies for the members. It is now early in the morning and I am exhausted.

April 10 Today was a big day. The vote in favor of issuing the subpoena on the President was 33 to 3, with 14 Republicans joining the Democrats. [Two of the members did not vote.] Since Rodino had finally overruled Doar and agreed to permit St. Clair to represent the

President, Frank Polk and I were fairly confident going into the meeting that most of the Republicans would vote for the subpoena.

Even so, when the meeting began I was astounded when Rodino did what I thought was a dumb thing. It was certainly not in the scenario that he had planned with me and Dan Cohen. He attempted to limit the debate on the subpoena to only thirty minutes, far less than the normal time. This would give each of the thirty-eight committee members less than one minute. The motion prevailed by a party-line vote of 21 to 17. This really irritated a number of Republicans—and justifiably. Larry Hogan of Maryland hollered in outrage. Most of the other Republicans also shouted their resentment against Rodino and the Democrats for cutting off their right to debate.

I will never know why Rodino did that. I don't think he was shaving points, or maybe he was. Maybe he had an appointment early in the day and was anxious to go home for the Easter recess, which began this afternoon. Who knows? At any rate the rancor it created needlessly endangered Polk and McClory's efforts to get Republican votes for the subpoena.

Fortunately, it all ended well. Delbert Latta offered a motion to recess and reconvene at 1:30 to permit the Republicans to prepare and offer an amendment to make the subpoena more specific. Rodino could not deny the request.

During the recess, Doar told Rodino he was going downtown to meet a friend for lunch. It was probably fortunate. Rodino agreed to follow the advice of Brooks, Edwards, McClory, Polk, and myself to accept the Latta amendment and to give the members five minutes each for debate.

In the end, Latta and 13 other Republicans voted with 21 Democrats to issue the subpoena on the President. Latta and most of the Republicans publicly commended Rodino for his wisdom in affording the President representation by counsel. With the strong bipartisan vote, the great wound that Doar had driven into the committee's side has been healed—I hope.

April 11 After the vote yesterday, Frank Polk jokingly made the observation that he and I were unappreciated because the bipartisan artistry of our staff work seemed to be effortless. In the *Washington Post* today, Rodino is the hero of yesterday's performance in uniting the committee. Like Frank, I am very pleased. As I see it, Brooks and O'Neill—with the help of Edwards, McClory, and even Latta—worked together to thrust greatness on Rodino.

It is the first day of Easter recess—a beautiful spring day on the Blue Ridge. The redbuds and dogwood blossoms are out and a white-tailed doe and fawn are grazing nearby. I have been here in my hammock under a hickory tree with my tape recorder, reflecting on all of this. As I see it, the vote yesterday was an affirmation of both the cynicism and idealism of democracy. Although we criticize our congressmen for being political, the Constitution requires them to get themselves elected every two years—thus encouraging them to become political animals. The political animal protects itself by looking out for itself more than for its party and its president. Yesterday the fire-eaters separated themselves from Rodino and Doar to protect themselves from public criticism, which is what Latta and the Republicans did by separating themselves from Nixon.

The Easter recess was hardly a rest for most members of the committee. They returned to their districts having to explain the status of the impeachment proceedings. Since the Watergate Committee had deliberated for only one week before issuing its subpoena for the White House tapes in July 1973, many of the Democrats were worried about how to explain why the Judiciary Committee—which had begun its inquiry in October 1973—had delayed issuing its subpoena until April 1974.

As Howard Fields of the United Press later wrote: "The most satisfied person on Capitol Hill at the beginning of the recess period was Peter Rodino. Although a vote to subpoena evidence that almost everyone agreed should be supplied was something less than a vote to impeach the President of the United States, it had the effect of a steam locomotive beginning to move away from the station platform. It wasn't moving very fast, but it was finally chugging in some direction."

The public opinion polls were now reflecting national impatience with our foot-dragging. Thus, the fire-eaters were pleased to be able to tell their constituents that the subpoena had been issued. They were even more pleased to announce that, when Congress reconvened, the committee was scheduled to begin hearings at which Special Counsel Doar would "present the case against Nixon."

12

THE "CASE"—
IN THIRTY-SIX VOLUMES

After President Nixon resigned, the final official report of the House Judiciary Committee stated, "In a status report to the Committee on March 1, 1974 the inquiry staff reported on investigations in six principal areas [including allegations of presidential misconduct relating to]: domestic surveillance . . . intelligence activities . . . the Watergate break-in . . . improprieties in connection with the personal finances of the President . . . use of agencies of the executive branch for political purposes . . . and other misconduct."

To the extent the report implied that Doar had either begun or even planned to begin any investigations of his own of these matters, it was at best misleading.

Well after Nixon's resignation, in *How the Good Guys Finally Won*, Jimmy Breslin revealed that from the very beginning Doar had made "a major decision not to undertake any investigation of his own." And in 1976, Doar's confidante Renata Adler characterized the failure of the inquiry staff to do their own investigation as an intentional "charade."

But during the 1974 Easter recess, the public and most members of the House expected that at the hearings scheduled to begin on May 7, Doar would present the evidence against Nixon that had been uncovered by the "full and thorough" investigation that Rodino had promised. But as soon as Congress was back in session, behind-the-scenes maneuvering began. Howard Fields reported that on April 22, "the first day after the recess, St. Clair called Doar and asked for a five-day extension of the April 25 deadline for complying with the subpoena that had been served on the President on April 11. Doar, Rodino, and ranking Republican Ed Hutchinson agreed to the extension in secret without the approval of the committee—although it was leaked to the public by the White House the next day."

Even though the inquiry staff had not done any original investigations on any of the fifty-five specific allegations covered in its status report of March 1974, on April 23 Doar and his staff give the committee members a status report recommending that we drop eighteen of the allegations. The report summarily concluded that we should disregard all allegations involving the secret bombing of Cambodia, the dismantlement of the Office of Economic Opportunity, and impoundment of funds. As a result, various Democratic members who believed passionately in the appropriateness of these charges became irate.

Doar's recommendations made such a stir among members such as Drinan, Conyers, and Holtzman—whom Rodino had privately nicknamed "the bomb-throwers"—that Rodino feared he would lose if he were challenged by them and the issue were put to a vote in the caucus. To placate these members, Rodino agreed to retain all of the original allegations, but got word to the Republicans that these charges would be dropped.

During the first week after recess, the resolution granting additional funds for the inquiry was also debated on the House floor. During the debate, Del Latta pointed out that committee members themselves had made no major decisions and provided no direction for the staff. Latta was right. In agreeing to a secret investigation by the staff, the committee Democrats, with the exception of Rodino, had excluded themselves from active participation in the inquiry.

After extensive pleading by Rodino and pressure from Tip O'Neill, Wayne Hays did not carry out his earlier threat to denounce the inquiry staff for squandering its first $1 million. Instead, he attacked Nixon for "stonewalling," and voted with the Democratic majority to give the Judiciary Committee another $967,000. That day, Hays also proudly displayed a new watch that he was wearing. It had a caricature of Nixon as Mickey Mouse on its face—with eyes that shifted back and forth with the seconds. Across the face were the words, "I am not a crook."

On Monday, April 29, the President appeared on national television in a "report to the American people on Watergate and impeachment." Regarding the subpoenaed White House tapes, Nixon turned dramatically from the television cameras, pointed to large blue-bound volumes on a table behind his desk, and said, "Here are more than twelve hundred pages of transcripts of private conversations I participated in, plus transcripts of other conversations which were not covered by the subpoena. . . . I shall invite Chairman Rodino and ranking minority member Congressman Hutchinson of Michigan to come to the White House and listen to the actual full tapes of these conversations."

The President appeared confident and open, and seemingly ready to argue his case personally in the court of public opinion, as well as through James St. Clair at the anticipated televised public hearings. The country was relieved—the issues of impeachment were at last going to be resolved in an open manner.

Once again, we were all to be rudely disappointed.

April 29 Rodino had asked me and Doar to be in his office to listen to the President's speech tonight. After the speech Rodino made no comments. He then checked out the news analysis on every channel. After that the first thing he did was to phone Lois. He then asked Doar and me for our advice on how to respond to the President's failure to provide the actual tapes to the full committee.

Doar's advice was simply to put the question of whether Nixon was in noncompliance to a vote of the committee. Rodino cringed. I agreed with Doar, but I added that we shouldn't just put the question of compliance to a vote. The important thing was to show that we had the will to enforce the subpoena. Doar seemed to agree. Rodino began to talk about the dangers of a party-line split, and then left.

When Doar and I were alone I made the point that since the President was now publicly defending himself on TV, it was more important than ever that we begin public evidentiary hearings quickly. At this, Doar became very angry, saying that he was willing to take that kind of talk from some of the members, but was not willing to take it from me. He is adamantly opposed to public evidentiary hearings.

As I see it, without open public hearings we may get an impeachment resolution out of the committee, but not by a large vote, and we may well not even get the impeachment resolution out of the House. Tonight I feel the odds are 70-30 in favor of Nixon.

April 30 The President's speech was a masterpiece of political maneuvering and may begin to turn the tide in his favor. I told Rodino that I knew he and Doar disagreed with me, but I felt it was necessary now more than ever that open investigative hearings get underway.

Rodino wants me to "lay off" the subject. He and Doar now insist on a closed-door presentation of evidence. At Doar's suggestion, Rodino is even considering sequestering all of the members of the committee in hotel rooms to prevent them from leaking information.

I am distressed. Madison, Jefferson, and Edmund Burke must be rolling in their graves. Rodino has asked Doar to find out the weekly price of sequestering the committee members in a hotel.

Alone with Rodino today, I reminded him again of his earlier observation that *parliament* and *parlare* have common Latin roots. I argued, "To impose restrictions of secrecy when the American public has a right to know the truth about Watergate would be unacceptable. And to impose gag rules on members of Congress with respect to so called "evidentiary materials" after the President has agreed that he will make transcripts of his private White House conversations public is ridiculous." His reply was, "You may be right. I haven't fully made up my mind. I'll think about it some more."

May 1 Don Edwards called me very early in the morning. He expressed deep concern that unless the inquiry staff was developing a real case the impeachment will not fly. He is also deeply concerned that there are no plans to question live witnesses. He believes that the committee certainly ought to call Elliott Richardson to testify, as well as Agnew, Haldeman, Dean, and others. He asked me to come up to his office for some coffee. Ailsa was also there. He asked me for my frank assessment.

I told Don how I feel about all of the institutional defects that the President is in the process of exploiting—and also told him how I feel about Doar's plans: "While thirty-eight members of Congress are sitting around believing they are going to be served a real meal, Doar plans to serve them dehydrated pablum. Doar's efforts have been continuously to isolate the committee from the evidence. This has been done in the name of confidentiality, but it also serves Doar's purpose of allowing him to maximize his control over the proceedings."

Edwards said that he was deeply disturbed, and that I had added nothing to his concern that was not already there. He told me that the night before he and Edie had dinner with Woodward and Bernstein. They had impressed on Edwards how vast the facilities available to the Judiciary Committee are in comparison to their own limited facilities as reporters.

We have now spent $1 million on collecting information which is already in the public record but which Doar treats as "confidential." Doar has investigated nothing, and we are now starting to spend another $1 million on a non-investigation.

Richard Nixon and his cohorts have been engaged in an all-out war to emasculate the Congress and the committee. Nixon's war against us has been somewhat open and notorious. But the impeachment inquiry staff in its own insidious way is making every effort to emasculate the Judiciary Committee. God only knows the extent to which Doar will continue with Rodino's approval to usurp committee powers.

May 2 In the morning I received a call from Rodino. He is prepared to accept Nixon's proposal that only he and Hutchinson listen to the subpoenaed White House tapes. I said that I didn't think the Democratic members of the committee would accept such terms. He disagreed rather sharply and insisted that most of them would approve. His plan is to refer the problem to Kastenmeier's subcommittee. Now that the full committee is beginning to come apart at the seams, Rodino is trying to pass the buck to Kastenmeier to deal with the can of worms of evaluating the flawed procedures recommended by the inquiry staff.

At Kastenmeier's request, Doar sent Joe Woods and Hillary Rodham to confer with me as well as with Frank Polk, Sam Garrison, and Bill Dixon. I started to go over their suggested rules of procedure. To me the draft procedures prepared by Woods and Rodham were a sleight-of-hand exercise to minimize the roles of St. Clair and the committee members. I immediately set Dan Cohen to work drafting various possible committee resolutions to vote on the question of Nixon's non-compliance.

Then I called Jack Brooks and suggested to him that he might want to introduce such a resolution. He was pleased. Brooks said, "For Rodino to accept a screening role for Congress is tantamount to removing the cornerstone of the Capitol."

Later in the afternoon, the Kastenmeier subcommittee had met to evaluate the procedures proposed by Woods and Rodham. Thank God that Ed Mezvinsky was there and that he and Kastenmeier began to grasp the significance of what Woods and Rodham were advocating. Mezvinsky raised this question: "When are the committee members themselves going to have access to the investigative material?" Woods and Rodham seemed surprised that such a question would even be asked. They answered that they had not yet addressed that. When the meeting broke up with nothing accomplished, Mezvinsky was holding his head in despair.

On the way back to my office, Dan Cohen summed up what was happening: "What they are trying to do is unconstitutional. The Constitution vested sole power of impeachment in the House. They are trying to rig it so that the sole responsibility is in the impeachment inquiry staff."

May 3 The Democratic caucus met today to decide what to do about the President's refusal to make the actual tapes available to the whole committee. It seemed to me that Rodino was unwilling to provide any leadership. He went around the room asking each and every member what they thought. In my view, the best recommendation came from Liz Holtzman. She suggested that the committee send a contempt citation against Nixon to the Speaker and request that action of the full House on the citation be deferred until our inquiry is completed.

All of the Democrats who spoke up were in favor of dramatic action. Edwards said, "Unless we take an active and aggressive action we will demonstrate to the whole world that we are gutless." He seemed ready for an open confrontation with Doar, coming out very strongly in favor of subpoenaing live witnesses. Edwards wants them called to testify as soon as possible. Doar sat stonefaced and said nothing.

John Seiberling, who had laryngitis, provided some comic relief. He was sitting next to Father Drinan. When Drinan launched into a tirade against Nixon for "rendering the committee impotent," Seiberling croaked out, "Why don't you excommunicate him?"

Barbara Jordan made a dramatic appeal to Rodino to exercise leadership by making a strong public statement rejecting the President's proposal.

After going round and round, Rodino asked Doar for his advice. Doar refused to take a position and said that the question of what to do about the the President's action was for the committee to decide.

When Rodino came to me, I agreed with both Don and Liz. Holtzman smiled at me—for the first time since she came to Washington.

In the end, the committee decided on a formal finding that the President was in noncompliance with our subpoena.

May 4 This morning I went for a walk in Shenandoah National Park and then chopped some wood. I have been mulling over the events of the past week, and I am incensed with Doar and some of his top assistants such as Joe Woods and Hillary Rodham. It seems to me that Haldeman and Ehrlichman are crude amateurs at arrogance in comparison to the more polished and sophisticated arrogance and deceit of some of Doar's assistants.

May 5 Some other things happened during the past week that I have not yet recorded. Bernie Hellring was in town and came to my office. He had previously had a discussion with Rodino to see what he could do about a problem confronting Addonizio. Hughie is being kept in a maximum security cell under a classification based on the notion of making him into an example because of the nature of his crimes as a Newark government official. Bernie and Rodino are trying to use congressional influence to get Hughie moved into a less-oppressive environment. They have decided that Bernie should also talk to Kastenmeier [whose subcommittee had jurisdiction over federal prisons].

I had a dinner meeting on Thursday night with Dean George Alexander of the law school at the University of Santa Clara. Alexander is wooing me to join the faculty with a teaching requirement of only six hours per week. I have told Tip O'Neill and Don Edwards that I will not continue as chief counsel under Rodino's chairmanship once the impeachment inquiry is over.

May 6 The first day of evidentiary hearings scheduled to begin tomorrow has been canceled. I still have not heard from Doar as to when he will be ready to begin.

I called Dick Cates at his apartment. Dick was more disturbed than I have ever known him. He said, "I am praying," and he meant it literally. He has been given no look at the final product of any evidentiary material that Doar intends to present. Dick says, "I am standing by in case the committee needs my kind of lawyer." My fears are that Dick will never get a chance to present a real case, even on the obstruction of justice charge.

May 7 Rodino phoned me at 7:30 this morning. St. Clair is demanding that we begin public hearings promptly. Rodino says that he now reluctantly agrees with Brooks and me to begin the hearings on Thursday afternoon, but he still agrees with Doar that no live witnesses are to be called to testify.

Tonight when I left the Capitol to walk home, I bumped into Tip O'Neill. We chatted for a few minutes. He asked me to tell him in confidence how I felt about what was happening, and I expressed my apprehensions to him as best I could: "Who is going to make the case, and when, and if there are to be no live witnesses, how many 'yes' votes can we get?"

He was very worried—and pleased that I was worried, that we both have a lot to worry about. As he got into his car he said, "Take it easy—and thanks."

It was an eventful evening. As I was walking up Independence Avenue, Chuck Morgan and his wife Camille stopped and gave me a ride. Chuck gave me a lobbyist pep talk—urging me to start an investigation of the Department of Justice, including Earl Silbert, Henry Peterson, and Elliot Richardson. I told him he was preaching to the choir, and that he should be lobbying Rodino and Doar.

May 8 Tomorrow at 2 P.M. the committee begins its evidentiary hearings. I feel exhausted and somewhat strange. I cannot afford to dwell on my thoughts—and my fears—about the importance of this process.

This morning at the Democratic caucus, Rodino announced his plans to close the hearings and impose confidentiality on the members. He hadn't given any of us forewarning, and the caucus was a donnybrook. Many of the Democrats were rebellious and did not want to comply with the restrictions advocated by Doar and the inquiry staff.

Everyone was nervous. We went around and around on the subject of whether the hearings should be closed. Some of the fire-eaters are beginning to separate themselves from Rodino and Doar. Rangel, Conyers, and Waldie in particular were opposed to closed hearings. But no one other than Brooks is willing to go to the mat with Doar and Rodino. The caucus acquiesced in closing tomorrow's hearing, and Brooks walked out in disgust.

Tonight I think that Dick Cates is right; the best thing to do is pray.

On the morning of May 9, a long line of spectators stretched outside of Room 2141 of the Rayburn Building. Inside, a mob of reporters and TV cameramen milled about. When Rodino arrived, the klieg lights went on. Peter sat in his leather chairman's chair, pounded his gavel to convene the hearing, and then entertained a motion to close the hearing. The motion was passed, the klieg lights went off, and the room was cleared of spectators and newsmen. The doors were locked, the hearing room was swept for electronic bugs, and the hearings began in "executive session."

To the disappointment of the networks and the public, the mahogany doors of Room 2141 remained locked and the proceedings secret for the next six weeks. During that period, no live witnesses were called and no testimony, sworn or otherwise, was heard from anyone other than Doar or his staff. The "testimony" consisted of the inquiry staff simply reading aloud from photocopies of documents obtained by the Ervin Committee, the Watergate Special Prosecutor, and other bodies that had not conducted an impeachment investigation. At the end of the six weeks, the documents were published and released to the media en masse in the form of thirty-six volumes.

Two years after Nixon's resignation, Renata Adler, praised Doar for his strategy of secrecy and delay. Adler's contention was that the non-investigation orchestrated by Doar was a "valuable charade" in that it allowed Doar and a smaller group to do the important work. As Adler described the non-investigation: ". . . the machine itself, firmly required to be directionless, produced, naturally enough, no investigation, and in the end no case. It is commonly said that 'the case' is in those thirty-odd staff volumes. Only by people who have not read them: hardly anyone has read them."

Investigative journalist Victor Lasky was less laudatory. After interviewing a number of committee members as well as conducting several years of research on the closed-door hearings, Lasky wrote in 1977:

> ·. The thirty-eight members of the Judiciary Committee sat behind closed doors and listened to Doar drone out evidence. What Doar and his staff were doing was pulling together a vast amount of material from numerous sources: the Senate Watergate Committee, the Joint Committee on Internal Revenue Taxation, the Internal Revenue Service, grand juries and·other congressional fact-finding committees. All this information was compiled in thirty-six black loose-leaf notebooks. . . . Which is why, in the end Doar earned the title pinned on him by a detractor, "The World's Greatest Archivist."
>
> Even Democratic members were appalled. "If these meetings were ever televised, the country would impeach us," said one [Jack Brooks]. "This isn't an investigation, it's a compilation," said another [Walter Flowers]. And the Republicans agreed. "Damned dull," said Robert McClory of Illinois. . . . Congressman McClory put it this way, "I kept waiting for the bombshell to appear, and it never appeared." Even Democrats agreed that not one piece of evidence had been produced—no "hand in the cookie jar" or "smoking gun"—which would show

conclusively that the President was guilty of a crime, or at least a broader "impeachable offense."

The impeachment forces were worried. Some worried out loud. As Ed Mezvinsky said somewhat incoherently, "This is it, this is the crunch. When we put the package together. Are we equipped to do it? Can we pull it off? That's the question now. I'm very concerned about that."

But seeking new material would have meant calling witnesses; and this Rodino and company wanted to avoid at all costs. Thus none of the principal Watergate figures were interrogated by Doar. . . . The failure to do more original digging drew the fire of Charles Wiggins, the Republican congressman who [later] brilliantly argued the President's case during the public debate. Concerning Doar's presentation Wiggins said ". . . you don't start your case by calling a transcript. You have to call witnesses."

When the secret hearings were finally concluded, *Washington Post* reporter William Greider, who eventually became editor of *Rolling Stone*, wrote, "Even the most bullish Democrats conceded that their investigations did not produce a thundering consensus that Nixon should be removed from office, the kind of compelling evidence which would remove all doubts about the outcome."

Ed Mezvinsky was later publicly to describe how worried he and other Democrats had been about the work of Doar and the inquiry staff. At first Mezvinsky had relied heavily on the flawed advice of Doar, Nussbaum, and Rodham. He had accepted Rodham's flawed assertions that it would be unprecedented to give the President's counsel the right to cross-examine witnesses. In a memoir published in 1977, Mezvinsky admitted how he had ill-advisedly spoken out against the President's counsel:

> My voice became louder as my speech quickened. "I really resent the thought of what's happening because we are trying to be objective, we are trying to run a fair investigation, and now I think we see a political storm trooper coming in here to represent him [Nixon]."

Later in the same memoir, Mezvinsky wrote about the closed-door period:

Some of the majority members began to talk of our somehow hiring a special prosecutor or a kind of task force, to make sure that the "case" against Nixon was vigorously pursued. What bothered people like John Conyers, and even those of more calm demeanor like Barbara Jordan, was that John Doar's presentation was so slow and careful that he would never get around to "making his case." For days, that phrase was popular. Several members also expressed concern that the "faceless forty"—the lawyers on the inquiry staff who were gathering the material that eventually made its way into our black books—were too research-oriented, and not sufficiently experienced in the preparation of a case that builds toward a showing of strong guilt such as in the preparation of a criminal case, or as in this situation, a bill of impeachment.

I suffered the same frustrations about the tedious pace of the presentation, but my continuing close contact with Bernie Nussbaum reinforced my faith in our staff. Once, in early May Bernie patiently heard me out as I went over my concerns that we were not developing the kind of evidence that would be needed. Then he looked at me for a moment and said, "Don't worry Ed, we've got a case." I knew I couldn't press him on the point—there had already been a big flap over leaks to the press from someone either on or with the committee—but I thought about his comments a lot in the next few weeks.

For years to come, everyone on Capitol Hill who, like Ed Mezvinsky, knew Bernie Nussbaum and Hillary Rodham in the spring of 1974 had a lot to think about. Nussbaum was the only one of the forty lawyers recruited by Doar who had extensive experience in litigating issues of fact. Doar had placed Nussbaum in charge of investigating the facts relating to Watergate and five other areas of presidential misconduct.

On Burke Marshall's recommendation, Doar had assigned Rodham to work closely with Nussbaum on procedural rules for presenting evidence to Congress. In the name of security against leaks, Doar and his key aides kept secret that there was no original investigation by the inquiry staff. In implementing their hidden agenda, Doar and Nussbaum, with Rodham's help, were misleading, if not deceiving, Congress.

13

THE SECRET HEARINGS

On the morning of May 9, 1974, the day the Judiciary Committee began its secret hearings, an editorial calling for Nixon's resignation appeared in the country's most powerful Republican newspaper, the *Chicago Tribune*. Previously, the famous Hearst paper had been staunchly pro-Nixon. The *Tribune* now stridently denounced the President as "immoral," lacking "concern for high principles," "devious," "vacillating," and displaying "dismaying gaps in knowledge." Before Rodino gaveled open the May 9 hearing, Bob McClory and Tom Railsback, both Republicans from Illinois, showed Rodino a copy of the editorial. McClory said, "Let's make the case and get it over."

As early as December 1973, when the impeachment inquiry's first funding resolution had been brought up on the House floor, Rodino and Jack Brooks, as well as Frank Polk and myself, were aware that McClory was ready to vote "yes" on impeachment and was waiting impatiently for Doar and Jenner simply to make the case. We suspected that Railsback, who was a very junior Republican, would follow McClory's lead. On May 7, two days before the *Tribune* demanded that Nixon resign, Railsback had told journalist Elizabeth Drew what he thought about Nixon:

> He's sounding the death knell for the [Republican] Party. He's killing the Party. Have you seen the latest poll? Fifty-two percent would vote for the Democratic candidate for Congress, twenty-nine percent for the Republican. It's devastating. It's worse than '64. . . . The American people are going to take out their wrath on the Republican candidates what they can't do to the President."

During the weeks of secret hearings, Railsback suffered tremendous psychological strain. The more Doar and Jenner failed to make an evidentiary case, the more speechless Tom became—literally. He actually lost his voice, the causes of which, he acknowledged, were "probably psychosomatic." During the same period, Ed Hutchinson, the committee's ranking Republican, also suffered from what may have been a stress-induced illness. He stopped attending the secret hearings and was at one point hospitalized. Under the seniority system, Bob McClory became the de facto leader of the committee Republicans.

At the start of the closed-door hearings, there were only three committee members actively pressing Doar and Jenner to make the case expeditiously and make Jerry Ford President as soon as possible: Brooks, McClory, and Railsback.

As for Rodino, the opening of the secret hearings coincided with a political uprising in Newark that seemed consistent with the White House's carrot-and-stick tactics to induce Rodino to shave points to help the President. On May 8, John McLaughlin appeared on nationwide TV to proclaim that the President had given America "outstanding moral leadership." The next morning, just before the hearings opened, Rodino received a distress call from Tony Siriano of his Newark office. McLaughlin had incited the New Jersey Right to Life Committee to make Rodino aware of the political clout Nixon had in Newark. The Republican-dominated anti-abortion activists were starting demonstrations and distributing literature urging their members to vote against Rodino in the upcoming Democratic primary—and accusing him of being in league with pro-abortion Democrats who were anxious to impeach Nixon.

Within just another few days, most of the Democratic members of the committee were demoralized by Doar's presentation, as was later reported by both Ed Mezvinsky and Victor Lasky. Even the liberal fire-eaters, who for partisan political purposes wanted to keep Nixon in office, did not want him to be exonerated by Doar's failure to make a case for impeachment. Those Democrats who had hoped to impeach Nixon soon, such as George Danielson of California, were becoming sympathetic to Railsback's condition. Danielson was more confident of reelection than Railsback was, yet he was not without his own anxieties. One of the most stout-hearted Democrats—and a former FBI agent—Danielson described his reaction this way: "This impeachment thing makes me sleep like a baby. I wake up every two hours and cry."

By the second week, a bipartisan rebellion arose against Doar's exclusive custody of the "evidentiary materials." Without fanfare or media attention, Brooks and McClory quietly put together enough votes to give the regular committee staff, headed by me and Frank Polk, access to some of the inquiry staff's secret files. Rodino also reluctantly agreed to let individual members seek help and advice on the impeachment inquiry from Frank and me as well as other regular staff members.

Frank and I were now able for the first time to review the report of the Watergate grand jury that Special Prosecutor Jaworski had transmitted to Doar for presentation to the committee. Jaworski was a Texan and knew Jack Brooks socially. He had told Brooks that the report he had given Doar "wrapped up a case against Nixon, like a package from Neiman-Marcus." Under the confidentiality rules imposed by Rodino and Doar, Brooks had not seen the report either, and he was anxious to at least have Frank and I read it. (We were still restricted from making copies.) After reviewing the report, my belief was confirmed that Doar, Nussbaum, and Rodham were misreading the law, and in doing so were disregarding evidence of Nixon's participation in criminal conspiracies.

It was not until 1976 that Jaworski went public with the truth about the grand jury's report, which had been meticulously sanitized out of Doar's thirty-six volumes. In his book *The Right and the Power* Jaworski included a chapter entitled "The Case Against the President." Without mentioning Doar's flawed legal theories, the chapter opened with two paragraphs correctly summarizing longstanding legal precedents that Doar, Nussbaum, and Rodham had obfuscated. In an analysis of basic principles of criminal law worthy of a law school textbook, Jaworski pointed out certain well-recognized rules:

> . . . one who learns of an ongoing criminal conspiracy and casts his lot with the conspirators becomes a member of the conspiracy. Once the existence of a conspiracy is shown, slight evidence may be sufficient to connect a defendant with it. But one does not become a member of a conspiracy simply because of receiving information regarding its nature and scope; he must have what the courts describe as a "stake in the success of

the venture." He "must in some sense promote the venture himself, make it his own, have a stake in its outcome. . . ." Although
one member of the conspiracy must commit an overt act, it is
not necessary that every conspirator do so.

Implicitly refuting what I had characterized as Doar's "Nuremberg defense," the Jaworski grand jury report specifically charged
Nixon with acting as a co-conspirator in the obstruction of justice in
the Watergate case proscribed by Section 1510 of the U.S. Criminal
Code. In his summary of the grand jury report, Jaworski noted:

> The available evidence reasonably indicated that the
> President participated in a conspiracy to violate certain other
> statutes in addition to those specifically charged in the indict-
> ment, and that he fairly could be held culpable, as a principal
> and on a theory of vicarious liability, for additional substan-
> tive offenses.
> There was evidence that the President conspired with oth-
> ers to violate 18 U.S.C. 1503—obstruction of justice—via the
> means set out in the coverup indictment. This included paying
> of funds and offers of clemency and other benefits in order to
> influence the testimony of witnesses, making and facilitating
> the making of false statements and declarations, obtaining
> information about the ongoing investigation of the Justice
> Department for the purpose of diverting or thwarting the inves-
> tigation.
> There was evidence that the President conspired with oth-
> ers to violate 18 U.S.C. 1623—perjury—which included the
> President's direct and personal efforts to encourage and facili-
> tate the giving of misleading and false testimony by aides.
> There was evidence that the President conspired with oth-
> ers to violate 18 U.S.C. 203(d)—bribery—by directly and indi-
> rectly suggesting and impliedly offering something of value—
> money and clemency in the case of Howard Hunt and/or a par-
> don in the case of some aides—with the intent to influence
> their testimony before courts, grand juries, and congressional
> committees.
> There was evidence that the President conspired with oth-
> ers to violate 18 U.S.C. 1505—obstruction of congressional
> committee—by corruptly endeavoring to influence testimony

of various persons before the Senate Watergate Committee. . .

At the very least, evidence establishing that Nixon was a member of a conspiracy that had as its means or objects violations of these statutes would also establish violations by Nixon of the particular statutes themselves on the theory of vicarious liability. In addition. 18 U.S.C. 2 provides that one who "counsels, induces or procures" the commission of an offense such as bribery, obstruction of justice or of a criminal investigation, or perjury by another is "punishable as a principal."

Jaworski's accurate formulation of the case against Nixon directly contradicted Doar's bizarre theory that as head of the executive branch, the President could not constitutionally be charged with entering into a criminal conspiracy with his subordinates.

Rather than allow even Dick Cates or any of the other lawyers on the inquiry staff to study the report in its entirety, Doar ordered that it be kept under lock and key and made available only in fragments. And in the materials prepared for presentation to the committee, the grand jury report was broken down into small needles buried amongst the evidentiary haystacks.

When I was finally able to review the report on May 13, I was relieved to note that it more than confirmed the professionalism of the legal analysis of known evidence that Bill Dixon, Dick Cates, and William Dobrovir had evaluated prior to Doar's appointment. I recalled that on his very first day on our payroll Doar had denounced Bill Dixon as incompetent for having tentatively reached the same conclusion regarding bribery charges against Nixon reflected in Jaworski's report. Doar had refused even to look at the Dobrovir brief, and wanted to fire Dick Cates for having advised Rodino that there was already enough evidence on the public record to convict Nixon for conspiring to obstruct justice.

A few days after Frank Polk and I read Jaworski's report, Dick Cates told me in confidence that he was returning to Wisconsin and his private practice. Doar and Nussbaum had excluded him from even preparing the documents and summaries of information being presented at our hearings. They had even instructed him that he was not to read the grand jury report in its entirety, and tried to limit him to one small fragment. He had ignored their orders and had read the entire document. I felt badly for Dick. Perhaps Bernie Hellring and I had put him in an untenable position by persuading

Rodino to keep him on the inquiry staff under Doar's supervision as one of Rodino's extra lines in the water. By now as I saw it, Doar and Nussbaum were themselves guilty of obstructing the Judiciary Committee's investigation. I had also decided that Rodino was no longer worthy of sufficient respect to enable me to remain as chief counsel under his chairmanship. I gave Rodino private notice that I would be leaving the committee staff by the end of the year. I also confided in the members of a small group that had started to confer on impeachment matters, which included Brooks, McClory, Polk, and Edwards. I continued to talk into the tape recorders that I kept at home and in my weekend cottage, filling tape after tape with my evaluations and perceptions of the inmpeachment inquiry, which Henry Hubbard of *Newsweek* dubbed "the tortoise on the hill."

May 19 On Thursday a very important development took place. On behalf of the President, St. Clair presented to the committee his request that further impeachment proceedings be entirely open. I see this as a very well-aimed and dangerous torpedo.

Jack Brooks, Frank Polk, and I had lunch together on Friday and discussed this problem at some length. We agreed that if we put Doar's presentation on national TV, everyone will lose except the President. If we go public, that is exactly what Nixon wants.

With Rodino's approval, the TV people are erecting a giant platform outside the Rayburn Building and are removing the back wall of our hearing room so the cameras can be behind the committee looking at Doar presenting the case against Nixon. Rodino has also agreed to allow the media to replace silver water pitchers by the members' desks with jugs that do not reflect the TV lights. The media is already announcing that there will be gavel-to-gavel coverage. The danger is enormous for the following reasons: If the committee continues in the manner that Doar has started—reading aloud from the "pablum books"—the effect would be a national calamity. It would have the disastrous effect of boring the public to tears. All of the members would look bad—sitting like bumps on a log, playing no active role, and expressing no moral outrage. The Democratic members would look particularly bad—docilely tolerating evil without a peep.

The public would immediately get the picture for what it is. They would hear and see Doar droning on and on with a lot of disjointed facts about a lot of people other than Nixon, and would hear no evidence incriminating Nixon. St. Clair would then get national TV coverage by publicly exposing the painful truth. The awful truth is that despite $2 million of taxpayer money and a staff of more than forty lawyers, Doar's six months of investigations have uncovered nothing new. Contrary to Rodino's fine words at the start of the inquiry, Doar has in fact left *all* the stones unturned. In contrast, St. Clair so far has successfully defended Nixon with a small staff of seven lawyers borrowed from the Justice Department and the White House.

Under the circumstances, Brooks and I have decided to work next week to keep the hearings closed, hopefully with help from McClory and Frank Polk. It will be interesting to see what the outcome of this will be.

Today I watched *Face the Nation*. Jim Naughton referred to the Judiciary Committee members as putty in the hands of John Doar and the inquiry staff. I believe that is correct. There is a part of me which thinks that maybe it would be good to open the hearings and let the torpedo hit the ship and let the committee members who refuse to listen to Brooks and McClory wake up to the fact that the committee as an institution has been emasculated by Rodino and Doar.

May 20 When I arrived at the office I was astounded to see that the entire hearing room had with Rodino's approval already been taken over by the media. The scaffold outside the building was finished, and the wall was broken through to allow the cameras in back of us, as well as to the right and left and in front of us. I met Peter Hackus of NBC in the hearing room and chided him about this. I pointed to one of the cameras and said, "That's the same camera that helped Jack Ruby murder Oswald and spared the country a public trial." Peter got the point right away and laughed.

Brooks, McClory, Polk, and I have been pondering all day on how to avoid the vote tomorrow on opening Doar's presentation to a public hearing with TV coverage. We considered a variety of parliamentary maneuvers, but came to the conclusion that we should avoid anything sophisticated or tricky. What we need to keep the hearings closed are votes. Brooks and I are sure only of Edwards's vote. To keep the hearings closed, the Republicans will have to vote to deny the President's request for public hearings.

Frank and I spent an hour or two mapping out our strategy. Later in the day Frank told me that he had been fairly successful in explaining to the Republican members why they should vote to keep the hearings closed. Brooks and I also did our best to explain to the entire committee the dangers of opening the hearings. We reminded them that Dick Cates, whom we had counted on to put the case against Nixon together, had resigned from the staff.

John Conyers in particular agreed with us. He called me up to his office for some wine, some jazz, and a protracted conversation about all of the problems we were facing. He then said he would get to work rounding up Democrats to attend a rump meeting tomorrow morning in Brooks's office.

May 27 I am sitting in a deck chair with a fine view of the Shenandoah River, reflecting on what hopefully has been a turning point in the impeachment proceedings. Things went even better at the meeting Tuesday than Brooks and I had hoped. The hearings remained closed. Brooks and I were vindicated. Only a month ago, when McClory and Polk, with our help, had fought to allow Nixon to be represented by St. Clair, Rodino had accused us of being "puppets on St. Clair's string." This past week McClory and Frank had done a masterful job. The Republican members lined up solidly to support McClory's efforts to defy the White House and St. Clair and keep the hearings closed.

As for the Democrats, only two were ready to expose Doar's presentation to the public. One was Rodino and the other was Wayne Owens, a freshman from Utah who had formerly been a staff aide to Ted Kennedy. Rodino didn't even want to put the matter to a vote. He knew he would lose.

Doar was permitted to go on reading all thirty-six volumes of documents aloud without making a case. But the politics of impeachment had changed. In Hutchinson's absence McClory was now leading the committee's Republicans. He was cooperating with Brooks to force Rodino to make the case against Nixon and put Jerry Ford in the White House.

14

IMPEACHMENT IS POLITICAL

By the end of the Memorial Day weekend, a disquieting truth became clear to the committee Democrats. With the possible exception of Ed Mezvinsky, who had trusted Bernie Nussbaum, everyone was certain that the inquiry staff had done no investigation of its own.

Neither Republicans nor Democrats took seriously Doar's rationalization that the impeachment inquiry was "nonadversarial and nonpolitical," for it was an absurd claim unrelated to the realities of the situation. Freshman Republican Bill Cohen of Maine (who later became Senator) echoed the sentiments of most, if not all, of the committee members about the nature of the impeachment process when he discussed his thoughts about the chances for impeachment with Elizabeth Drew:

> If I had to predict, I would say he's going to make it. There's not enough time. We haven't heard enough evidence yet. And there's going to be unbearable pressure exerted. There's St. Clair saying the Judiciary Committee has all the evidence to find the President innocent. It's Orwellian. We're caught in the catch phrases, the symbols, the emotions, the media, the Presidency, the life forces that drive people. It's not a judicial decision, it's a political one. I think you'll hear more and more about how impeachment will tear the country apart. It will if they keep saying it will.
>
> But we live by symbolism and catch phrases, and we're stuck with them.

Cohen's perceptions of impeachment as a broad political process was consistent with that of the Judiciary Committee's most conservative Democrat, Walter Flowers of Alabama: "I think the broad view is the right view, and Jerry Ford wasn't all wrong when he said [at the time of the Douglas impeachment inquiry] that an impeachable offense is whatever a majority of the House of Representatives says it is."

Flowers was a good friend of fellow Alabaman Charles Morgan, whose sentiments about impeachment were also unabashedly political. During his long campaign for impeachment, Morgan had, in Alabama plain talk, told me, Flowers, and everyone else on Capitol Hill who would listen to him that "the House could be forced to act against Nixon in self-defense. The people could make them move, and sooner or later congressional cowardice might do Nixon in."

Morgan was right. By requiring House members to run for reelection every two years, the founders made fear of defeat at the polls an omnipresent driving force. As an aide to former Representative Ed Willis of Louisiana once told me, "Ninety-nine out of every one hundred congressmen fear voters more than they fear God. If they have to choose between saving their political asses and their immortal souls, they will favor their asses."

With that in mind, the committee Democrats recognized the California Democratic gubernatorial primary on June 4 as a political bellwether. Jerry Waldie, who authored the principal impeachment resolution and led the fire-eaters, was defeated by Jerry Brown. In the Democratic cloakroom, Waldie explained his defeat with black humor: "The people have spoken. Goddamn the people."

Like the rest of the fire-eaters, Waldie had supported the Rodino-Doar strategy of delay, rejecting the impeach-him-promptly political advice of the more populist Jack Brooks and Chuck Morgan. He had openly defied Tip O'Neill by trying to delay Jerry Ford's confirmation as Vice President, and had initially supported Rodino's efforts to deny Nixon representation by counsel at our hearings. Democratic voters, who were generally pro-impeachment, saw him as a "Washington foot-dragger who was more smoke than fire in the battle against Republican conservatives." So the Democrats in California decided that they didn't want him as their challenger to Governor Ronald Reagan.

After his primary loss, Waldie joined forces with O'Neill, Brooks, Edwards, and Conyers to wrest control of the impeachment inquiry from Rodino and Doar and make the long forestalled case against Nixon. Waldie and most of the Democrats now agreed with Brooks that Doar was not only boring them but was also demeaning them by requiring them to don earphones and listen for hours to every word of the White House tapes that we had been able to obtain. A more efficient use of time would have been to provide accurate written transcripts, which would have been much more comprehensible and could be studied thoroughly in less time.

In addition, Rodino had permitted Doar to assign Rodham to help censor the tapes to eliminate so-called "inflammatory" material, including profanity and so-called ethnic slurs. Holtzman was incensed by the censoring and wanted to hear the unexpurgated recordings. Mezvinsky also argued passionately that copies of all of the tapes should be made available for public listening. But Rodino and Wiggins combined forces to get enough votes to maintain the censoring, to keep the censored tapes secret from the public, and to allow Doar to drone on and on.

Even some of the Republicans who had been pleased that Doar and Jenner had abstained from investigating Nixon were beginning to fear the anti-Nixon voters in their party. Like Barry Goldwater, Melvin Laird, and Elliot Richardson, many of the Judiciary Committee Republicans had wished that Nixon would resign. One Republican House member was quoted in the press:

> The light dawned that it was counterproductive to try to get a group together to ask him to leave. At least Republican members have gone back to reading the transcripts [of the Nixon tapes] and saying, "Come on Judiciary, find something and get it over." More and more people think he is guilty. I think the feeling among the Republicans is that we were made to look like jackasses by the Democrats. The Democrats are motivated by a desire to string it out. . . . His White House people come here looking for support. Most of us tell them to go away. We didn't stand up for him. I'm not sure that the White House got the message though. I don't think they understand anything at all.

Although the source was anonymous, the sentiments could have been McClory's or Railsback's.

There is an adage amongst criminal defense lawyers that "delay is on the side of the defendant." Even if delaying the impeachment or resignation of Nixon was in danger of killing the Republican Party, as Railsback had put it, Nixon had staunch defenders on the committee. A group led by Charles Wiggins of California and nicknamed the "stalwarts" by the press had decided that because of Doar's failure to make the case or even conduct an investigation they had a special responsibility to defend Nixon to the end. They argued that the President was dealing effectively with pressing international affairs while the Democrats were trying to impede him—and that the domestic economy was being intentionally neglected by the Democratic Congress so the blame would fall on the President.

The White House strategy was to accuse the Judiciary Committee Democrats of "wallowing in Watergate." Washington journalist Elizabeth Drew was now forecasting that Nixon might prevail: "Something else seems to be in the air. The President's extraordinary durability is making an impression. It appears to have self-fulfilling effects: he might endure; therefore what side does one want to have been on in this ultimate struggle over power? Nixon is still the President, and is still feared."

During that period, confusion reigned at every meeting of the Democratic caucus, the Republican caucus, or the full committee. The President had not complied fully with our first subpoena for tapes, and had refused to comply with a second subpoena. Vice President Ford justified the President's noncompliance on the grounds that the committee was still conducting its inquiry in secret and had no plans to call any live witnesses to testify on the charges that Democrats had been making for months. To the chagrin of pro-impeachment Democrats, who now included Waldie, Edwards, Kastenmeier, Conyers, Rangel, and Holtzman, Rodino joined forces with the stalwarts to muster enough votes to defeat motions by Waldie and Conyers to cite the President for contempt. Even a more tepid motion by Railsback to ask the courts to enforce our subpoenas was resoundingly rejected.

By now, according to my head count, every member of the committee except Rodino was in favor of rejecting Doar's recommendation that we hear no testimony from live witnesses. But each committee member was an attorney and had his or her own list of proposed witnesses based on his or her own blend of legal and political considerations. To contribute to the turmoil, the inquiry staff in-group had Rodham prepare memoranda recommending procedures that would require witnesses—if they were called—to be interrogated by the inquiry staff only. We were now faced with the problems of getting some form of bipartisan agreement among the disparate committee members as to which witnesses should be called, whether they should be deposed prior to public hearings, and who was going to cross-examine them.

During the turmoil Rodino handled his frequent TV and press interviews with a skill and finesse that served to exacerbate the dissatisfaction of the other Democrats. He presented himself as a judicious chairman who was determined to be fair to the President, and created the impression that his younger Democratic colleagues, such as Waldie and Conyers, were hotheads whose rush to judgment he was appropriately resisting. Behind the scenes, Rodino was still resisting O'Neill and had advised Tip that the soonest he and Doar would be finished with the committee's inquiry would be August 15, and so the debate on the House floor would have to be postponed until then.

O'Neill recounted this timetable to Seiberling and Mezvinsky, and the result was a rebellion. At the next Democratic caucus, Seiberling and Mezvinsky were beside themselves. Almost in unison they screamed, "That's too late! That will kill it!" The closer we got to election time, the more members of Congress would want to put off a vote on impeachment until the next session. And since the House, unlike the Senate, is not a "continuous body," the whole process would have to start all over again. Nixon would be halfway through his term and presidential politics would be well underway for 1976. The chances of impeachment at that point were infinitesimal.

Delay, which started out as the strategy of Rodino and the pro-Kennedy fire-eaters, was now clearly on the side of the defendant. Led by Wiggins, the stalwarts seemed likely to prevail in defending the President from impeachment.After the first week of secret hearings, bipartisan leadership in accelerating the process in defiance of Rodino and Doar was coming mostly from Democrat Brooks and Republican McClory—with McClory ready to take even stronger action than Brooks. McClory and Frank Polk had read Jefferson's manual, which was still part of the official rules of the House. McClory had decided on a procedure that had deep roots in the eighteenth century and the earlier traditions of Parliament. As Jefferson had put it, the rules of the House affirmed and reconciled "the rights of the many, of the few, and of the one." Among the most cherished rights of any one member of the House was the right to have access to facts in the possession of the president.

Even if every other member of the Judiciary Committee were to acquiesce in Doar's non-investigation and in the President's non-compliance with our subpoenas, McClory had a right to introduce a privileged motion on the House floor that could force a showdown between the President, who wanted to withhold information, and the people's representatives, who had a right to the information. Jefferson had entitled the procedure a "motion for a resolution of inquiry." The motion had fallen into disuse over the years, for it had the effect of challenging committees that were engaged in bipartisan coverups. That was exactly what McClory wanted to do—challenge the bipartisan coverup being fostered by Rodino and committee members who were willing to remain passive.

Bob McClory was a deeply religious man, who in May had believed that he had a moral responsibility to help thrust greatness on Rodino by forcing him to do the right thing. By early June, McClory was ready to defy Rodino openly

June 4 Yesterday Frank Polk came to my office to let me know that McClory had decided to pursue a strong course of action, had been conferring with Frank about it, and had asked Frank to confer with me in the hope that I would recommend the strategy to Jack Brooks.

McClory is considering a three-pronged attack on Nixon. One, a motion for a resolution of inquiry, which would take control of the inquiry away from Doar and Rodino. Two, a motion for a contempt citation against the President. Three, a motion to censure the President.

I phoned Brooks immediately. First I thanked him for a book on gardening he had sent me. Then I told him that Frank was with me and was hoping to work out an alliance. With Frank on an extension, the three of us discussed McClory's approach and agreed tentatively that it was a good idea. Brooks made the observation that to do anything like that on the House floor would be so disruptive for Doar and Rodino that they simply would not know how to handle it. Brooks and I agreed with McClory's suggestion that we sleep on it for a few days before deciding how best to proceed.

June 6 Frank Polk told me that both John Rhodes [Minority Leader] and Les Arends [Republican Whip] called McClory today to try to order him to turn off his plans for a resolution of inquiry. Frank told me that he had advised McClory, "Of course they would try to prevent you from doing that, because they don't want the responsibility of having to decide the impeachment question in the full House. They prefer that the decision be made in the Judiciary Committee." I think Frank is right. McClory's action would be so gutsy that it would probably also shake up Tip O'Neill, who also wants to make Rodino bite the bullet and resolve the matter in the Judiciary Committee.

I asked Frank whether he thought McClory's desire to move for a resolution of inquiry was motivated by courage or cowardice. The two of us meditated a bit and decided that it was a combination—with courage predominating. McClory understands the extent to which the committee has been emasculated. Having taken a strong position against the President, he is now fearful that Wiggins and the stalwarts will prevail, and is afraid that the White House will retaliate against him. Interesting how the system is designed so that members of Congress are sometimes motivated by political fears to show courage. Of course, as Frank puts it, "If McClory presses for a resolution of inquiry and loses, he will go down in flames for his kamikaze approach." With Rhodes and Arends opposed to a resolution of inquiry, my guess is that Frank will probably help McClory understand that for all of his boldness it is likely that he will lose.

It is significant that at the hearing today McClory announced that Hutchinson is recuperating and will be back in a few days. Brooks made a remark to me that "Hutchinson is finding out what McClory is up to—and that's why Hutchinson is coming back."

Also, the press is getting more and more critical of not only Rodino but the entire Congress. Joe Kraft had a column asking, "How many times does the President have to streak before the Congess has the courage to say that he has no clothes?" Father McLaughlin at the White House retaliated, saying it is Rodino who is the emperor with no clothes, keeping our hearings closed to cover our failure to make a case against Nixon.

June 8 I am very fearful. When this is over I hope that we can go back to the eighteenth century, where we belong. The founders viewed the executive branch as the authoritarian branch. The question now is whether the Congress is even a co-equal of the President.

I have come to believe more in a supreme being. I realized this yesterday morning walking to the Capitol. I began to think that, because of god knows how many human frailties that contribute to our dilemma, there does not seem to be a way that the various characters playing out this drama can rise to the occasion and do what has to be done in a noble, responsible way. I felt a need to pray, and I prayed.

June 10 Frank Polk again asked me to play the broker's role between McClory and Brooks to find out if Brooks would be willing to cosponser McClory's resolution of inquiry. When I discussed it with Brooks, he decided against McClory's idea, mostly because he does not think that he and McClory can get enough votes to get such a bold measure passed, and that to lose on the House floor would be counterproductive.

I did not ask Brooks, and he has not told me, but I suspect that Brooks has talked the idea over with Tip O'Neill. Without the support of O'Neill and Rhodes, there is no way that Brooks and McClory can get the votes for their plan. As Brooks put it, "If Bob McClory and I were to lose on a resoluion of inquiry there would be nothing we could do but turn our backs on impeachment and walk away in tears."

Remarkably, within an hour after my telephone conversation with Brooks, the White House took the offensive against Rodino so strongly that I recall Clark Clifford's warnings that our phones were tapped. Every reporter on Capitol Hill had a White House press release announcing that Nixon, who was leaving on a tour of the Middle East, had sent a long letter to Rodino giving all the reasons why he was not complying with our subpoenas—including Rodino's refusal to open the hearings to the public and hear testimony from live witnesses.

After receiving the President's letter, Rodino immediately called me to round up the committee Democrats to come to a caucus at 5:30. I suggested that before the caucus we have copies of the letter sent to all the committee members so they could study it. He agreed and said he would instruct Doar to have copies made and distributed.

When the caucus began, most of the members did not have copies. Rodino and Doar had aspparently decided that if the members went to the caucus having read the letter, they might have come up with some considered suggestions as to what to do—suggestions that might be inconsistent with Doar's recommendation that we simply ignore the letter. Instead of distributing copies, Rodino read it aloud.

During the caucus I felt very uneasy and very disgusted. Most of the members just sat there. Seiberling fell asleep—probably more from fear than boredom. No one displayed much dissatisfaction, except Waldie and Conyers who again pressed Rodino to agree to a motion to cite Nixon for contempt. Nothing really positive or constructive came out of the meeting.

While the Democrats were caucusing the President was en route to the Middle East. He had timed his letter to Rodino well. Accompanied by Secretary of State Kissinger, he began what he called "A Journey for Peace." With overseas media coverage by the nation's most highly respected political commentators, Nixon was refurbishing his image as a master of foreign policy. Joseph Alsop, who enjoyed a national reputation as a trustworthy news analyst, was now reporting that in the court of public opinion the Democrats were losing the impeachment case against the President.

Meanwhile, the Judiciary Committee Democrats, whom Nixon had charged with "wallowing in Watergate," were in turmoil. Their special counsel and his hundred-member inquiry staff had failed to interrogate even one live witness under oath or conduct any investigation of his own. At this late date, there was no case for impeachment.

15

STOP THE LEAKS!
CALL THE WITNESSES!

En route to the Middle East on their journey of peace, the presidential party was followed by an entourage of nationally prominent TV commentators. Kissinger in particular took advantage of the media facilities to wage a political war against the Judiciary Committee Democrats back in Washington.

For more than a year, liberal antiwar Democrats had been condemning Nixon and Kissinger for having established the White House "plumbers" to plug leaks to the press of the secret bombings of Cambodia. Now, in June 1974, it was Nixon and Kissinger's chance to play the advocates of the people's right to know. They denounced the Judiciary Committee for conducting secret hearings and refusing to call live witnesses requested by St. Clair. They reminded newsmen that St. Clair was one of the lawyers who two decades earlier had defended liberals against vilification by Republican Senator Joe McCarthy. Conservative journalists began to characterize the Judiciary Committee as a Star Chamber. Even journalists who supported impeachment began to refer to the congressional Democrats—who appeared unwilling to present their case openly to the people—as "craven."

On Capitol Hill, Senator Russell Long's assistant, Wayne Thevenot, had a Cajun maxim for political strategy: "When you fight with alligators, take them on one at a time." This strategy was not unknown to Father McLaughlin and Henry Kissinger. They used their worldwide media forum to single out one committee Democrat in particular, Joshua Eilberg of Philadelphia. Josh was chairman of our

173

Subcommittee on Immigration and International Law, and was one of the most docile and politically vulnerable of the Democrats.

The Jewish Eilberg found himself under attack from Rabbi Baruch Korff, head of the National Citizens Committee for Fairness to the President. Korff was working closely with McLaughlin to organize religious groups to defend the President from impeachment. At a luncheon just before the President's departure for the Middle East, Korff read a resolution of his committee affirming "Faith in God and country, in constitutional government, and in our beloved President, who is one of the strongest links in the chain of the presidency." To a crowd of 1,400 cheering guests, the President assured Korff, "I shall do nothing to weaken this office."

Nixon had described Korff as "my rabbi" and Korff was proudly reminding voters in Eilberg's district that Kissinger was appointed by Nixon to be the "first Jewish Secretary of State in American history." But many of Eilberg's Democratic constituents regarded Kissinger as a quisling. As they saw it, Kissinger had joined with the White House "Germans"—Kleindienst, Haldeman, and Ehrlichman—to foster the Gestapo-like tactics of plumbers Howard Hunt and Gordon Liddy.

A popular joke among Jewish Democrats at that time was that Israel's Prime Minister Golda Meir, herself a former school teacher from Minnesota, had in her foreign minister Abba Eban (a Welsh Jew formerly known as Aubrey Evans) a Jewish diplomat who was smarter than Kissinger. Meir had said, "At least Abba Eban speaks English without a German accent." In a newsletter to his constituents, Eilberg had reminded them that on Kissinger's recommendation, the President had established the plumbers, who had engaged in at least seventeen illegal wiretaps—including on one of Kissinger's own Jewish aides, Morton Halperin.

On June 11 Kissinger launched a media attack on Eilberg. At a stopover in Salzburg, Austria, Kissinger appeared on primetime television and announced to the world that he would resign unless his name was cleared on the wiretapping charges alleged by Eilberg. In his clipped accent Kissinger said, "I have believed that I could help the President to heal divisions in this country. I can do this only if my honor is not at issue. If that condition cannot be maintained I cannot perform my duties. I do not believe it is possible to conduct the foreign policy of the United States under these circumstances when the character and credibility of the Secretary of State is at issue."

As a news story, the evidence that Kissinger had directed illegal wiretaps of journalists and of even his own aides was quite stale. The *New York Times* had broken the story a year earlier, based on a statement that Nixon himself had made. In November 1973, before Doar had been appointed, William Dobrovir had made public a legal brief concluding that the seventeen documented wiretaps were criminal violations of the United States Code. (This was the same brief that Doar had refused to look at on his first day as special counsel.) Other facts previously extensively reported included a lawsuit by Morton Halperin charging the Secretary of State with illegal wiretaping. (Many years later, the suit was settled in Halperin's favor with an apology by Kissinger.)

In attacking Eilberg for "leaking" news that had been in the public record for more than a year, Kissinger struck a public relations blow against the Judiciary Committee that Rodino could have easily deflected. All that would have been necessary to defend Eilberg was a simple truthful statement—a statement that Rodino refused to make. There was nothing in our so-called confidentiality rules that deprived Eilberg of the right to remind his constituents of information that was already on the public record. Instead, Rodino agreed publicly with Kissinger that such leaks "demeaned the committee" and advised the media that he was ordering them to be "stopped immediately."

Since Rodino publicly chastised Eilberg, the *New York Times* also sided with Kissinger. The *Times* ignored the fact that in 1973 it had scooped its competitors with documented evidence of the illegal wiretaps. The *Times* agreed with Rodino and wrote, "The leakers, apparently impatient with the rules of secrecy adopted by the committee and presumably anxious to 'get the President' are subjecting him to trial by the court of public opinion based upon fragmentary and unrebutted evidence and analysis."

To make matters worse for the committee Democrats, after discrediting Eilberg as a "leaker," the White House and the Republican stalwarts attacked other Democrats as similarly shameless. They accused the Democrats of violating the secrecy rules by leaking a series of memoranda prepared for them by Bill Dixon, who had resigned from Doar's staff and returned to his prior role as chief counsel to Kastenmeier's subcommittee. Dixon's conclusion that there was evidence to incriminate the President had been reached in the Dobrovir brief that had been made public by Ralph Nader a year earlier. Dixon had done little more than draw on additional information that Nixon himself had entered into the public record when he published transcripts of his tapes. When Rodino publicly chastised Dixon for even writing the memoranda, a cartoonist depicted the committee as a ship that was beached on dry land with water spouting through holes in its side, with Rodino on the bridge shouting "Stop the leaks!" Another cartoon depicted Rodino scolding Father Drinan, saying "I will never confess anything to you again."

Never before in the history of impeachments in the United States or England had legislators been gagged from advocating their own positions until after an inquiry staff made its findings and advised them how to vote. Yet, the public was being misled. With the aid of flawed legal memoranda written by Rodham and endorsed by Doar, Rodino was posturing. Using false legal analogies, he compared the committee members to jurors, who are required to be passive and silent in public until the end of a trial. He compared his own role to that of an impartial judge ordering the jury "until all the entire presentation of evidence is completed you are not to draw any conclusions, enter into any deliberations with each other, or talk to the press or each other or any one else about the evidence in this case."

However, under centuries of precedents, House members were not barred from public charges before all of the evidence was in. In fact, Drinan and Waldie had publicly charged Nixon with impeachable offenses even before the official inquiry had begun. Yet under the Rodham-drafted procedures presumably recommended by Burke Marshall, members of the committee as well as the President's counsel were given even fewer rights than jurors in a court case—who are not barred from hearing the testimony of live witnesses for and against the accused. With Rodino and Doar resisting public hearings and condemning the Democrats for leaking information to the press, Washington pundits were beginning to consider impeachment as a lost cause.

Remarkably, the strongest defender of the committee Democrats during that period was Republican Senator Lowell Weicker of Connecticut. As a member of the Senate Watergate Committee, Weicker had also been attacked by the White House for leaking information that was damaging to the President. Weicker praised Eilberg, Dixon, and the pro-impeachment Democrats by emphasizing that Congress was not a passive body created to keep secret the misdeeds of the President.

All of the Judiciary Committee Democrats were both lawyers and legislators. They were fully aware that one of their major duties was to exercise diligent public oversight over the executive branch. They now found themselves politically gagged and tied behind a wall of secrecy—a wall that Doar had erected to conceal his abdication of reponsibility to investigate a President whom the Watergate grand jury had named as a criminal co-conspirator.

By now, Jack Brooks had had his fill of criticism by the media for the delay and by Kissinger for leaking "scurrilous lies." One of the most unfair criticisms of Brooks himself was that while Rodino was scrupulously impartial and fair to Nixon, Brooks was shamelessly partisan. For a few days, Jack Brooks—for the first time in the years I had known him—was in a state of depression. But he recovered quickly and exploded. He was ready to lead a committee revolt against Rodino.

June 12 We had another day of Doar-Jenner pablum today. I was very dismayed by the general feeling of melancholia among the Democrats. I had a talk with Jack Brooks this morning before the hearing. He told me, "I felt like crying last night. The only thing I could do was to go home and play with my kids and forget about it." Later, during a recess, we went to the men's room. In front of some of the other members waiting to use the urinals, he said to me aloud: "I don't feel like I ought to stay here. I'm really wasting my time. I ought to give you my proxy and go home." I said, "I don't want your proxy, because I don't think that members of Congress have a right to vote. I don't think your proxy is worth anything." He laughed half-heartedly, shrugged his shoulders, turned to one of our listeners and said, "You see, he has it right."

Tonight I feel badly. I may have increased Brooks's despondency.

June 14 This morning I was sitting in my office with Jim Cline and Dan Cohen. The three of us were all shaken up by Doar's failure to develop the impoundment issue yesterday. I got a call from Jack Brooks. He was shouting into his phone. "Listen, I want to talk to you before I go home to Texas. I want to make sure that you have a good Father's Day. I want you to go to your cottage in the mountains and have a good rest—and enjoy the weekend, 'cause I'm making you a promise. Starting Monday it's all over. I got the votes. Maybe I don't have all the votes, but I got enough, and I'm not gonna take any more of this shit—not from John Doar and not from Peter Rodino. They've fucked around long enough with me. I'm gonna give them a fight like they've never had. I'll use knives if I have to—and goddamit if I have to I'm gonna take those thirty-six books of pablum on Monday and announce to everybody that Peter Rodino has fucked up, just like that!"

Brooks talked continuously for about twenty minutes, going from having a catharsis to reassuring me that he was going to lead a revolt against Rodino and Doar. He also explained that every one of the subcommittee chairmen [Edwards, Kastenmeier, Hungate, Conyers, and Eilberg] agreed with him and were urging him to lead a revolt against Rodino by having Dick Cates assigned back to the position on the regular staff which he had originally held, freed from supervision by Doar. Brooks said, "I want Dick Cates back here to help you. And if I don't get Dick Cates back, goddamit, we're gonna do this thing without him. Goddamit, that son of a bitch, that Doar, has instilled in that whole fucking staff of his a contempt for me, a contempt for this place! They are just . . . Well, forget it." He paused, breathing hard, then said, "I've got enough votes now to raise holy hell, so have a good weekend and I'll see you June 16."

June 16 When I got to the office this morning Mary Sourwine [our office manager] gave me an astounding report. She told me that John Doar's nephew as well as several of his children have been put on the payroll.

Then I went to Brooks's office. To my surprise he had a three-or-four-page plan all typed up, he has rooms available for his own staff to work, has a computer rig available, and several staff people all lined up, ready to go. We went over his plan briefly. We see it exactly the same way. We have to call live witnesses, question them under oath, let St. Clair cross-examine them, let the members cross-examine them, let the members draft articles of impeachment, and allow amendments to be offered—everything that Rodino and Doar oppose.

He called Don Edwards in and the three of us chatted about it briefly. Edwards agrees with the plan and is sure that all of the other subcommittee chairmen will, too—with the possible exception of Eilberg. I know Eilberg fairly well and am sure he will also agree.

After my meeting with Brooks, I went to the cafeteria for coffee with Frank Polk. Frank says the Evans and Novak column in yesterday's *Post* was correct—that the Republican line is hardening and we could end up with a very close party-line vote. Frank thinks that to tell Rodino to stop listening to Doar and to comply with the Republicans' request for live witnesses would be like telling a man on a tightrope that he is going in the wrong direction.

I was back in my office for only a few minutes when Gary Hymel from Tip O'Neill's office called. He said that Tip is very shaken because Rodino told Speaker Albert that he cannot get impeachment articles to the House floor until August 24 at the earliest. The Speaker called Tip and told him that he had to do something. Tip wanted to talk to me in his office right away before he spoke to Rodino.

When I got there, O'Neill sat me down by his desk. He asked me if wanted some cream and sugar with coffee. Then he said, "Tell me the whole story, just as you see it. What the hell is going on in the Judiciary Committee?"

We talked for several hours. First, I summarized my perceptions about the defects of Rodino having refused to create a manageable sub-committee to direct the investigation, instead delegating all of the responsibility to Doar. There has been no investigation. Doar in cahoots with Burke Marshall and Kennedy. Doar and the pablum books. Doar sanitizing all the meat out of the case, even the report of the grand jury.

Then we talked about the Republicans' misconceptions that the Democratic leadership has orchestrated all of this to put the Republicans in a noose by presenting a case that is so tepid and improper that Republicans cannot vote for it. O'Neill knows that John Rhodes has been advising the Republicans that they cannot vote "yes" unless they are thoroughly convinced that there is a proper case.

At one point, Tip put his hand to his head and said, "Jesus Christ! You mean we're gonna have a political impeachment along party lines!"

I told him that wasn't necessarily so—that Jack Brooks was working on a plan to get bipartisan support. The plan would comply with St. Clair's request for live witnesses, including John Dean, and would also permit the members, not Doar, to make the case.

Tip went out to the floor to vote. When he came back he said that he had talked to Brooks and was in agreement with him. He had also talked to Edwards. We talked further about Brooks's plan—he's not concerned with procedural details, and is willing to leave them to Brooks and me. We agreed that the process has to be institutionalized, meaning it has to be a process of the committee and of the House; that the reponsibility for impeaching a President cannot be delegated; that the honor and dignity of the House of Representatives is at stake.

When I left, Tip put his arm on my shoulder and said, "I'm grateful." I answered, "And I'm grateful to you."

16

THRUSTING GREATNESS ON RODINO

In the Democratic cloakroom, Brooks articulated his impeachment strategy in Shakespearean as well as Old Testament terms.
He said, "We shouldn't disgrace Rodino unless we have to. We
should thrust greatness upon him." And he was still carrying around
his Biblical flashcard with its quote from Jeremiah: "Cursed be he
who doeth the work of the Lord with a slack hand. And cursed be he
who keepeth his sword back from blood."

It was not only Democrats who were clamoring for impeach-
ment. Robert Welch, founder of the ultraconservative John Birch
Society, had characterized Nixon as "the most disingenuous and
slipperiest politician that ever showed up on the American scene. .
. . To conquer the world has been Nixon's aim for twenty years."
When a delegation of fundamentalist clergymen met with Senator
Barry Goldwater, their spokesman said, "Senator, all of us know that
Nixon is a liar! If he is not impeached, how can we teach the ten
commandments in our Sunday schools?"

Congressman Barry Goldwater, Jr. was a very close friend of
John and Maureen Dean. The Goldwaters were confident that Dean
was telling the truth and that Nixon was a liar. The Goldwaters also
shared their views with their fellow Arizona Republican, Congressman John Rhodes—who had become Vice President Ford's successor as House minority leader.

Rhodes was now having daily private meetings with Tip O'Neill,
and was soon persuaded that O'Neill was not in favor of Rodino's
strategy of delay—that the House leadership wasn't trying to keep
Nixon in the White House to assure electoral gains in 1976. The

Republican leadership then switched their tactics. A number of Judiciary Committee Republicans had previously supported the Rodino-Doar strategy since it kept Nixon in office. With Nixon refusing to resign, and Wiggins and the stalwarts encouraged by Doar's failure to make a case, Rhodes and O'Neill—like McClory and Brooks—were in agreement that the Judiciary Committee Democrats should make their case shortly after July 4. This would give House Republicans such as McClory, and Railsback—who wanted to make impeachment bipartisan—the opportunity to vote "yes." Above all, it would then give the House and Senate the opportunity to make Rhodes's mentor, Jerry Ford, President—and give Ford and Rhodes more than two years to restore confidence in the Republican party before the 1976 elections.

There was a popular maxim in the Capitol that O'Neill and Rhodes understood and practiced: "The House cannot be driven. It can only be led." Unlike generals in the military or executives in a corporation, O'Neill and Rhodes could not "order" members of their parties to follow the party line. They had to lead by example. Therefore, they both supported calling John Dean as a witness and permitting cross-examination by St. Clair. When Rodino tried to argue with O'Neill that Doar's legal staff considered such an approach unprecedented, O'Neill replied, "Pete, you got thirty-eight members of Congress on your committee and every one is a lawyer. The votes on your own committee are probably thirty-seven to one against you."

After June 16, when Brooks and all five subcommittee chairmen revolted against Doar's recommendations, control of the impeachment inquiry was taken away from Rodino. With the bipartisan encouragement of O'Neill and Rhodes, committee members on both sides were free to work their will. Doar completed his reading of the documents on June 24. On that afternoon the committee voted to issue more subpoenas and to permit St. Clair to present his defense later that week. On the same day, the Democrats had a caucus to consider whether to make all thirty-six of Doar's volumes public by releasing them to the press before the committee voted on articles of impeachment.

June 24 Rodino now says that to make the books public before the committee votes on articles of impeachment is exactly what he and Doar have always had in mind. At a caucus of the Democrats he argued, "The case is in the books, and once we give the books to the press the press will make the case for us—and we will not be accused of being partisan."

Most of the Democrats, including Brooks, disagreed. Brooks fears that the press will report the truth—that there is nothing new in the books and that the Democrats have done nothing but blow smoke for six months. But Brooks, Conyers, Eilberg, and Hungate have a good reason to release the pablum books. As Brooks puts it, "If we don't get ourselves out of the secrecy swamp that Rodino has led us into, the Republicans will continue to accuse us of leaking lies every time we mention any evidence that is already in the public record."

Rodino asked for a show of hands of those that were opposed to releasing the books. Edwards, Flowers, Jordan, Mann, and Thornton were opposed. Mann spoke first. He admitted he had some difficulty in articulating his feelings against releasing the books, but that it seemed underhanded. Then Ray Thornton, who usually was reticent, spoke so honorably and eloquently that a hush came over the room. He said, "I believe we have a very solemn responsibility to make our own conclusive judgment about whether the President of the United States should be removed from office—and that it would be professionally and morally wrong for us to try the impeachment case in the press or release evidentiary materials prior to judgment."

Barbara Jordan then said, "Amen! There is nothing that I can add to that." Rodino then asked Doar for his opinion. Doar was stonefaced, and said only, "I understand you Mr. Thornton, but I disagree."

Barbara, who was sitting across from me, then asked for my opinion. I said, "I don't want to detract from Mr. Thornton's statement by adding a crass political note, but in addition to being improper to try the case in the press, it will make it more difficult for us to get Republicans to vote 'yes' on articles of impeachment."

I explained further: "Bob McClory and Frank Polk tell me that the Republicans are convinced that we have a strategy of intentionally making the case inconclusive—in order to make them vote 'no' and crucify themselves at the polls by keeping Nixon in office until after the congressional elections." The day ended with the Democrats not reaching a final decision.

June 25 At a business meeting of the full committee, the members voted 22 to 16 to release the materials that Doar has presented in secret since May 9. But one good thing has come out of Thornton's opposition to the release. He has framed the issue squarely by asserting that the committee members have a responsibility to resolve the question of the

President's guilt or innocence before voting "yes" or "no" on articles of impeachment.

Now that every member of the committee knows that Doar's thirty-six volumes do not make the case, Doar and Nussbaum have come up with a tongue-in-cheek, flawed legal argument to cover up their non-investigation. Rodino is now arguing with a straight face, "The constitutional authority of the committee is limited to determining what the factual questions are. The committee does not have the authority to answer the question of whether the President is guilty or innocent of an impeachable offense."

Ray Thornton has articulated the fallacy in that argument eloquently. Like Doar and Nussbaum, Thornton is a former prosecutor [he was Attorney General of Arkansas], and he knows what every responsible prosecutor is supposed to know: before you prosecute someone in court you are supposed to collect sufficient evidence to convince yourself of his guilt. Like Thornton, other Democrats on the committee who are former prosecutors—George Danielson and Charlie Rangel—have also told me how shocked they are by the non-investigation. The horrible reality is that Doar and Nussbaum—whom Doar put in charge of the factual portion of the inquiry—have intentionally failed to meet their professional responsibility to investigate the President. Having failed to put together appropriate evidence of Nixon's guilt, the House would be acting irresponsibly by voting to impeach Nixon without first granting St. Clair's request for testimony by live witnesses.

With the issue of the release of Doar's documents resolved, but over opposition of Thornton and other Democrats, the committee was faced with an even more vexing problem. St. Clair had sent a formal letter to Rodino reiterating his request that six witnesses be called. First on the list was John Dean. The others were former Attorney General John Mitchell; former Chief of Staff John Haldeman; John Bittman, who was the attorney for convicted Watergate burglar Howard Hunt; Fred LaRue, who had been Mitchell's aide on Nixon's reelection committee; and Paul O'Brien, a reelection committee attorney. With the exception of O'Brien and Bittman, all of the witnesses for the "defense" had already been convicted or at least indicted by the Watergate Special Prosecutor for participating in felonious conspiracies involving obstruction of justice.

With the Republicans all supporting St. Clair's request, Rodino, Doar, and Nussbaum lobbied the Democrats intensively to deny the request and to refuse to call any live witnesses. Just as they had when they argued against permitting St. Clair to represent the President, they once again claimed that the Republicans, such as Railsback and McClory, who supported the request were "puppets on St. Clair's string." Rodino, Doar, and Nussbaum also argued that every one of the witnesses requested by St. Clair would only hurt the case for impeachment—that even Dean would testify that he had no knowledge that Nixon had either ordered the Watergate break-in or had specifically directed the payment of hush money to Hunt. Indeed, St. Clair himself had pointed out that Dean had already testified that Nixon had not ordered the payment of the hush money to Hunt and that the matter was "left hanging."

To support their contention that Dean's testimony would hurt the case for impeachment, Doar and his aides reiterated the flawed legal argument that Doar had advanced during the secret hearings—that as leader of the executive branch the President could not be charged with participation in a criminal conspiracy, and could only be charged with the criminal acts of his subordinates that he specifically directed. But by now every subcommittee chairman had become aware that Jaworski had named the President as a co-conspirator in the obstruction of justice in the Watergate case. Brooks summed up the sentiment of most, if not all, of the pro-impeachment Democrats when he told Rodino, "If Doar advances that crazy argument one more time you ought to take a knife and cut his tongue out."

Most, if not all, of the Democrats also recognized that McClory and Railsback were ready to vote to impeach Nixon but would be hard put to explain their votes to their Republican constituents if they voted to prevent St. Clair from cross-examining Dean—the one Republican who had given direct evidence to the Watergate Committee that Nixon had committed a felony. And some of the Democrats—such as Thornton, Flowers, and Mann—represented districts that were far more conservative and pro-Nixon than McClory's Illinois district. With every Democrat on the committee now in disagreement with Rodino's resistance to calling live witnesses, Rodino agreed reluctantly to permit Ray Thornton to make a motion on June 27 to call a list of witnesses, including Dean. The motion prevailed by a vote of 33 to 5.

Rodino was piqued. The media was beginning to report that Nixon and St. Clair were now winning on key votes and were more in control of the committee than he was. However, the truth was that Nixon was losing Republican votes. It was not Nixon who was gaining control of the committee, it was a coalition headed by Brooks and McClory and backed by O'Neill and Rhodes.

Later that day, Rodino walked into his outer office where three newsmen—Sam Donaldson of ABC and Jack Nelson and Paul Huston of the *Los Angeles Times*—were waiting in the hopes of interviewing him. Without getting any agreement that his comments were off the record, he told the reporters that all twenty-one Democrats and five Republicans were ready to vote to impeach Nixon. He gave the reporters a list that included conservative Democrats Walter Flowers of Alabama, Ray Thornton of Arkansas, and James Mann of South Carolina, as well as Republicans Caldwell Butler of Virginia, McClory and Railsback of Illinois, Hamilton Fish of New York, and William Cohen of Maine. The next morning Rodino's head count was printed in the *Los Angeles Times* as a major scoop. The media dealt with the story as a radical departure from Rodino's prior representations of himself as judicious and impartial. As national news the story discredited Rodino and all of the members he identified as ready to impeach Nixon even before open hearings and a public debate had begun.

Tip O'Neill was distressed, and not only because Rodino had discredited himself and the committee. For O'Neill, whose well-known maxim was "All politics is local," Rodino had weakened the cause for impeachment by exposing key committee members to political injury in their districts.

In Tuscaloosa, the pro-Nixon press reported that Rodino had said Flowers had committed himself to vote for impeachment before all the evidence was in. Flowers was irate. He complained to O'Neill, "How do you expect to get my vote if you allow Rodino to embarrass me like that?" O'Neill summoned Rodino to the Speaker's office for a highly confidential meeting.

Rodino was ashen when he left the Speaker's office. He spent the rest of the day drafting a statement for delivery on the House floor:

> "I want to state unequivocally and categorically that this
> [news story] is not true. There is no basis in fact for it whatso-
> ever. . . . None of the House members have discussed a vote
> with me, and were it otherwise, I want to assure the House that
> I would not be sitting as chairman of the committee. I would
> withdraw myself from that capacity."

The statement only served to decrease his stature on Capitol Hill. For the rest of the week, Peter shunned discussion with the press as well as with his colleagues.

On Monday, July 1, the confidence of the House in Rodino's leadership of the committee was put to a test on the House floor. Even though a bipartisan majority on the committee had overruled his oppositon to calling live witnesses, Rodino was still refusing to permit committee members to question the witnesses. Under procedures apparently recommended by Burke Marshall and drafted by Rodham, Rodino had introduced a resolution on the House floor to leave the questioning of witnesses entirely to Doar and the inquiry staff on behalf of the committee.

The resolution required an unprecedented suspension of House rules that had been enshrined for almost two centuries in Jefferson's manual, and its passage required a two-thirds vote. Without the active support of O'Neill or Rhodes, the resolution came up twenty-five votes short.

Brooks and McClory were pleased, and regarded the vote as a bipartisan victory. The Democratic members were unleashed to make the case for impeachment, and McClory and the moderate Republicans were ready to vote "yes."

However, the media described the vote differently. Rising TV stars Sam Donaldson and Connie Chung characterized it as "partisan." Howard Fields wrote: "The vote was a strong rebuff of Rodino. That meant that each committee member would be allowed to question witnesses and it also meant that Rodino's wishes for a bipartisan impeachment were in great jeopardy. It was a bad, partisan beginning for July, the month that was to climax the impeachment inquiry."

The media pundits who were describing Brooks as shamelessly partisan and Rodino as striving for a bipartisan majority were ignoring the political skills of Brooks and McClory, who were committed to saving Rodino from himself by shaking the committee loose from its self-imposed shackles of secrecy. Also, as Tip O'Neill saw it, if Rodino and Doar had their way on the live witnesses, there would have been no way that articles of impeachment would have been adopted in the Ninety-third Congress.

Walter Flowers, who had been politically wounded a few weeks earlier by Rodino's outburst to Sam Donaldson, shared O'Neill and Brooks's view. Although Flowers's public image was that of country boy, he had studied in London and was a George Orwell fan. In the Democratic cloakroom he commented on the media's skewed characterizations of Rodino and the other Democrats: "Even though we still have ten years to go to reach 1984, the media liberals have already mastered the art of 'Newspeak.'"

In an insidious way, the media pundits had been misled by the six months of secret hearings. On July 1, 1974, when the first live witness was scheduled to testify, Doar's thirty-six volumes had not yet been released. The media was unaware of Rodino's true views or that Doar's volumes were not based on any original investigation. Doar had compiled them only to raise questions and to avoid a resolution by the committee of whether any impeachable offenses were committed.

That Rodino knew and approved of Doar's strategy from the very beginning was recorded in my diary:

June 23 It is a very rainy day and I feel very apprehensive. Rodino called me a little while ago from New Jersey to go over the agendas for our business meetings. We spoke for more than an hour.

I went over with Rodino very exactly the same perceptions I had given Tip O'Neill. I discussed the Republican fears that the case was not really being made in the committee and that the Democrat's strategy is simply to determine whether or not there are serious questions which ought to be resolved in a Senate trial. The more we talked the more it became apparent that the Republican fears are thoroughly justified. Rodino does have the wrong perception of our responsibilities.

I tried my best to retain my composure and to reason with him. I explained that, based on all of my research, I have the opinion that the House has a prosecutorial role and has a responsibility to determine for itself whether Richard Nixon should be removed from office, and to answer that question in the affirmative before sending articles of impeachment to the Senate—just as a prosecutor in a criminal case has a responsibility to investigate the defendant's conduct before the trial begins.

Rodino answered, "If you are talking about the possibility of the House making that kind of determination, you can forget it. Nixon will not be impeached. We have not approached it that way. If we were going to approach it that way we would have had to start from the beginning with the notion that we had a responsibility to get to the bottom of the case."

May the Lord have mercy on Peter Rodino's soul! This is the same Peter Rodino who stood piously in the well of the House eight months ago and pledged that under his chairmanship we would conduct a thorough and complete investigation of the allegations against Richard Nixon.

By July, other lawyers on the committee's permanent staff who had been studying the details of Doar's six weeks of secret presentation had professional misgivings about the thirty-six volumes about to be published under the committee's official imprimatur.

July 2 I had a conversation with Doar concerning the publication of his books and how the committee staff's names should be listed in the masthead of each volume. He suggested that my name and those of the other lawyers on the permanent staff be in their conventional place in the masthead, above his name and those of the impeachment inquiry lawyers to demonstrate that I had overall staff responsibility.

I decided to put this up to a vote of the permanent staff lawyers at a meeting in my office. Jim Cline, Alan Parker, Dan Cohen, Bill Dixon, and I voted unanimously not to allow our names to appear on the masthead.

I for one would find it repugnant to have my name used in any way to imply my endorsement of any of the thirty-six volumes. I see them as professionally and morally flawed.

17

LIVE WITNESSES AT LAST

D ue to bipartisan efforts of Judiciary Committee members backed by the House leadership, the committee scheduled the testimony of ten live witnesses beginning July 2, 1974. John Dean was sixth on the list, and was scheduled for July 11.

Although all the precedents made it clear that impeachment does not require proof of a statutory crime, St. Clair's contention was that unless the President actually committed a felony as defined in the United States Code, he ought not to be impeached. With the exception of Dean, none of the ten witnesses was prepared to provide hard evidence that the President had committed a statutory felony.

As attorneys themselves, all of the committee members knew that St. Clair's defense of Nixon would turn on whether or not he could destroy Dean's credibility. Ed Mezvinsky's perception of the testimony of the first five witnesses was not atypical of the members:

> About halfway through the testimony of the witnesses, I began to wonder if it was worthwhile. The Republicans had insisted that—out of fairness to the President—we call witnesses, and we had to call ten, not just the five that Doar's staff considered necessary. But after we had listened to the first five—Alexander Butterfield, Fred LaRue, Paul O'Brien, William Bittman, and John Mitchell—I was at a loss to explain what they were adding to either side's view of the inquiry. . . .
>
> The remaining witnesses [except for Dean] served only to buttress the opinion of many members that we never should have called witnesses in the first place.

189

As was well known to the public long before our inquiry staff was put together, John Dean's televised testimony before the Ervin Committee in April 1973 was tantamount to a confession that he and the President had conspired together to obstruct justice in the prosecution of the Watergate burglars. The Dobrovir brief of November 1973—which Dick Cates had relied on and which Doar had refused to look at—had been sent to every member of the Judiciary Committee long before Doar's appointment. Expressed simply: If Dean was telling the truth, then Nixon was guilty of at least one felony—participation in a conspiracy to obstruct justice.

The Dobrovir brief had accurately summarized a factual and legal basis for relying on Dean's prior testimony. As Dobrovir had pointed out, the first break-in and wiretap was on May 27, 1972. On June 17, a second break-in and wiretap took place, which was detected and led to the arrest of Howard Hunt, Gordon Liddy, and five others. By November 1973, five of the defendants had pleaded guilty, and the remaining two were tried by a jury before Judge John Sirica and convicted.

Although Watergate prosecutor Archibald Cox had ascertained that Nixon had met with Haldeman and Ehrlichman as early as June 20, presumably to discuss Watergate, Dean was not present at that meeting. According to Dean's testimony, the President's aides had begun an unlawful conspiracy to obstruct the prosecution of the burglars immediately after the first five burglars were arrested on June 17. There then followed what is in summary the Watergate coverup: false testimony, concealment of evidence, offers of clemency to the defendants, payments of at least $450,000 in hush money to keep the arrested burglars from incriminating the White House, and misuse of the FBI and CIA to impede the prosecution of the burglars. Dean also admitted his own participation in the conspiracy and in October 1973 pleaded guilty to a felony charge. In his testimony before the Ervin committee, Dean specifically charged that the President participated in the coverup from September 15, 1972—a charge that the President denied throughout the impeachment inquiry.

With respect to Dean's anticipated testimony of July 11, 1974, since Nixon had not yet released the famous "smoking gun" tape of June 20 (which indisputably established his participation in the coverup just three days after the arrest of the burglars) the resolution of the question of the President's complicity in the coverup depended squarely on whether the Judiciary Committee believed the President's public denials or the sworn testimony of John Dean.

By the time Dean was to testify before the Judiciary Committee, the fact that he had not lied to the Ervin Committee about the President's participation had already been established to the satisfaction of Archibald Cox, Leon Jaworski, and the Watergate grand jury—all of whom had concluded that as a matter of law the President was in fact a co-conspirator. This was the conclusion that Charles Morgan and the ACLU had publicly asserted as early as February 1973, long before impeachment had become politically viable.

Thus, if the legal analyses of Morgan, the ACLU, Dobrovir, Cates, Cox, Jaworski, and the regular staff of the House Judiciary Committee were sound—and the President could be charged constitutionally with participating in a conspiracy—the only appropriate defense that St. Clair could hope to assert against the criminal charge of conspiring to obstruct justice was to prove by cross-examination that Dean was not credible and had lied when he incriminated the President.

However, St. Clair and his legal team also knew that Doar and his staff were on record in support of a legal argument that St. Clair had not been brazen enough to argue. This was the "Nuremberg defense" —the notion advanced by the German defendants at the Nuremberg trials that a nation's high command cannot be charged with entering into a conspiracy with subordinates. If the Judiciary Committee members were not prepared to refute Doar and his staff, to impeach Nixon required proof that Nixon had personally directed the coverup.

On the morning of July 11 when Dean, surrounded by a mob of reporters and cameramen, arrived at Room 2141 of the Rayburn Building, he was neatly dressed as always. He wore a brown suit, blue shirt, and green tie. He had been in the room countless times during the years he had served as the committee's minority counsel. Of course, today he was sitting at the witness table, with James St. Clair waiting to cross-examine him.

Doar was permitted to question Dean for about two hours in the morning. After lunch St. Clair was given three hours to cross-examine, and after that each of the members was to be allowed five minutes for their own questions.

In his cross-examination, St. Clair exhibited all of his skills as a seasoned trial attorney. He questioned Dean on the finest points in

the hope of showing that Dean had made prior inconsistent statements before either the Ervin Committee or the grand jury.
However, Dean easily convinced most, if not all, of the members
that there were no inconsistencies between his testimony that
morning and his prior testimony of more than a year earlier—and
that he had a phenomenal memory. At one point when Dean
responded that he didn't have a good memory of the exact words
used by the President with respect to a minor incident, St. Clair
became contentious and said, "I would like to ask you a little bit
about your memory. Do you have a good memory?" Dean replied,
"I would say it is a good memory, yes." St. Clair snarled, "Well, when
you testified before the Senate committee you said you had a very
good memory, didn't you?" Dean's cool reply caused St. Clair to
squirm and the committee to admire the dry wit of its former
minority counsel: "I believe I indicated I had a good memory, but it
was not a tape recorder."

Several years later, after Nixon resigned, Leon Jaworski commented on St. Clair's cross-examination of Dean:

> St. Clair, while proclaiming the President innocent of
> wrongdoing to the committee, so far as I could ascertain had
> not made as much as a dent in the hard evidence. . . . St. Clair
> was reflecting the President's apparent contempt for that body.
> But the hard evidence in the committee's hands was of the kind
> that reasonable men had acted upon from the beginning of our
> system.

For me, John Dean's appearance had a profound personal
impact.

July 11 John Dean began his testimony today. His trial on a felony
charge is still pending. . . . Shortly before the hearing I saw him coming
down the hall to my office accompanied by some U.S. Marshals [who
had been assigned to protect him under the Justice Department's witness protection program]. I felt that I wanted to express something to
him. I didn't quite know what to say. I put my arm on his shoulder and
he put his arm on my shoulder.

I invited him to make himself comfortable in my office, which I
made available for him and his counsel, Charlie Shaffer, for their own
use all day. He said the only request he had was for a plan to help him

avoid getting photographed while getting in and out of the hearing room. Shaffer disagreed, and advised Dean that he ought to get photographed, although Dean had the final word.

We chatted briefly—mostly small talk and reminiscences of earlier and better days. I bummed a cigarette and jokingly reminded him of the agreement we had made several years ago to pay $10 to whichever of us could give up tobacco the longest.

Rodino came into my office to say hello to John. He agreed with Shaffer about John being photographed, and also made it clear that he would like to be photographed with John in the hearing room.

During the lunch break, we went back to my office. I suggested that he might prefer to have lunch alone with his counsel. He said no, he would like to talk further. I asked Mrs. Chellman [my secretary] to get food and coffee. We reminisced a bit about our prior work together on civil rights issues during the Johnson administration. Then he seemed distressed and became very serious. He talked about his experiences in the Nixon White House: "There are still things that I have not testified about—that are speculations and things of that sort. What has come out publicly so far is just the tip of the iceberg. But let me just tell you this. When I was first placed in the witness protection program, a Justice Department official had warned me that they were in fear for my life. They were afraid that the President's friend Bebe Rebozo would arrange to have me encased in concrete and buried at the bottom of the seas off the Bahamas."

When the hearings finally concluded it was rather late. Dean was in a hurry to avoid the press and get out. I shook his hand, but he was preoccupied and unresponsive. As we parted, I said, "Good luck, John."

On the conclusion of Dean's testimony, it was clear that the committee had at last established a record adequate to impeach the President for at least one of the statutory crimes analyzed in the Dobrovir brief. As for the other felonies, the record set forth in Doar's documents was inconclusive and inadequate. Thus, the week of live testimony could be viewed as a victory for Brooks and O'Neill in that impeachment on at least one felony charge seemed assured. However, if Rodino was in fact shaving points with Doar's help, it was also a large victory for them. He and Doar had knocked out twenty-eight felony charges.

18

ARTICLES OF IMPEACHMENT

*A distillation of the thought of many members
from many areas, and of differing political philosophies.*
—Representative William Hungate

Since the House of Representatives is a political forum, the
adoption of articles of impeachment is a political act with all
the clashes of competing interests that entails—and more so.
What most members of the Judiciary Committee were unwilling to
reveal publicly was their fears and anxieties about the effects that an
eventual vote on impeachment might have on their own political
futures as well as on their own images of themselves. The public
rarely knows about this, for the face that our representatives put
on their behind-the-scenes negotiations for the media is one of
calm, rational discourse. Thus, it was behind the closed doors of
party caucuses and private conversations that the slings and arrows
of impeachment politics were most in evidence.

On the night before John Dean's testimony, the committee
Democrats were in even more turmoil than usual. Of the twenty-one
Democrats, three were not certain to vote for impeachment: Walter
Flowers of Alabama, Ray Thornton of Arkansas, and James Mann of
South Carolina. All three represented districts that had given Nixon
overwhelming majorities over McGovern in 1972. Added to the sev-
enteen Republicans on the committee, it was possible that an
impeachment resolution could be defeated in committee, 20 to 18.

The Democrats caucused in my office, with the members seated on sofas or in chairs around the walls. Peter Rodino sat behind my desk, with me beside him. The door was locked and no official records were kept.

July 10 The caucus tonight was extraordinary. One of the most moving speeches I have ever heard was made by Jim Mann, who arrived late. He spoke softly with great dignity and morality, and implored the northern liberals to give him and other southern Democrats a chance to help them and to help the country. He said that the committee was too caught up in details, and couldn't see the forest for the trees. He wanted a chance to confer privately with the Republicans.

Before Mann began, Rodino had recommended that we break up into small task forces to work on separate pieces of the documents in Doar's volumes. He also recommended that the members themselves not attempt to draft articles of impeachment, but rather should rely on Doar's staff to do the drafting. Elizabeth Holtzman complained that Doar had not provided any drafts, despite a promise to do so.

The junior members were expressing their fear that the impeachment case will not fly, and were worrying about how to explain their failure to their liberal constituents. Before the caucus, Barbara Jordan had told myself and Ed Mezvinsky that Richard Nixon is the safest man in the United States.

Mezvinsky was distressed by our failure to develop a case for tax fraud. He added, "Yes, the King is safe in his castle, but goddammit, why are we building moats for him!"

In his statement at the caucus today, Mann said softly, "With all of the talk here tonight about political problems, let me point out to you that of the 435 congressional districts in the United States, my South Carolina district was number one in terms of support for Nixon in the last election. I have the most heavily concentrated pro-Nixon district of any member of Congress, including the most conservative Republicans. But what I believe is at stake here is more important than my reelection. What is at stake is our way of life and the very structure of our government. If we are going to impeach Nixon, we will have to stop studying the trees and look at our whole country. To do that we have to get together with the Republicans and let it all hang out."

Jim's speech had left the other members silent. I was hoping that Peter and Doar might agree with Mann and suggest that we get together with the Republicans, but both remained silent and Doar seemed bored. Even though I was seated alongside Rodino, I raised my hand and asked to be recognized. Rodino was surprised. Seiberling, who had already started talking, stopped and said, "Go ahead."

I made a statement about the two different perceptions of the impeachment process. "One is that our responsibilities are limited to determining if there are factual questions requiring resolution in a trial by the Senate. That is the perception of our chairman and of the inquiry staff.

"Most of the Republicans have a different perception, which frankly I share. In my view, before the committee votes to impeach the President, we have a moral responsibility to make a compelling case that he is guilty. As I see it, it is because of this difference in perception that the Republicans are fearful that we have a political strategy which is less than honorable."

Walter Flowers agreed with me and said, "Jerry has told it like it is. Come on! Let's talk turkey, goddammit! Let me tell everyone here tonight that I'm not gonna vote to impeach the President unless I can base my vote on a deep personal conviction that he is guilty. I will not vote to impeach him unless a strong case is presented against him in terms of his actual guilt, rather than some frivolous notion that we are only supposed to ask questions and not provide answers."

Since the hour was quite late, it was quickly agreed that Mann, Flowers, and Thornton should try to arrange a closed-door meeting with some of their Republican friends on the committee, and that Doar should provide drafts of articles of impeachment that make a case and are not limited to raising questions.

After the caucus broke up, Doar left. Rodino stayed in my office to talk to me. His reaction to my statement was consistent with his practice of always having more than one line in the water. He shrugged his shoulders and said, "Who really knows? Maybe you're right. If after this is over you should decide that you don't really want to become a law professor, I hope you will stay on as my chief counsel."

The next day, after Dean's testimony, Mann made arrangements for the three southern Democrats to begin having regular meetings with Republican Caldwell Butler of Virginia as well as northern Republicans Railsback, Fish, and Cohen. They agreed to work together and also tentatively agreed to vote as a bloc. However, Wiggins, leader of the stalwarts, soon got wind of the group's existence.

July 16 Today Wiggins played a master stroke. He succeeded in getting Railsback to publicly identify the four Republicans and three southern Democrats as the "swing seven" who could determine the final outcome. Then Wiggins publicly expressed confidence that all four Republicans will stay with their party and defend their president. This means that Nixon, Kissinger, Father McLaughlin, Rabbi Korff, and every other anti-impeachment advocate can now direct their troops of lobbyists and supporters to aim their political rifles at the same four Republicans and three Democrats whom Rodino had recently embarrassed by telling the media that they were already committed to impeachment.

My fear tonight is that some or all might succumb to political intimidation. If that happens, the vote for impeachment will be something like 23 to 15. That's not quite good enough to avoid being characterized by the media as "party-line politics as usual," which could dangerously polarize the country.

Charles Colson testified today, just about a week after he started a one-to-three-year prison term for conspiring to obstruct justice. He didn't tell us anything new other than that he has found God in prison and has been born again. This produced some bipartisan humor. Caldwell Butler chided Father Drinan [out of earshot of Colson and the reporters], "Hey, to tell us if his religious conversion is for real, we should swear you in as an expert witness and get your professional opinion." Drinan shot back, "Okay, but first I'd have to check his contributions to the Baptist church."

Also, George Danielson, who has publicly announced that he will vote to impeach, told me this joke, "This impeachment thing is like making love to a gorilla. You can't stop until the gorilla is ready."

That is enough for tonight. I am very weary. Oh yes, one more thing. During a recess, Henry Smith [Republican from New York] and I were joking about collaborating to produce a Broadway musical to be called *High Crimes and Misdemeanors,* in which Nixon will be backed by a chorus of White House plumbers in the theme song "I Am Not a Crook." Charles Colson will sing, "Grab 'em by the balls, and their hearts and minds will follow." John Dean will be joined by a chorus of Democrats singing "Nixon's the one!"

I think there is probably a lot of grim political wisdom in all of today's humor. I think it was James Madison who warned of the dangers of dark secrets that can turn democracy into a "farce or a tragedy, or perhaps both."

On Wednesday, July 17, the committee heard its last witness. Herbert Kalmbach, a political fundraiser for Nixon who had already pleaded guilty to violations of the Federal Corrupt Practices Act, had come from a prison cell in the custody of federal marshals.

On Thursday, July 18, St. Clair was permitted to sum up his defense of Nixon. Consistent with Doar's theory that the President could not be charged with participating in a conspiracy, St. Clair argued that Nixon had not personally directed the payment of hush money to Howard Hunt.

July 18 Doar summed up his presentation this morning at 10:00. To my surprise, at about 9:00 Rodino came up behind me in the hallway outside my office and gave me a very friendly pat on the shoulder. He asked me to come with him to a meeting with Doar. At the meeting he referred to a copy of the summary that Doar had previously given him. I have never before seen Rodino express so much anger at Doar. I wonder whether it wasn't a show for my benefit.

Rodino said he was looking for a hard-hitting, succinct summary of what the whole case was about, and that Doar's summary "didn't cut the mustard." Doar stormed out of the room.

When Doar delivered the statement about a half hour later, he began by introducing about four pounds of documents that he had handed out to the members. Then he read his prepared summary and added, "Members of the committee, for me to speak like this, I can hardly believe I am speaking as I do or thinking as I do . . . I realize that most people would understand an effort to conceal a mistake. But this was not done by a private citizen and the people who are working for the President are not private citizens. This was the President of the United States. What he decided should be done following the Watergate break-in caused action not only by his own servants, but by agencies of the United States, including the Department of Justice, the FBI, the CIA, and the Secret Service.

"It required perjury, obstruction of justice, all crimes. But most important, it required deliberate, continued, and continuing deception of the American people.

"It is that evidence that we want to present to you in detail and to help and reason with you, and this summary of information is the basis, or a work-product, to help you."

I was very impressed. It had an emotional impact. It struck the right notes. It was on a high road and it did fly.

As Jack Brooks and I agreed afterward, it may be that this was the only time during the whole proceeding that Doar really flew. But there remains one major criticism: Doar still insists that the President cannot be charged with participating in a conspiracy.

Under pressure from Tip O'Neill, Rodino had finally scheduled committee debates on articles of impeachment for the following Wednesday, July 24. Henry Smith's nervous humor about the entertainment value of Watergate undoubtedly grew out of a major decision that had been made to amend House rules to permit congressional debates to be televised. Rodino and Doar had hoped that the rules change would increase the committee members' reliance on the inquiry staff to make the case and draft the articles of impeachment. Thankfully, the opposite occurred.

Realizing that their performances would be witnessed by huge TV audiences, the Democratic members decided to rely on their own talents. Disregarding Rodino's advice, Jack Brooks and Jim Thornton had each already started to draft proposed articles. Don Edwards and Brooks formed a whole team comprised of committee members and permanent staff members. The "swing seven" started by James Mann also started drafting its own articles, coordinating its work with the Edwards-Brooks team as well as with Doar.

Among themselves, the "swing seven" had an extraordinary combination of legal and political skills. Three of them had had years of experience as trial lawyers. Thornton had served as a federal prosecutor and later as Attorney General of Arkansas. Butler had been a practicing attorney and litigator in Virginia for twenty-two years. Mann had been both a prosecutor and a practicing civil litigator in South Carolina—and had served in the Army throughout World War II, coming out as a lieutenant colonel. Bill Cohen, in addition to being a former practicing attorney, was a poet and probably the best-read member of the House. Hamilton Fish was a Harvard graduate, and was the fourth generation of his family to serve in Congress. Walter Flowers was a rare combination of practical "good ol' boy" politician and intellectual who had a Phi Beta Kappa key and had done graduate studies at London University. Tom Railsback had such extraordinary political skills that, although he was a Republican, he had the full support of the AFL-CIO.

From Saturday, July 20, until after the televised hearings began

on the night of July 24, members of the two drafting groups seques-
tered themselves from media coverage. First they considered the
question of whether Nixon had in fact conspired with Dean and others to obstruct justice as alleged by Dean and charged by the
Watergate grand jury. Most, if not all, of the members of both drafting groups rejected Doar's contention that the President was constitutionally shielded from being charged with such participation.
The experiences of two of the Democrats, New York City-born
Charlie Rangel and Alabama-born Walter Flowers, made their views
particularly persuasive.

Rangel had been a federal prosecutor in New York and Flowers
had served as a military intelligence officer. Both had practical experience with "plausible deniability"—a doctrine which high-ranking
drug dealers as well as high-ranking intelligence officers often
asserted when their subordinates were charged with crimes. Doar's
Nuremberg defense was essentially one of several variations of the
flawed plausible deniability doctrine.

Both drafting groups also took a high-road constitutional approach
to impeachment. They concluded that, aside from the obstruction of
justice charge, Nixon should be impeached for violating his oath of
office to defend the Constitution and faithfully execute the laws of
the United States.

Having confidence in their abilities, both drafting groups
rejected the draft articles prepared by Doar for a variety of reasons,
but primarily because they perceived that Doar still saw the committee's responsibility and authority as limited to submitting issues
of fact for resolution by the Senate. Over Doar's objections, each of
the proposed articles that the two drafting groups agreed on concluded with a sentence that was traditional, having appeared in
prior impeachments. It left no doubt as to the House's prosecutorial role: "Wherefore, Richard M. Nixon, by such conduct, warrants
impeachment and trial and removal from office."

While the articles were still being drafted, Pearl Chellman prepared a notice for my signature formally advising all committee
members that on Wednesday, July 24, at 7:30 P.M., there would be a
meeting to consider "whether the House of Representatives should
exercise its constitutional power to impeach Richard M. Nixon,
President of the United States." For me, signing that notice was a
moving experience.

July 23 Ed Mezvinsky was with me when I signed the notice. I was glad he was there. Before signing it I told him, "My grandfather arrived at Ellis Island as an illiterate harnessmaker. He would have never believed that his name would be affixed to a document like this. If he were still alive he would caution me. I can hear him now saying, 'You can get into a lot of trouble for something like this.'" Mezvinsky, who is the son of a Russian Jewish immigrant, said he knew exactly what I meant.

On July 24, the committee met at 7:30 P.M. For the first time in history, a congressional debate and roll call vote was recorded on television, and the coverage lasted until July 30. During that week, the committee adopted three articles of impeachment, all by fairly substantial bipartisan majorities.

Article I was the obstruction of justice charge drafted largely by the "swing seven" in consultation with the Edwards group. It passed on July 27 by a vote of 27 to 11.

Article II was the high-road abuse of constitutional powers article, also drafted largely by the "swing seven" and the Edwards group. It passed on July 29 by a vote of 28 to 10.

Article III charged the President with unlawfully refusing to comply fully with the committee's subpoenas. It was proposed by Bob McClory. Despite vigorous opposition from both Rodino and Doar, it passed on July 30 by a vote of 21 to 17.

During the proceedings, the committee also considered two other proposed articles. One charged the President with unlawful secrecy in concealing the bombing of Cambodia. It was defeated by a vote of 26 to 12. The other charged Nixon with criminal tax evasion. It too was defeated by a vote of 26 to 12.

The televised proceedings reached an estimated 90 million viewers over a period of some thirty-eight hours of broadcast coverage.

After the articles of impeachment were adopted by the committee, Tip O'Neill scheduled a debate by the full House to begin in two weeks. The general mood in the House and throughout the country was that impeachment was a foregone conclusion.

But major questions persisted. Would Nixon resign? If not, how long would a Senate trial take? And if there was a Senate trial, would the Senate undertake the investigation that Doar had intentionally avoided?

19

THE "SMOKING GUN"
AND THE DISAPPEARANCE
OF HALE BOGGS

July 24, 1974 was an historic day because of another event that was somewhat eclipsed by the opening of the impeachment debate. At 11 A.M. the Supreme Court met to announce their decision in *United States v. Nixon*. The case had been brought by Special Prosecutor Leon Jaworski to compel the President to turn over White House tapes that Nixon's counsel argued were shielded from disclosure by executive privilege.

Just two blocks away from the Rayburn Building—where the congressional drafting teams were feverishly preparing articles of impeachment—the traditional cry went out: "Oyez, Oyez, Oyez . . . God Save the United States and this honorable court." Then Chief Justice Warren Burger, who had been appointed by President Nixon, gave a simple history of the case and announced that eight of the court's justices had ruled against the President—with Associate Justice William Rehnquist, who had previously served in the Nixon Justice Department, having recused himself from the case.

One of the tapes covered by the court's order, that of June 23, 1972, was assumed correctly by Robert McClory to be a "smoking gun" which would conclusively establish from the President's own lips that he had participated in a conspiracy to obstruct justice in the Watergate case. When McClory had received word of the Supreme Court's decision, he had called Rodino and requested that the impeachment debate scheduled to open that evening be postponed to give the committee time to review the new evidence, which

202

McClory felt would nail down the obstruction of justice article still being drafted. Rodino refused, and the televised debates went on as scheduled. (Under the circumstances of incomplete evidence, McClory had refused to vote "yes" on Article I. However, he had voted for Article II and had aggressively lobbied Democrats and Republicans alike to support Article III.)

Almost simultaneously with the opening of debate, St. Clair announced that Nixon—"a firm believer in the rule of law"—would comply with the Supreme Court's order, adding that "the time-consuming process [of preparing the evidence for submission to the court] will begin forthwith."

On August 2, Charles Wiggins, the leader of the stalwarts, was summoned to the White House and permitted to review a transcript of the smoking gun tape.

On August 5, the transcript was released to the public. It more than corroborated Dean's incrimination of the President as a co-conspirator. It showed that as early as three days after the break-in the President had personally directed Haldeman to press the CIA to instruct the FBI to turn off its investigation of the burglars in the interest of national security.

Wiggins appeared on television that same day to announce that if the President did not resign, he would vote to impeach him. He said, "The magnificent career of public service of Richard Nixon must be terminated involuntarily." The nine other stalwarts withdrew their support for Nixon and announced that they were changing their votes on Impeachment Article I to "yes," making the final committee vote for impeachment on the obstruction of justice charge unanimous.

On August 8, Nixon and Jerry Ford met before noon briefly in the Oval Office. Immediately after the meeting, United Press White House correspondent Helen Thomas reported that the President had decided to resign. Minutes later Minority Leader Rhodes confirmed the news to Tip O'Neill and the members and staff of the Judiciary Committee. He said, "I feel relief, sorrow, gratitude, and optimism." That night, Nixon spoke to the nation on television, stating, "It has become evident to me that I no longer have a strong enough political base in the Congress. . . . Therefore I shall resign the presidency effective at noon tomorrow."

On August 9, eleven days before the Judiciary Committee was to file its articles of impeachment with the full House, Jerry Ford became President. Frank Polk and I watched on television as Chief Justice Burger administered the oath of office that the fallen President had violated. In a brief inaugural address—which he labeled as "just a little straight talk among friends"—he reminded us for a moment of the modest and affable Jerry Ford who as minority leader had said, "I am a Ford, not a Lincoln." Since he was not elected, he asked that the people "confirm me as your President in your prayers."

The next day, Frank Polk and I met for lunch and discussed our reactions to Nixon's resignation and Ford's inaugural address. We agreed that in a very profound sense the nightmare of Watergate seemed to be over at last—and as congressional staffers we could turn to all of the pressing committee matters that had been neglected by our preoccupation with the White House horrors. But we both still had disquieting fears that the root causes of the Watergate cancer had never been dealt with. True, the Constitution had worked, but perhaps only miraculously—and there was a serious question as to whether as a precedent our failure to conduct an investigation had not weakened the impeachment clause.

For most of the committee Democrats, the smoking gun tape had raised disturbing questions that were rarely discussed, since most of us feared the answers. The tape revealed more than the incriminating fact that Nixon had ordered Haldeman to direct the CIA to impede the investigation of Watergate. It also suggested evidence of government-sponsored crimes during the Kennedy administration.

The June 23 tape had a particularly jolting effect on me. During the course of the impeachment inquiry, Congresswoman Lindy Boggs had made a discreet and poignant request of Rodino and me that in the context of the smoking gun tape had ramifications even more grotesque than the coverup of Watergate. Lindy had requested that the impeachment inquiry be expanded to include the mysterious disappearance of her husband Hale—who had formerly been a member of the Warren Commission as well as Tip O'Neill's predecessor as majority leader. A few months after the Watergate break-in, and less than three weeks before Nixon's landslide reelection 1972, Hale had been reported missing in a small plane in Alaska. His body was never found.

After Hale's disappearance, Lindy and Hale's brother, a Jesuit priest in New Orleans, were fearful that he had been murdered because of his inside knowledge about the role of the FBI, CIA, and organized crime in events leading up to the Kennedy assassination—knowledge that he had acquired as a member of the Warren Commission and that might also have some relevance to Watergate.

Congresswoman Boggs had expressed her fears to Congressman Bill Hungate as well as to me and Peter Rodino in the strictest confidence. It had fallen to my lot to gently inform her that we could not comply with her request for an investigation. After reviewing the smoking gun tape, Lindy Boggs's request for a congressional investigation seemed more reasonable than ever, but there was no likelihood of our ever commencing such an investigation in the Ninety-third Congress. The funds for the impeachment inquiry had been depleted and Doar and his staff were seeking employment elsewhere. Other matters required more immediate attention by the committee's permanent professional staff.

Following the assassination of President Kennedy in Dallas on November 22, 1963, both Richard Helms of the CIA and J. Edgar Hoover of the FBI became fearful that a thorough investigation by the Warren Commission of the Kennedy assassination would lead to public awareness of government-sponsored assassination programs, domestic surveillance, and illegal wiretapping. Their fears were exacerbated when Black Muslim leader Malcolm X began preaching sermons characterizing the fallen president as both a racist and assassin who had already had three rulers of third-world countries assassinated and had been attempting to assassinate Castro. (After making his now-famous sermon in which he claimed that the Kennedy "chickens have come home to roost," Malcom X was excommunicated by the Black Muslims. Soon thereafter, he himself was assassinated.)

We also know now that, like Malcolm X, President Johnson believed that his fallen predecessor had approved the CIA-sponsored project that led to the killings of the Dominican Republic's Generalissimo Trujillo in 1961 and South Vietnam's President Diem in 1963 (only a few weeks before Kennedy's own assassination). Yet, ironically, the Warren Commission, formed by President Johnson, was compromised by its reliance on the FBI and the CIA, which did everything possible to prevent the truth from coming out.

When the Warren Commission was established, its members included, among others, Hale Boggs, Jerry Ford, and former CIA Director Allen Dulles. Its staff also included Albert Jenner, who a decade later became minority counsel to the impeachment inquiry. We now know that the official report of the Warren Commission was intentionally sanitized by both the CIA and the FBI to exclude any mention of anti-Castro plots or other illegal activities approved by the Kennedy Justice Department—which at that time employed Burke Marshall and John Doar in high positions.

We also now know that, after the Warren Commission filed its report with President Johnson, Hale Boggs went to the White House and in confidence told Johnson of the efforts of Robert Kennedy in particular to have Castro assassinated. Boggs, who was from New Orleans, had apparently learned of the plots from at least two sources. One was House colleague Gillis Long, Democrat from Louisiana, who had previously been employed in New Orleans by Howard Hughes as an aide to Robert Maheu—the former FBI agent who had helped the CIA recruit Mafia hitmen for the project. Another of Boggs's close confidants and sources of sensitive information was New Orleans District Attorney James Garrison, who had investigated the assassination in 1967 and was being denigrated by the CIA and FBI for his efforts to prove that Oswald was not the lone assassin.

From his experience on the Warren Commission, Hale Boggs became even more aware than most congressmen of the illegal wiretapping and domestic surveillance programs of the FBI. In 1971 Boggs had made an extraordinary speech on the House floor. The then-majority leader accused the Department of Justice of using "Gestapo-like" police-state tactics that included bugging the offices and homes of members of Congress and other political leaders— and in some cases using illegally obtained information to blackmail public officials. Boggs prophetically blamed the erosion of the rule of law in the executive branch on his own personal fear and the fear of Congress in general of assuming its constitutional responsibilities:

> Our apathy in this Congress, our silence in this House, our very fear of speaking out has watered the growth of a vine of tyranny which is ensnaring that Constitution and Bill of Rights which we are sworn to uphold. . . . While America's sons have faithfully manned the watchtowers of freedom around the globe, the liberty of our own lives has been yielding steadily before the power, prerogatives, and privileges of government.

I point no fingers and place no blame elsewhere. What has occurred could not have occurred without our consent and complicity here on Capitol Hill.

After enumerating a wide variety of criminal acts either directed or sanctioned by the Department of Justice over the entire Cold War, Boggs observed that "1984 is closer than we think." Then he criticized the Kennedy administration and Attorney General Robert Kennedy as much as the Nixon administration and Attorney General John Mitchell: "I have seen every postwar president, Democrat or Republican, except Lyndon Johnson, tacitly acknowledge this new character of the Department by installing their campaign managers or political party chairmen as Attorney General or Deputy Attorney General."

The next day, apparently due to the success of Justice Department disinformation efforts, most of the reporters who covered Capitol Hill gave the story of Boggs's speech their own inside-the-Beltway spin. Based on information from anonymous "reliable sources," it was reported that Boggs was drunk. But those of us who knew Boggs and were present at his speech knew that he was not drunk.

The unreported truth was that when Boggs made the speech he was undergoing psychiatric treatment for manic depression, and the CIA and FBI were concerned that his judgment had become sufficiently impaired to endanger national security.

Hale Boggs had already proved himself to be Congress's highest-ranking outspoken opponent of the lawlessness that had been deeply rooted in the Department of Justice and the CIA ever since the secret Houston-Rogers memorandum of agreement in 1954. Whether the sole member of the Warren Commission to speak out against government-sponsored crimes had been murdered during the Watergate period, as feared by his widow and his brother, still remains a mystery.

As for the sham impeachment inquiry that followed Watergate and Boggs's disappearance, major mysteries also remain. Many of the stones covering up high crimes and misdemeanors were intentionally left unturned. However, we do know now that the sham impeachment inquiry investigation—as orchestrated by Peter Rodino, Burke Marshall, John Doar, Bernard Nussbaum, Hillary Rodham, and others—protected not only Nixon. It also protected many officials of the Kennedy Justice Department from being embarrassed by public disclosure of what Nixon referred to on the smoking gun tape as "one hell of a lot of things."

Even though Nixon had resigned, under the impeachment clause of the Constitution he could still be tried and convicted by the Senate with the result that he would be forever after barred from holding public office. Although Senate Majority Leader Mike Mansfield as well as a number of House members urged the House leadership to present the articles of impeachment to the Senate, Rodino was unwilling. He instructed Doar to work out a procedure to delay filing the committee's report and to avoid the result being urged by Mansfield on behalf of the Senate Democrats.

The procedure that Doar worked out was somewhat unorthodox. After preparing a draft of that portion of the report traditionally published under the imprimatur of the committee chairman, he first sent it to Burke Marshall for review. Since I and key members of the committee's regular staff had refused to have our names affixed to his thirty-six volumes of "evidence," he did not give us the opportunity to review the report before Rodino signed it and filed it with the Clerk of the House. But he affixed our names below those of his staff on the committee masthead preceding the report.

The procedure Doar worked out for filing the articles were also unorthodox. If the House approved the deftly worded resolution that accompanied the committee's report on the articles of impeachment, it would simply accept the report as an official House document without setting a Senate trial in motion. The resolution also stated that the House "takes notice" that the committee had been directed to conduct an investigation and then commended the committee for its "conscientious and capable efforts in carrying out" its responsibility.

On August 20, Doar's resolution was brought up on the House floor and approved by a vote of 412 to 3. The official impeachment inquiry was over.

Within a matter of minutes, we had one more major new assignment. When the House Doorkeeper bellowed a cry of "Mr. Speaker! A message from the President of the United States," Jerry Ford's nomination of Nelson Rockefeller to be his Vice President was officially submitted to the House. After it was referred to the Judiciary

Committee and the staff commenced its investigation of Rockefeller, the House took a three-week recess.

On September 8, the final political bombshell of Watergate exploded. President Ford granted Nixon a "full and complete pardon" of any and all prior criminal acts, known or unknown. To quell the public unrest created by the pardon, Ford agreed to appear personally before the House Judiciary Committee to testify about the circumstances that had led to the pardon. In the very hearing room where articles of impeachment had been adopted in July, the Committee was given Ford's assurances that the pardon had not been granted pursuant to a political deal between him and Richard Nixon, who by then was a recluse at San Clemente.

After our hearings on the pardon, we concluded the investigation and confirmation of Nelson Rockefeller as Vice President. Rockefeller took the oath of office on December 19, 1974. A few days later, I left Washington to take up a teaching position at the University of Santa Clara.

20

A QUESTION OF MORALITY

What is morally wrong can never be politically right.
—Abraham Lincoln

O n the eve of the opening of the Judiciary Committee's televised impeachment debate of July 24, 1974, my relationship with Peter Rodino was strained but still cordial. He turned to me with an eleventh-hour assignment: "Write a statement for me to open the debate."

In framing the issues to be resolved by the Congress, the statement that I drafted—and which Rodino delivered eloquently—drew on a quotation from the eighteenth-century British conservative, Edmund Burke. In the House of Commons, Burke had successfully impeached mad King George III's minister, Warren Hastings—who as Governor General of the East India Corporation was charged with obstructing justice, operating brothels in Bengal, and other high crimes that offended the moral standards of British statesmen. In opening the impeachment in the House of Lords, Burke stated:

> It is by this process that magistracy, which tries and controls all other things, is itself tried and controlled. Other constitutions are satisfied with making good subjects. This is a security for good governors. It is by this tribunal that statesmen who abuse their power are accused by statesmen, and tried by statesmen, not upon the niceties of a narrow jurisprudence, but upon the enlarged and solid principles of state

morality. It is here that those who by the abuse of power have violated the spirit of the law can never hope for protection from any of its forms. . . .

With the Hastings impeachment still pending in the House of Lords while our founders were drafting the impeachment clause of the Constitution, Burke's "state morality" standard was translated into American jurisprudence in the form of the "Madisonian" standard—which does not require proof of a statutory crime. For Madison as for Burke, a "high crime" was an immoral abuse of power by a high-ranking government official. Thus the core of a successful impeachment charge in the Nixon case was a finding that the President had failed to meet the moral standards that are expected of those who hold high office in a democratic society.

As I saw it, since the abuse of power standard was essentially a standard of political morality and did not require evidence of guilt beyond a reasonable doubt of the commission of a statutory crime, it would be easier to prove in an evidentiary sense. However, although Doar and his key aides were not able to refute the constitutional soundness of the state morality standard, it became painfully clear to me that their advice to Rodino differed radically from mine.

Recognizing that the statesmanship standard relieved impeachment proponents of the burden of proving that Nixon had committed a statutory crime, Doar and his closest aides felt that the standard also gave Nixon a defense that would not be available in the criminal courts. What Doar seemed to fear most was that a Senate trial based on a state morality standard might vindicate Nixon if he could show—or perhaps even threaten to show—that in handling Watergate his acts were no more immoral or illegal than the acts of prior presidents, especially John Kennedy. As Nixon well knew, at the height of the Cold War, top officials of the Kennedy administration had not only engaged in wiretaps and burglaries, but had even sanctioned murders in the name of national security.

Did Nixon have such a politically or legally viable defense? Obviously, he felt that he did. In May 1977, Nixon made his first national appearance since his voluntary exile to San Clemente in the summer of 1974 in a series of televised interviews with David Frost. The former president stated, "I did not commit, in my view, any impeachable offense. . . . I can only say that while technically I did not commit a crime, an impeachable offense . . . these are legalisms.

As far as the handling of this [Watergate] matter is concerned, it was so botched-up. I made many bad judgments. The worst ones, mistakes of the heart rather than the head."

At one point in the interview, Nixon explained the basis of his defense:

> When the president does it, that means that by definition it is not illegal. . . . If the president approves an action because of the national security, then the president's decision in that instance is one that enables those who carry it out to carry it out without violating a law. Otherwise, they're in an impossible position.

It was a political defense that was commonly asserted on the highest levels of government during the Cold War. It was also a doctrine that often shielded CIA operatives from prosecution for acts which were defined as felonies under our criminal law but which presidents had approved in the name of national security.

Did Doar know that Nixon had such a defense against a wide variety of charges of presidential misconduct? And did Doar intentionally structure the impeachment inquiry to avoid the possibility of a debate on the state morality of Nixon as compared to that of John Kennedy? It was not until late September 1974, almost two months after Nixon's resignation, that it first became apparent to me—if not to most of the members of the Committee—that the answer to both questions was "yes."

The revelation was provoked by a personal letter that Charles Wiggins sent to Peter Rodino on September 26, 1974, with copies sent to "All Judiciary Committee Members":

> Within the past few days, some disturbing information has come to my attention. It is requested that the facts concerning the matter be investigated and a report be made to the full committee as it concerns us all.
>
> Early last spring when it became obvious that the committee was considering presidential "abuse of power" as a possible ground of impeachment, I raised the question before the full committee that research should be undertaken so as to furnish a standard against which to test the alleged abusive conduct of Richard Nixon.

As I recall, several other members joined with me in this request.

I recall as well repeating this request from time to time during the course of our investigation. The [impeachment inquiry] staff, as I recall, was noncommittal, but it is certain that no such staff study was made available to the members at any time for their use. . . .

Wiggins further advised Rodino that he had just learned that Doar had commissioned such a study to be undertaken at committee expense by a team of professors who completed and filed their reports with Doar well in advance of our public hearings; and that the report was not made available to members of Congress, but was later published commercially. Wiggins also requested that Rodino inform himself and the other committee members about such information as when the reports were received by Doar, what were the terms of the commission, by whom and by whose authority, and the content. Wiggins ended his letter pointedly:

I am troubled especially by the possibility that information deemed essential by some of the members in their discharge of their responsibilities may have been intentionally suppressed by the staff during the course of our investigation. Also, we must resolve the question of whether the staff possesses a literary property right in nonpublic information collected during the course of our investigation.

On October 3, 1974, ignoring Wiggins's request that all members of the committee be given the benefit of his answers, Rodino wrote a four-page personal reply to Wiggins. He explained that the report was received by Doar in July and attempted to explain why its existence was kept secret from the committee:

Hillary Rodham of the impeachment inquiry staff coordinated the work. . . . After the staff received the report it was reviewed by Ms. Rodham, briefly by Mr. Labovitz and Mr. Sack, and by Doar. The staff did not think the manuscript was useful in its present form. . . .

In your letter you suggest that members of the staff may

have intentionally suppressed the report during the course of its investigation. That was not the case.

As a matter of fact, Mr. Doar was more concerned that any highlight of the project might prejudice the case against President Nixon. The fact is that the staff did not think the material was usable by the committee in its existing form and had not had time to modify it so it would have practical utility for the members of the committee. I was informed and agreed with the judgment.

From Rodino's letter and the later writings of Renata Adler, we now know that, early in 1974, Doar had given Rodham a secret assignment that was not to be disclosed to the committee members even after the committee's self-imposed exclusion from access to the inquiry staff's confidential files was terminated. Rodham was assigned to work with Yale professor C. Vann Woodward—who was a colleague of Burke Marshall—to help him prepare a highly sensitive historical account of abuses of presidential power that both Doar and Republican special counsel Albert Jenner had agreed was essential. The report was given the title *Responses of the President to Charges of Misconduct Including Accusations of High Crimes and Misdemeanors from George Washington to Lyndon Johnson: An Authoritative History Requested by Counsel John Doar for the Impeachment Inquiry Staff Investigating Charges Against Richard M. Nixon.*

With Rodham's help, Woodward and a team of twelve scholars completed the report and submitted it to Doar in secrecy prior to July 2, 1974, the date on which the Judiciary Committee began its first evidentiary hearings in anticipation of the impeachment debate scheduled to begin July 24. Two years after Nixon's resignation, Albert Jenner, Doar's Republican counterpart, was to say of the Woodward report, "We've kept it top secret. It was something we relied on very heavily."

Despite the efforts of Doar, Jenner, and Rodham to keep the report secret from the committee, the possibility that such a report might exist and might aid Nixon's defense occurred to Wiggins, who was the President's chief defender on the committee. Wiggins inquired of Doar as to whether such an investigation had been undertaken, and insisted that if the inquiry staff failed to make such a study, such failure would be unforgivable. However, the first time the contents of the Woodward report became known to any member of Congress was when Dell Publishing Company later sold it commercially in book stores.

In an effort to explain that Doar, Jenner, and Rodham were well-intentioned in keeping the taxpayer-financed Woodward report secret from Congress until after the House had voted to accept the committee's impeachment report, Renata Adler later stated that the need for secrecy on the project "illustrates the virtual impossibility at the time of conducting almost any impeachment research project. It has to do with the 1976 report of the Church Committee." Without reminding her readers that the Church Committee had publicly reported that political assassinations and covert wars had become official instruments of foreign policy in the Kennedy administration, Adler went on to say that Doar knew that such a report could be put to good use by Nixon's lawyers. Adler stated that Doar commissioned the report from outside the staff and kept it under wraps in case St. Clair used the defense on his own.

Summarized in brief, the President might have chosen to defend himself by arguing—as did his subsequent defender Victor Lasky and others who have struggled to restore his credibility—that the cancer on his presidency "didn't start with Watergate." If Adler is to be believed, Doar's reason for misleading Wiggins and the entire Congress by withholding the Woodward report was that to do so might generate a debate that Doar and Jenner wanted to avoid—a debate in which the misconduct of prior presidents might be relevant.

Thus the explanation of why Doar, Nussbaum, and Rodham kept the Woodward report secret appears to be essentially the same as the explanation of why they refused to conduct any original investigation of their own. For Doar to have conducted a thorough and complete investigation of Watergate would have exposed the immoral and unlawful abuses of power that had became systemic in the Department of Justice under Attorney General Robert Kennedy.

In my view, on a pragmatic level all of us who participated in the impeachment process are indebted to the inquiry staff to the extent that the non-investigation of Watergate did in fact avoid a Senate trial to determine whether Nixon's responses to charges of misconduct were as acceptable as the responses of his predecessors. For the Democrats as well as the Republicans who were proponents of Nixon's impeachment, it has been particularly pleasant to have avoided the agony of a Senate trial and at the same time enjoy the accolades in national best-sellers such as Jimmy Breslin's *How the Good Guys Finally Won.*

Yet there is more to the history of the Ninety-third Congress than most commercially popular journalists and historians are willing to confront—perhaps from fear of being considered unpleasantly cynical. Sadly, my own view is that on a long-term basis, the impeachment charade, being ethically flawed, did harm to our future national life and the credibilty of the current leaders of both political parties.

That President Nixon escaped the need to assert a defense in a Senate trial has left unresolved major questions about the roots of the corruption that led to Watergate and about our ability to eradicate them. The portion of the official impeachment report that I view as most consistent with my own current perceptions is that provided by Representative John Conyers, who labored unsuccessfully to prod the committee chairman and the inquiry staff to investigate Nixon's misconduct and eventually became exasperated by the committee's failure to enforce even one of our subpoenas. In a separate opinion in 1974, the Michigan congressman—who twenty years later became the committee's ranking Democrat—stated:

> It has frequently been said . . . that the committee's impeachment inquiry and the President's subsequent resignation demonstrate that "the system works." But such satisfaction or complacency is misguided. . . . If the system has worked, it has worked by accident and good fortune. It would be gratifying to conclude that this House, charged with the sole power of impeachment, exercised vigilance and acted on its own initiative. However, we would be deluding ourselves if we did not admit that this inquiry was forced on us by an accumulation of disclosures which, finally and after unnecessary delays, could no longer be ignored. . . .
>
> And most importantly, the President himself documented his words and actions through his secret taping system, without which our inquiry might never have begun. The President himself did more than anyone or anything to insure his removal from office.
>
> Perhaps ironically, and certainly unintentionally, we have

ourselves jeopardized the future of the impeachment process.
. . . Now with our inquiry as a precedent, future Congresses
may recoil from ever again exercising this power. They may
read the history of our work and conclude that impeachment
can never again succeed unless another president demon-
strates the same, almost uncanny, ability to impeach himself. If
this is our legacy, our future colleagues may well conclude that
ours has been a pyrrhic victory, and that impeachment will
never again justify the agony we have endured.

With the advantages of more than two decades of hindsight to
complete the historic record, my own view is that the "unnecessary"
delays were in fact intentional—as was the failure to investigate the
charges of President Nixon's misconduct. Both were violations of
the spirit, if not the letter, of Section 1505 of Title 18 of the United
States Code—which makes it a felony to obstruct a congressional
investigation. For a congressional staff itself to impede an investigation is at best an immoral abuse of power.

Another sad legacy of Watergate, Camelot, and the Cold War in general is that the moral flaws of the Nixon impeachment inquiry have
until now been kept secret from most of the public. There are
Democratic and Republican leaders alike who would now have our
children believe that whatever his transgressions in Watergate,
Richard Nixon was a "statesman," and that the Kennedy presidency
maintained a level of idealism worthy of emulation by students of
government who would pursue careers in public service.

Ironically, my own efforts to define an acceptable standard of
"state morality" for my naval and government service date back at
least to 1951. Then, at the University of Freiburgh in the center of
Germany's Black Forest, I met Herbert Mast, a fellow student. A former Luftwaffe war hero, he had grown up in the Hitler Youth. As
our prisoner of war, Mast had become an avid reader of American
newspapers, before eventually enrolling at Freiburgh's officially
"denazified" law school.

At a beer hall discussion of the immorality of the Third Reich, he
cited a recent *New York Times* article by George F. Kennan, former
U.S. Ambassador to the Soviet Union. Kennan warned that totalitarian threats to our national security are not only an external danger:

They represent a danger within ourselves—a danger that something may occur in our own minds and souls which will make us no longer like the persons by whose efforts this republic was founded and held together, but rather like the representatives of that very power that we are trying to combat: intolerant, secretive, suspicious, cruel and terrified of internal dissension because we have lost our own belief in ourselves and in the power of our ideals. The worst thing that [the enemies of our freedoms] could do to us, and the thing we have most to fear from their activities, is that we should become like them.

It appears to me that Nixon and the Kennedys had become "like them." Ambassador Kennan and others like him had a moral vision that I and other Capitol Hill supporters of Cold War policies too often denied to ourselves.

In 1928, before the rise of the Third Reich, Supreme Court Justice Louis Brandeis cautioned an earlier generation of government lawyers:

The government is the potent omnipresent teacher. For good or ill it teaches the whole people by its example.

Crime is contagious. If the government becomes a lawbreaker, it breeds contempt for law; it invites every man to become a law unto himself; it invites anarchy.

To declare that the end justifies the means—to declare that the government may commit crimes—would bring terrible retribution.

Today, with the Cold War ended, more of us are coming to an awareness that in the name of the "public good," our highest officials have committed secret crimes, including murders—and with the help of Congress have lied to cover them up. Perhaps the rising tide of disaffection with Congress, the White House, and both political parties will elevate our state morality—and reduce the present dangers that secret crimes hatched in government offices will breed contempt for law, invite anarchy, and bring terrible retribution.

EPILOGUE

In 1974, recent Yale graduate Bill Clinton visited his friend Hillary Rodham in the offices of the House Judiciary Committee. As Bernard Nussbaum was to recount years later to the *New York Times*, Hillary introduced Bill this way: "He's soon going to become governor of Arkansas—and eventually President of the United States."

At that time all three lawyers shared common interests in Arkansas politics as well as the fortunes of the Camelot government-in-exile. Placed on the impeachment inquiry staff by Burke Marshall, Nussbaum was a member of a law firm founded by Herbert Wachtell—who as a former counsel to Arkansas Congressman Oren Harris had investigated political corruption during the Eisenhower administration.

At the time of Watergate, the Wachtell firm was already expanding its practice, but in a sense was still not as well established as its major competitors, which included the following:

- The Washington law firm of Clark Clifford—who as Harry Truman's Counsel had helped to establish the CIA in 1947
- Donovan & Leisure (Wachtell's leading and more dominant New York competitor) which was founded by "Wild Bill" Donovan, of OSS fame—who was also a founding father of the CIA
- Fulbright & Jaworski, the Texas-based law firm of ABA President Leon Jaworski, who was to replace Archibald Cox as Watergate Special Prosecutor and whose multinational law firm had ties

219

to defense and intelligence-related industries that dated back to World War II
- Davis & Cox, which was cofounded by Archibald Cox's brother, Maxwell—who represented the Howard Hughes enterprises, the largest CIA contracting conglomerate of all
- Hale & Dorr of Boston, whose senior partner Joseph Welsh, assisted by James St. Clair, had been retained by the Eisenhower administration to defend the Army from charges of Communist infiltration brought by Senator Joe McCarthy—the firm that was later to grant a leave of absence to St. Clair to defend Nixon against impeachment charges ·
- Jenner & Bloch of Chicago, which was founded by·Albert Jenner, who had served on the staff of the Warren Commission and took a leave of absence from his lucrative practice to serve as the Republicancounsel on the impeachment inquiry staff

After the impeachment staff was disbanded in 1974, the staff's John Doar joined Donovan & Leisure. Albert Jenner returned to his Chicago practice representing such multinational defense companies as General Dynamics. Nussbaum returned to New York, where he helped Wachtell rival Donovan & Leisure.

By the time Bill Clinton was elected President in 1992, Nussbaum had ascended to superstar status among New York's top corporate litigators. His hourly fee was $500, and his annual earnings were reported in the $1 million range.

Hillary Rodham was twenty-seven when the impeachment inquiry staff was disbanded. Since she was still a relative neophyte in law, she had no prospects of moving directly into a lucrative private practice representing multinational corporations. On her last night on the House Judiciary Committee's payroll, Rodham had dinner with a few of her younger staff colleagues at the A.V. Ristorante, a moderate-priced pasta bistro near Capitol Hill. She confided in her friends that she was still undecided as to whether to marry Bill Clinton—who was then in Little Rock beginning his climb up the political ladder by planning a campaign for Attorney General.

By the next morning Rodham had made her decision. She took the train down to Little Rock, Arkansas. In 1977, when her husband became Attorney General, Rodham joined the Rose law firm as an associate. In 1979, the year her husband became the nation's youngest governor, Rodham became a Rose partner.

In 1992, Hillary Rodham Clinton rode back up to Washington, D.C. on a bus—the caravan that had taken her and Bill Clinton around the country on a Harry Truman-like campaign for the presidency.

Once in the White House, the Clintons embarked on a course that was reminiscent of some of the questionable policies of prior administrations. Clinton promptly named Nussbaum as White House Counsel, and also gave high government positions to several of Hillary's law partners. Even before choosing an Attorney General, he appointed Rose partner Webster Hubbell as Associate Attorney General, suggesting that, through Rodham and Nussbaum, Hubbell would be higher in the White House pecking order than the Attorney General. (Later, Hubbell was indicted and compelled to resign, and he pleaded guilty to charges of fraudulent billing practices while business manager of Rose.)

Vincent Foster, another Rose partner and close friend of Rodham's, was made Deputy White House Counsel, and was later alleged to have committed suicide while in possession of files relating to the financial mismanagement of the White House travel office, as well as personal files of the Clintons relating to their roles in the infamous Whitewater matter.

Following Foster's suicide, Nussbaum too was forced to resign after a March 4, 1994 *New York Times* editorial stated:

> It is, of course, long past time for Mr. Nussbaum to be dismissed. He seems to conceive of his being "the President's lawyer" as a license to meddle with the integrity of any federal agency. First, he and his staff tried to involve the Federal Bureau of Investigation in a politically inspired White House purge of employees of its travel office. When Vincent Foster, the deputy counsel, committed suicide, Mr. Nussbaum interfered with the investigation by the National Park Service and transferred secret files to Mr. Clinton's private lawyer.
>
> All this paints a picture of a White House dedicated to short-cutting justice if that is what it takes to shield the financial affairs of Mr. Clinton and his wife from scrutiny. This president desperately needs first rate legal advice and a staff that is under someone's management control. . . .

On March 11, 1995, in an op-ed article entitled "The First Lady-ship," *Times* editor A. M. Rosenthal also criticized Rodham:

> In concept, the First Ladyship is an affront to American democracy. . . . In practice it skews the administration of government, evades anti-nepotism statutes and avoids the responsibility that should go with authority. . . . It is the only political post that demands the essential qualification of being married to a particular man at a particular time in his life. . . .
>
> Seen and used as a job . . . the First Ladyship has become a government center. In lieu of salary it provides the jobholder with staff, luxury, and that most important of all perks, power.

In 1993, with Nussbaum as White House counsel, Rodham embarked upon a project that was reminiscent of her 1974 apprenticeship on the impeachment inquiry staff. She became head of a vast government task force on health care that operated in secret. The alleged illegality of this, and the alleged conflicts of interest of some of the members of the task force, was first made public in a complaint filed in the same courthouse where the Watergate burglars and many of President Nixon's aides had been prosecuted twenty years earlier. The court action was entitled *Association of American Physicians and Surgeons, Inc. (AAPS), American Council for Health Care Reform, and National Legal & Policy Center v. Hillary Rodham Clinton et al.*

The complaint and following legal actions publicized a number of disturbing facts about the health care task force. Initially, Ira Magaziner, a senior advisor to the president and executive director of the task force, had announced that the First Lady was forming a working group of 100 participants with a projected budget of $100,000. Later, the budget estimate was raised to $325,000. The final bill for the task force, according to the Government Accounting Office, was $9.6 million.

The reason for this inflation was that the task force ultimately comprised twelve "cluster groups" made up of some thirty-eight subgroups. By the end of May 1973, the staffing of the group had increased to more than 600 people. Besides normal staff salaries, the plaintiffs alleged that substantial sums were paid in violation of conflict of interest requirements to individuals who were also on the payrolls of private sector health care businesses and were friends who had made campaign contributions.

When, on February 10, 1993, the AAPS asserted their right under federal sunshine laws and the Federal Advisory Committee Act to attend the meetings of members of the task force, Nussbaum replied that the sunshine laws did not apply to meetings comprised solely of federal employees:

> The Act does not, and was not intended by Congress, to apply to the health task force—comprised solely of Cabinet secretaries, senior White House officials and the First Lady. The participation of the First Lady on the task force does not trigger application of the Act.

Two weeks later, the AAPS filed their complaint in court. In response, Rodham and her co-defendants filed a sworn declaration by Magaziner representing to the court that only full-time employees of the federal government were participants on the task force. In fact, many participants were from the private sector with financial ties to special interest groups. Under penalty of perjury, Magaziner also represented that all participants had been subjected to restrictions against conflicts of interest, when in fact most had ignored the restrictions and failed to comply with the disclosure regulations. The trial judge eventually determined that Magaziner's sworn declaration was "misleading at best."

After the health task force had completed its work and been disbanded, a three-judge panel of the U.S. Court of Appeals ruled that, in spite of the anti-nepotism statute, Rodham was a de facto federal official for the purpose of the sunshine laws. The reason given was that Congress has for years authorized presidents to hire aides for their wives. However, the issue of whether Rodham was a federal official was really a red herring, as the court implied. It noted that the essential work of the task force had been accomplished by the 600 people in working groups which, the court noted, "seems more like a horde than a committee." The court remanded the case to the trial judge for extensive discovery proceedings in June 1993.

Further proceedings relating to the working groups were contentious and drawn out. In September, the plaintiffs filed a motion to compel the defendants to turn over documents that were still being withheld. On November 9, the trial judge lost patience and sharply criticized the defendants' tactics, stating that their discovery responses were "preposterous" and "incomplete," and that the First Lady's contentions were "meritless" and that she and the other defendants had "improperly thwarted the plaintiffs' legitimate discovery requests." Despite the court's order to release the working group documents, the First Lady and the other defendants all continued to stonewall.

In July 1994, the exasperated judge put an end to the stonewalling by threatening to cite Magaziner for contempt and ordering the case to be set for trial. In December—with the Clinton health care package already rejected by Congress—the First Lady and the task force decided to "moot the case out" by voluntarily releasing all of the then-stale documents of the working groups.

The court declared the case moot on December 21, 1994, noting that this also mooted out the question of Magaziner's contempt. The court stated one remaining question: "Did Mr. Magaziner commit the criminal offense of contempt of court—as well as possible perjury and/or making a false statement—when he signed a sworn declaration . . . that led this court to initially dismiss the claim for records of the interdepartment working group?"

The court referred the case to the Justice Department for a determination of whether to prosecute Magaziner for perjury or to seek an independent counsel to make such a determination. Eventually, U.S. Attorney Eric Holder, Jr., insisting that he had no conflicts of interest even though he was appointed by Clinton, decided to neither ask for a special prosecutor or file charges against Magaziner.

The misinformation and stonewalling of the First Lady and her key aides relating to health care are reminiscent of the deceptive actions not only of the Nixon White House but of the impeachment inquiry staff. When the result of this secretive operation—the Clinton health care package—was unveiled, Congress was essentially told to take it or leave it. They left it, bringing to mind Madison's declaration that "secrecy in a popular government is but a prologue to a farce or a tragedy, or perhaps both."

Thus, the Clinton presidency—with its high-ranking advisors who learned their political skills during the Watergate era—fell victim to the folly of using secrecy and deception to govern a freedom-loving people.

APPENDIX A

ARTICLES OF IMPEACHMENT

Resolution

Impeaching Richard M. Nixon, President of the United States, of high crimes and misdemeanors.

Resolved, that Richard M. Nixon, President of the United States, is impeached for high crimes and misdemeanors, and that the following articles of impeachment be exhibited to the Senate:

Articles of impeachment exhibited by the House of Representatives of the United States of America in the name of itself and of all of the epople of the United States of America, against Richard M. Nixon, President of the United States of America, in maintenance and support of its impeachment against him for high crimes and misdemeanors.

Article I

In his conduct of the office of President of the United States, Richard M. Nixon, in violation of his constitutional oath faithfully to execute the office of President of the United States, and, to the best of his ability, preserve, protect, and defend the Constitution of the United States, and in violation of his constitutional duty to take care that the laws be faithfully executed, has prevented, obstructed, and impeded the administration of justice, in that:

On June 17, 1972, and prior thereto, agents of the Committee for the Re-election of the President committed unlawful entry of the headquarters of the Democratic National Committee in Washington, District of Columbia, for the purpose of securing political intelligence. Subsequent thereto, Richard M. Nixon, using the powers of his high office, engaged personally and through his subordinates and agents, in a course of conduct or plan designed to delay, impede, and obstruct the investigation of such unlawful entry, to cover up, conceal, and protect those responsible, and to conceal the existence and scope of other unlawful covert activities.

The means used to implement this course of conduct or plan included one or more of the following:

(1) making or causing to be made false or misleading statements to lawfully authorized investigative officers and employees of the United States;

(2) withholding relevant and material evidence or information from lawfully authorized investigative officers and employees of the United States;

(3) approving, condoning, acquiescing in, and counseling witnesses with respect to the giving of false or misleading statements to lawfully authorized investigative officers and employees of the United States and false or misleading testimony in duly instituted judicial and congressional proceedings;

(4) interfering or endeavoring to interfere with the conduct of investigations by the Department of Justice of the United States, the Federal Bureau of Investigation, the Office of Watergate Special Prosecution Force, and Congressional Committees;

(5) approving, condoning, and acquiescing in the surreptitious payment of substantial sums of money for the purpose of obtaining the silence or influencing the testimony of witnesses, potential witnesses, or individuals who participated in such unlawful entry and other illegal activities;

(6) endeavoring to misuse the Central Intelligence Agency, an agency of the United States;

(7) disseminating information received from officers of the Department of Justice of the United States to subjects of investigations conducted by lawfully authorized investigative officers and employees of the United States, for the purpose of aiding and assisting such subjects in their attempts to avoid criminal liability;

(8) making false or misleading public statements for the purpose of deceiving the people of the United States into believing that a thorough and complete investigation had been conducted with respect to allegations of misconduct on the part of personnel of the executive branch of the United States and personnel of the Committee for the Re-election of the President, and that there was no involvement of such personnel in such misconduct; or

(9) endeavoring to cause prospective defendants, and individuals duly tried and convicted, to expect favored treatment and consideration in return for their silence or false testimony, or rewarding individuals for their silence or false testimony.

In all of this, Richard M. Nixon has acted in a manner contrary to his trust as President and subversive of constitutional government, to the great prejudice of the cause of law and justice and to the manifest injury of the people of the United States.

Wherefore, Richard M. Nixon, by such conduct, warrants impeachment and trial, and removal from office.

Article II

Using the powers of the office of President of the United States, Richard M. Nixon, in violation of his constitutional oath faithfully to execute the office of President of the United States and, to the best of his ability, preserve, protect, and defend the Constitution of the United States, and in disregard of his constitutional duty to take care that the laws be faithfully executed, has repeatedly engaged in conduct violating the constitutional rights of citizens, impairing the due and proper administration of justice and the conduct of lawful inquiries, or contravening the laws governing agencies of the executive branch and the purposes of these agencies.

This conduct has included one or more of the following:

(1) He has, acting personally and through his subordinates and agents, endeavored to obtain from the Internal Revenue Service, in violation of the constitutional rights of citizens, confidential information contained in income tax returns for purposes not authorized by law, and to cause, in violation of the constitutional rights of citizens, income tax audits or other income tax investigations to be initiated or conducted in a discriminatory manner.

(2) He misused the Federal Bureau of Investigation, the Secret Service, and other executive personnel, in violation or disregard of the constitutional rights of citizens, by directing or authorizing such agencies or personnel to conduct or continue electronic surveillance or other investigations for purposes unrelated to national security, the enforcement of laws, or any other lawful function of his office; and he did direct the concealment of certain records made by the Federal Bureau of Investigation of electronic surveillance.

(3) He has, acting personally and through his subordinates and agents, in violation or disregard of the constitutional rights of citizens, authorized and permitted to be maintained a secret investigative unit within the office of the President, financed in part with money derived from campaign contributions, which unlawfully utilized the resources of the Central Intelligence Agency, engaged in covert and unlawful activities, and attempted to prejudice the constitutional right of an accused to a fair trial.

(4) He has failed to take care that the laws were faithfully executed by failing to act when he knew or had reason to know that his close subordinates endeavored to impede and frustrate lawful inquiries by duly constituted executive, judicial, and legislative entities concerning the unlawful entry into the headquarters of the Democratic National Committee, and the cover-up thereof, and concerning other unlawful activities, including those relating to the confirmation of Richard Kleindienst as Attorney General of the United States, the electronic surveillance of private citizens, the break-in into the offices of Dr. Lewis Fielding, and the campaign financing practices of the Committee to Re-elect the President.

(5) In disregard of the rule of law, he knowingly misused the executive power by interfering with agencies of the executive branch, including the

Federal Bureau of Investigation, the Criminal Division, and the Office of Watergate Special Prosecution Force, of the Department of Justice, and the Central Intelligence Agency, in violation of his duty to take care that the laws be faithfully executed.

In all of this, Richard M. Nixon has acted in a manner contrary to his trust as President and subversive of constitutional government, to the great prejudice of the cause of law and justice and to the manifest injury of the people of the United States.

Wherefore Richard M. Nixon, by such conduct, warrants impeachment and trial, and removal from office.

Article III

In his conduct of the office of President of the United States, Richard M. Nixon, contrary to his oath faithfully to execute the office of President of the United States and, to the best of his ability, preserve, protect, and defend the Constitution of the United States, and in violation of his constitutional duty to take care that the laws be faithfully executed, has failed without lawful cause or excuse to produce papers and things as directed by duly authorized subpoenas issued by the Committee on the Judiciary of the House of Representatives on April 11, 1974, May 15, 1974, May 30, 1974, and June 24, 1974, and willfully disobeyed such subpoenas. The subpoenaed papers and things were deemed necessary by the Committee in order to resolve by direct evidence fundamental, factual questions relating to Presidential direction, knowledge, or approval of actions demonstrated by other evidence to be substantial grounds for impeachment of the President. In refusing to produce these papers and things, Richard M. Nixon, substituting his judgment as to what materials were necessary for the inquiry, interposed the powers of the Presidency against the lawful subpoenas of the House of Representatives, thereby assuming to himself functions and judgments necessary to the exercise of the sole power of impeachment vested by the Constitution in the House of Representatives.

In all of this, Richard M. Nixon has acted in a manner contrary to his trust as President and subversive of constitutional government, to the great prejudice of the cause of law and justice, and to the manifest injury of the people of the United States.

Wherefore Richard M. Nixon, by such conduct, warrants impeachment and trial, and removal from office.

Articles Not Approved

Cambodia Bombing In his conduct of the office of President of the United States, Richard M. Nixon, in violation of his constitutional oath faithfully to execute the office of President of the United States, and in disregard of his constitutional duty to take care that the laws be faithfully executed, on and subsequent to March 17, 1969, authorized, ordered, and ratified the concealment from the Congress of the facts and the submission to the Congress of false and misleading statements concerning the existence, scope, and nature of American bombing operations in Cambodia in derogation of the power of the Congress to declare war, to make appropriations, and to raise and support armies, and by such conduct warrants impeachment and trial and removal from office.

Emoluments and Income Taxes In his conduct of the office of President of the United States, Richard M. Nixon, in violation of his constitutional oath faithfully to execute the office of the President of the United States, and, to the best of his ability, preserve, protect, and defend the Constitution of the United States and in violation of his constitutional duty to take care that the laws be faithfully executed, did receive emoluments from the United States in excess of the compensation provided by law pursuant to Article II, Section 1, Clause 7 of the Constitution, and did willfully attempt to evade the payment of Federal income taxes due and owing by him for the years 1969, 1970, 1971, and 1972, in that

(1) He, during the period for which he has been elected President, unlawfully received compensation in the form of government expenditures at and on his privately owned properties located in or near San Clemente, California, and Key Biscayne, Florida.

(2) He knowingly and fraudulently failed to report certain income and claimed deductions in the year 1969, 1970, 1971, and 1972 on his Federal income tax returns which were not authorized by law, including deductions for a gift of papers to the United States valued at approximately $576,000.

In all of this, Richard M. Nixon has acted in a manner contrary to his trust as President and subversive of constitutional government, to the great prejudice of the cause of law and justice and to the manifest injury of the people of the United States.

Wherefore Richard M. Nixon, by such conduct, warrants impeachment and trial, and removal from office.

APPENDIX B

EXCERPTS FROM THE DOBROVIR BRIEF

[Originally published in November 1973 as *The Offenses of Richard M. Nixon: A Lawyer's Guide for the People of the United States of America*, written by William Dobrovir, Joseph Gebhardt, Samuel Buffone, and Andra Oakes.]

Introduction

The purpose of this paper is to set out certain offenses committed by President Nixon, both directly and through his official and unofficial White House and reelection campaign staff, personal advisers and employees. This analysis is confined to acts which are not only unconsitutional abuses of power but which are also indictable common crimes. It should be kept in mind, however, that impeachment may not be limited to indictable crimes, but that "high crimes and misdemeanors" may also include offenses against the Constitution and abuses of the office of the Presidency. Such offenses—like Presidential usurpation of the legislative or war-making powers of Congress—are uniquely related to the Presidency and are not included in the Criminal Code.

Part I is in the form of an indictment or articles of impeachment stating the factual charges to which President Nixon should be required to answer, and the criminal provisions applicable to each factual situation. Part II is a complete exposition in narrative form of the evidence presently in the public domain pertinent to the offenses charged. ....

I. Specification of Charges

... The following are 28 violations of law, committed or caused to be committed by Richard M. Nixon and/or his principal White House aides H. R. Haldeman, John Ehrlichman, John W. Dean III, and Charles Colson, and his principal campaign aides John N. Mitchell, Maurice Stans, and Herbert Kalmbach, in violation either of the U.S. Constitution or of specific criminal statutes.

All of these violations were committed or caused either by the President personally *or* by persons answerable to him. They are all included in this bill of particulars against Mr. Nixon himself because, whether or not he himself committed or caused a particular act, under the law that governs all Americans he is liable for the actions of those answerable to him.

1. Conspiracy. President Nixon, H. R. Haldeman, John Ehrlichman, Charles Colson, John Dean, John Mitchell, Herbert Kalmbach, and Maurice Stans, in concert with and abetted by others, conspired together to devise and carry out a plan or scheme to commit various crimes against numerous citizens of the United States who opposed the policies of Richard M. Nixon. President Nixon and his coconspirators thereby conspired to commit burglary in violation of 22 D.C. Code 1801; violated federal statutes making it a crime to wiretap, section 2510 et seq. of the United States Criminal Code (Title 18, U.S.C.); conspired to deprive citizens of civil rights in violation of section 241 of the Criminal Code; conspired to violate other federal statutes (e.g., the wiretap statute) in violation of section 371 of the Criminal Code; violated the President's constitutional duty to take care that the laws be faithfully executed, article 11, section 3; violated the First amendment rights of persons to freedom of speech, and violated the Fourth amendment rights of persons to be secure from unreasonable searches and seizures.

Pursuant to the plan or scheme specified in Count 1, President Nixon and his co-conspirators:

2. Illegal Wiretaps. Caused wiretaps to be placed on the telephones of seventeen persons without having obtained a court order authorizing the tap, as required by federal law; in violation of sections 241, 371 and 2510-11 of the Criminal Code.

3. Conspiracy to Suppress Free Speech. Caused harassment, by means of tax audits and other acts by the Internal Revenue Service, of named persons designated as political "enemies" of President Nixon for the purpose of inhibiting or preventing their exercise of First amendment rights, in violation of section 241 of the Criminal Code.

4. Conspiracy to Commit Burglary and Other Crimes. Caused the creation and adoption of a so-called "domestic intelligence plan" for securing information about American citizens, under which plan it was intended to commit unlawful acts of burglary, wiretapping, bugging and the opening of mail; in violation of sections 241 and 371 of the Criminal Code.

5. Burglary. Caused the creation of a "special investigations unit," called "the Plumbers," in which were employed, inter alia, G. Gordon Liddy and E. Howard Hunt, which carried out a burglary on September 3, 1972 of the office of Lewis Fielding, M.D. in Los Angeles, California, for the purpose of obtaining evidence for use in the trial of Daniel Ellsberg; in violation of sections 182.1, 459, 6020(j) and 647(a) of the California Penal Code and section 241 of the Criminal Code.

6. Obstruction of Justice. Attempted to influence a United States District

Court Judge, Hon. W. Matthew Byrne, in a matter then pending trial before him, to wit, the prosecution by the United States of Daniel Ellsberg for violation of the espionage statutes, by suggesting to Judge Byrne that he might be appointed as Director of the Federal Bureau of Investigation; in violation of sections 371 and 1503 of the Criminal Code.

7. Conspiracy to Commit Crimes to Influence the Election. Adopted a plan or scheme proposed by G. Gordon Liddy to employ various unlawful devices, including wiretaps, illegal entries, assault and battery and prostitution, to influence the results of the 1972 Presidential election in a manner favorable to Richard M. Nixon; in violation of section 371 of the Criminal Code.

8. Burglary. Caused the commission of two acts of burglary on May 27, 1972 and June 17, 1972, by the "Plumbers" into the offices of the Democratic National Committee in the Watergate Office Building, 2500 Virginia Avenue, N.W., in the District of Columbia, in violation of 22 D.C. Code 1801; the placing therein of a telephone wiretap in violation of section 2510 of the Criminal Code; in violation of sections 241 and 371 of the Criminal Code.

9. Obstruction of Justice, Perjury. Concealed the complicity of high officials of the White House staff and of the campaign Committee to Re-Elect the President in the acts specified in Counts 7 and 8, for the purpose of defeating and preventing criminal prosecutions by the United States, by (a) destroying documentary evidence, (b) concealing the existence of documentary evidence, (c) promising executive clemency and paying money and causing money to be paid to G. Gordon Liddy, E. Howard Hunt, Bernard Barker, Virgilio Gonzales, Frank Sturgis, James McCord and Eugenio Martinez to induce them, and which did induce them, to plead guilty to charges of burglary and to withhold testimony and to refuse to testify before a grand jury and at trial, (d) suborning perjury by Jeb S. Magruder at the trial of Liddy, et al.; in violation of sections 371, 1503, 1510, 1621 and 1622 of the Criminal Code.

10. Conspiracy to Defraud the United States. President Nixon, H. R. Haldeman, John Ehrlichman, Charles Colson, John Dean, Herbert Kalmbach and Maurice Stans, in concert with and aided and abetted by others, conspired to devise and carry out a plan or scheme to obtain money to spend for and in support of the reelection of Richard M. Nixon as President of the United States in 1972, in which they employed various unlawful means, to wit, obtaining campaign contributions from corporations and foreign nationals in violation of sections 610 and 613 of the Criminal Code, and soliciting and/or obtaining campaign contributions from individuals, political committees, corporations and foreign nationals in exchange for promises of governmental benefit and/or the withholding of governmental sanctions and/or the cessation of governmental law enforcement action; in violation of article II, section 4 of the Constitution and sections 201, 241, 371, 1503 and 1505 of the Criminal Code.

Pursuant to the plan or scheme specified in Count 10, President Nixon and his co-conspirators:

11. Illegal Campaign Contributions from Corporations. Solicited and obtained before April 7, 1972, campaign contributions from seven corporations, in violation of sections 371 and 610 of the Criminal Code, and by means of express or implied promises of governmental benefits and/or threats of the withholding of governmental benefits; in violation of sections 201, 371 and 872 of the Criminal Code.

12. Bribery, Fraud. Solicited a contribution of $200,000 to $400,000 and obtained a contribution of $100,000 from the ITT Corporation promised on July 21, 1971, and delivered on August 5, 1971 to support the Republican National Convention expected to be held in San Diego, California; by means of promises, express or implied, to obtain a decision by the Antitrust Division of the Department of Justice, which decision was obtained on July 31, 1971, to accept a consent decree which permitted ITT to retain the Hartford Fire Insurance Co., which the Antitrust Division had theretofore opposed by the filing and prosecution of a civil antitrust action in the United States District Court for the District of Connecticut; in violation of article 11, section 4 of the Constitution and sections 201, 271, 872 and 1505 of the Criminal Code.

13. Bribery, Fraud. Solicited and obtained a promise of a campaign contribution of $2,000,000 for President Nixon's reelection campaign from Associated Milk Producers, Inc. (AMPI), a dairy farm cooperative, in exchange for conferring on December 31, 1970, a governmental benefit on AMPI, to wit, the promulgation by President Nixon of reduced quotas for imports of dairy products; in violation of article 11, section 4 of the Constitution and sections 201, 371, 872 and 1505 of the Criminal Code.

14. Bribery, Fraud. Solicited and obtained from three dairy producer cooperatives a promise of contributions to President Nixon's reelection campaign and obtained at least $427,500 in such contributions, from March 22, 1971, to November 6, 1972, in exchange for conferring upon the three cooperatives on March 25, 1971, a governmental benefit, to wit, an increase ordered by the Secretary of Agriculture in the minimum price support level for dairy products for 1971-72 from $4.66 to $4.93 per 100 lbs. of fluid manufacturing grade milk; at a cost of $125 million to the Treasury of the United States and to the profit of the dairy industry of $500 to $700 million; in violation of article 11, section 4 of the Constitution and sections 201, 371, 872 and 1505 of the Criminal Code.

15. Conspiracy. Solicited and obtained from AMPI's political committee, TAPE, a contribution of $5,000, delivered on September 3, 1973, at a meeting which President Nixon attended, part of the funds obtained as specified in Count 14, expressly for the purpose of paying the costs of the "plumbers'" burglary of the office of Dr. Lewis Fielding specified in Count 8; in violation of sections 241 and 371 of the Criminal Code.

16. Bribery, Fraud. Solicited and obtained for the reelection campaign of President Nixon, from Robert Allen, President of Gulf Resources and Chemical Co., Inc., on April 3-5, 1972, a contribution of $100,000 of corporate funds in violation of section 610 of the Criminal Code, in exchange for the cessation and withholding, on March 29, 1972, of civil enforcement action by the Environmental Protection Agency of the United States Government to abate air and water pollution by Gulf Resources and Chemical Company's subsidiary Bunker Hill Company's lead and zinc smelter in Idaho; in violation of article 11, section 4 of the Constitution and sections 201, 371, 872 and 1505 of the Criminal Code.

17. Bribery, Fraud. Solicited and obtained for the reelection campaign of President Nixon, on April 9, 1972, from Dwayne O. Andreas, a contribution of $25,000, in exchange for conferring upon Andreas and other persons associated with him a governmental benefit, to wit, the approval by the Comptroller of the Currency of a national bank charter sought by Andreas and his associates, applied for on May 26, 1972 and approved on August 22, 1972; in violation of article II, section 4 of the Constitution and sections 201, 371, 872 and 1505 of the Criminal Code.

18. Conspiracy. Solicited and obtained the contributions specified in Counts 16 and 17 for the purpose, in part, of paying for the burglary of Democratic National Committee headquarters specified in Count 8, in violation of sections 241 and 371 of the Criminal Code and 22 D.C. Code 1801.

19. Bribery, Fraud, Illegal Foreign Campaign Contributions. Solicited and obtained for the reelection campaign of President Nixon, in April and in October, 1972, contributions totalling $25,000, from Nikos Vardinoyannis, a Greek national; in violation of Section 613 of the Criminal Code, and in exchange for conferring upon Vardinoyannis a governmental benefit, to wit, a, contract for $4.7 million in U.S. government funds to supply fuel for the U.S. Sixth Fleet in Piraeus, Greece; in violation of article II, section 4 of the Constitution and sections 201, 371, 872 and 1505 of the Criminal Code.

20. Bribery, Fraud. Solicited and obtained for the reelection campaign of President Nixon, in August, 1972, from officers of carpet manufacturing firms, Martin B. Seretean, Eugene T. Barwick and J. C. Shaw, contributions totalling more than $200,000 in exchange for conferring upon the carpet industry governmental benefits, to wit, a meeting at the White House with Charles Colson and other government officials, including officials from the Department of Commerce, and the withholding by the Department of Commerce of action opposed by the carpet industry, to wit, the introduction of a test for flammability of carpets more stringent and of higher safety than the current test, in violation of article 11, section 4 of the Constitution and sections 201, 371, 872 and 1505 of the Criminal Code.

21. Bribery, Fraud. Solicited and obtained for the reelection campaign of President Nixon, in June, July and August, 1972, from Ray A. Kroc, Chairman of the Board of McDonald's, Inc., contributions of $200,000, in exchange for permission from the Price Commission, first denied on May 21, 1972, then granted on September 8, 1972, to raise the price of the McDonald's quarter-pounder cheeseburger; in violation of article II, section 4 of the Constitution and sections 201, 372, 872 and 1505 of the Criminal Code.

22. Bribery, Fraud. Solicited and obtained for the reelection campaign of President Nixon, from the Seafarer's International Union, on November 2, 1972, a contribution of $100,000, in exchange for the conferring of a governmental benefit, to wit, the decision of the Department of Justice not to appeal dismissal of an indictment against the Union, filed on June 30, 1970,for violations of section 610 of the Criminal Code prohibiting campaign contributions by Unions; in violation of article II, section 4 of the Constitution and sections 201, 371, 610, 872, 1503 and 1505 of the Criminal Code.

23. Bribery, Fraud. Solicited and obtained for the reelection campaign of President Nixon, from Robert Vesco, on April 10, 1972, a contribution of $200,000, which was not reported to the General Accounting Office as required by law, in exchange for conferring upon Vesco governmental benefits, to wit, arranging a meeting between his attorney, Harry Sears, and federal law enforcement officials, to wit the Chairman of the Securities and Exchange Commission, and promises of other benefits, to wit, that John Mitchell and Maurice Stans would use their influence to prevent law enforcement action from being taken against Vesco; in violation of article 11, section 4 of the Constitution and sections 201, 371, 872, 1503 and 1505 of the Criminal Code.

24. Bribery, Fraud. Solicited and obtained, purportedly for the 1972 reelection campaign of President Nixon, in 1969 and 1970, contributions totalling $100,000 from Howard Hughes, in exchange for governmental benefits, to wit, the approval in 1969 by President Nixon, pursuant to authority conferred on the President by law, of the purchase by Hughes of Air West, a CAB certificated airline with international routes; and the withdrawal in 1970 by the Antitrust Division of the Department of Justice of its opposition to acquisition by Hughes of a seventh gambling casino in Las Vegas, Nevada; in violation of article 11, section 4 of the Constitution and sections 201, 371, 872, 1503 and 1505 of the Criminal Code.

25. Receiving Money Unlawfully Obtained. By the means specified in Counts 10-24 Richard Nixon received and obtained for his own use and benefit and did have the use and benefit, for the purpose of financing his campaign for reelection as President, of moneys illegally obtained as specified in Counts 10-24 to a total amount of $1,652,500, which he knew and/or had reason to know had been unlawfully obtained; in violation of article II, section 4 of the Constitution and sections 201, 241, 371, 872, 1503 and 1505 of the Criminal Code.

26. Conspiracy to Defraud the United States. President Nixon, H. R. Haldeman, Herbert Kalmbach, Frank DeMarco, Charles G. Rebozo and Robert Abplanalp, in concert with and aided and abetted by others, devised and carried out a plan or scheme personally to enrich President Nixon by abuse of the power and authority of his office as President; in violation of article II, section I of the Constitution, sections 271, 641, 1001 and 1505 of the Criminal

Code, and section 7201 of the Internal Revenue Code.

Pursuant to the plan or scheme specified in Count 26, the President and his co-conspirators:

27. Embezzlement, Fraud. Caused the expenditure of public funds, in the amount of more than one million dollars, for materials and labor to improve, adom and permanently increase the value of President Nixon's privately owned real property in San Clemente, California and Key Biscayne, Florida, in excess of expenditures authorized by law to provide for the security of the President; in violation of article II, section I of the Constitution and sections 371, 641 and 1505 of the Criminal Code.

28. Tax Evasion. Caused the filing of federal income tax returns on behalf of Richard M. Nixon, in which were claimed deductions from taxable income in an amount of approximately $570,000 for purported gifts to the United States of papers of Richard M. Nixon, which deductions were known to the co-conspirators to be unallowable because the gift of papers had not been timely made and consummated; in an attempt to evade or defeat the payment of federal income taxes and by reason of which Richard M. Nixon reduced his personal income tax for 1969 to $792.81 and for 1970 to $878.03, and thereby received in 1970 and 1971 large refunds of withheld taxes; in violation of section 7201 of the Internal Revenue Code and sections 371 and 1001 of the Criminal Code.

II. Summary of the Factual Record

Counts 1-9 charge a single plan or scheme, i.e., a conspiracy headed by the President, to deprive political opponents of their constitutional rights by various methods, some of which were themselves illegal. The plan began in 1969 when the President ordered domestic wiretaps without court order and the IRS was ordered to harass political enemies. The President himself ordered an admittedly illegal plan for domestic surveillance by means of wiretaps and burglaries and personally approved the creation of a new interagency intelligence unit to gather the same kind of information on political opponents. He personally approved the creation of the "plumbers," an extra-legal, private, White House operation headed by White House staff aide Egil Krogh. The President also personally approved the trip by two of the "plumbers," Liddy and Hunt, to "case" the office of Daniel Ellsberg's psychiatrist for an illegal entry and was to receive any information obtained by the entry. The President himself ordered his chief domestic aide, John Ehrlichman, to approach the trial judge, Judge Byrne, in the midst of the Ellsberg trial (which was of great importance to the President) about a promotion to the Directorship of the FBI.

All of the activities of the campaign group were directed by and known to the President's closest aides, Haldeman and Mitchell. The espionage plan that led to the Watergate burglary was approved by Mitchell, then Attorney General, and Colson, Special Counsel to the President, and was presumably known to Haldeman. Their illegal acts of wiretapping and burglary were intended to benefit Richard Nixon by ensuring his reelection.

Following the burglary, the effort to cover up White House involvement, by (a) buying silence with promises of money and executive clemency, (b) suborning the perjury of campaign officials Jeb S. Magruder and Herbert Porter, and (c) restricting the FBI's investigation (by invoking CIA involvement) deeply involved Mitchell, Haldeman, Herbert Kalmbach (the President's lawyer and long-time political associate, who raised the hush money) and White House Counsel John Dean. The President by his own admission participated in (c) (trying to hamstring the FBI) and by John Dean's testimony, contradicted by others, participated in a decision to make offers of money and executive clemency to keep the burglars quiet. And of course the President, whose reelection was at stake, was the principal beneficiary of the cover-up effort.

Counts 10-25 charge a second plan or scheme, created and carried out by the same persons, with the addition of others like Maurice Stans and Murray Chotiner, to collect a political campaign fund without precedent in history by the use of methods known to be in violation of law, including the corrupt bargaining of governmental benefits for cash.

The finance operation was first headed by Kalmbach, who was designated by Haldeman, speaking for the President, in January, 1971. Mitchell and Haldeman were involved and were kept informed from then on. Maurice Stans became finance chairman in February, 1972, but there is no indication that reports to the White House ceased, and the White House gave advice to Stans about funding problems. The President oversaw the whole operation; his private secretary, Rose Mary Woods, maintained a list of over-$1,000 campaign contributions. And, of course, the fund raising operation had as its sole purpose the support of President Nixon's reelection campaign—he was its chief, if not sole, beneficiary.

In the course of this operation Kalmbach and Stans solicited and obtained campaign contributions from corporations and unions and they and other fund raisers were able to trade immensely valuable government decisions for campaign contributions from powerful and interested economic interests.

Thus Robert Vesco paid $200,000 for promises by Mitchell and Stans to divert the SEC from investigating his financial dealings. A Greek oil dealer paid $25,000 and received a $4.7 million contract to fuel the Sixth Fleet in Piraeus. McDonald's hamburger chain's chairman paid $200,000 and received permission from the Price Commission to raise the price of their cheeseburger. Carpet manufacturers paid $200,000 and obtained a meeting with Colson and Commerce Department officials—set up by Stans—that resulted in the killing of proposed new, stricter safety/flammability standards for carpets.

Dwayne Andreas paid $25,000 (in cash, used to finance the Watergate burglary) and received approval of a national bank charter application in record time. Robert Allen paid $100,000, likewise used to finance the Watergate burglary, and obtained the dropping by the government of action against his company's pollution. The Seafarers Union paid $100,000 and obtained the dropping by the government of a prosecution for illegal campaign gifts the Union made in 1968. Howard Hughes paid $100,000 to C. G. Rebozo, Nixon's closest friend and obtained (a) approval by the President of his purchase of Air West and (b) approval by the Justice Department of his proposed purchase of another casino in Las Vegas.

President Nixon was personally involved in several of these transactions. Dairy interests wrote him a letter promising $2 million for his reelection campaign and asked for quotas on dairy product imports—which the President promptly imposed. When the Secretary of Agriculture refused to increase the 1971 price support for milk, long-time Nixon associate Murray Chotiner set up the channels for a flow of dairy money. After the flow began, dairy leaders met with Nixon and two days later the Secretary of Agriculture reversed himself. The dairy groups eventually paid $427,500 (of which $5,000, delivered virtually in Nixon's presence, financed the Ellsberg psychiatrist's break-in) for a decision that cost consumers $500 million.

ITT paid $100,000 (it had promised more) to help the Republicans hold their 1972 convention in San Diego. The company obtained, from the Antitrust Division of Justice, the dropping of a suit to stop ITT from acquiring the Hartford Fire Insurance Company, with the President telling Justice not to oppose bigness-as-such and to treat ITT "fairly." Nixon, Colson wrote, was "directly involved"; he discussed the ITT case with Mitchell and personally ordered Deputy Attorney General Kleindienst to delay the case.

Counts 26-28 charge the President with using his office to enrich himself personally by causing the government to spend money on his private estates and by taking an unallowable tax deduction. He knew what physical improvements were being made to the property, and could veto them; indeed the work was usually ordered or approved by Kalmbach or Haldeman. Like all other citizens he assuredly signed his own tax returns, in which he declared taxable income of around $7,000 on a salary of $200,000.

There are a number of points of overlap and intersection among these various acts. For example, the Watergate burglary, the last known overt act in pursuance of the plan to suppress dissent and opposition to the administration, was financed in part by campaign contributions apparently contributed out of corporate funds and "laundered" through foreign bank accounts, which funds appear to have been contributed in exchange for the dropping by the government of enforcement action against the corporate giver's polluting smelter in Idaho. Likewise, the burglary of the office of Daniel Ellsberg's psychiatrist carried out by the "plumbers," directed and employed by the White House, was in part financed by money contributed by dairy cooperatives who obtained a price support increase for dairy products with promises of contributions of $2,000,000 (less than 25 percent of which was actually delivered).

Of course the two organizations that carried out these acts the White House staff and the Committee to Re-Elect the President—were under the overall direction of and were ultimately responsible only to one man—President Nixon. Indeed, he has admitted "responsibility" for the acts of his subordinates. (President Richard Nixon, Statement of May 22, 1973. See *New York Times*, May 23, 1973, 28.) Moreover, the various acts were carried out directly by and under the direct supervision of the President's closest official and unofficial advisers. The President's personal attorney, Herbert Kalmbach, a political and personal associate of Mr. Nixon for twenty years, handled much of the campaign contribution solicitation personally and directed the entire operation until February, 1972, when Maurice Stans resigned as Secretary of Commerce to take formal charge. Kalmbach ordered and supervised installation at government expense of improvements at the President's estate in San Clemente, California, and his partner Frank DeMarco handled the President's tax avoidance device. Kalmbach was in charge of making payoffs to some of the burglars and wiremen who served as the White House "plumbers" and then were employed by the Committee to Re-Elect the President to burglarize the Democratic National Committee, and raised money to pay their legal fees and living expenses—or to buy their silence—after they were apprehended.

H. R. Haldeman, the President's chief of staff and the effective guardian of the President's time, appears to have supervised and was kept informed of campaign contribution affairs, likewise ordered property improvements at San Clemente, and was generally involved in the various devices used in efforts to suppress dissent. John Mitchell, the President's 1968 campaign manager, law and-order Attorney General and then 1972 campaign manager, approved illegal domestic wiretaps and the Liddy campaign espionage plan, was part of the campaign contribution collection operation and in furtherance of it made decisions at the Justice Department that favored big contributors.

All three of these men were the President's chosen instruments—his agents. As we shall see, he is criminally liable under the law for all the acts carried out in the conspiracy which he headed.

```
┌─────────────────────────────────────────────────────┐
│                   APPENDIX C                          │
│                                                       │
│          ROGERS-HOUSTON                               │
│                                                       │
│            MEMORANDUM                                 │
│                                                       │
└─────────────────────────────────────────────────────┘
```

Memorandum for: Deputy Attorney General, Department of Justice,
Washington, D.C.
Subject: Reports of Criminal Violations to the Department of Justice
Date: March 1, 1954

Attached is a memorandum for the record, addressed to the Director, of my
understanding of our conversation regarding the investigation of possible
criminal activities arising out of our activities. If you find no objection to this
statement, please return and we will retain it in our files for future guidance.

Lawrence R. Houston, *General Counsel*

Memorandum for: Director of Central Intelligence
Subject: Reports of Criminal Violations to the Department of Justice
Date: February 23, 1954

    1. From time to time information is developed within the Agency indicating
the actual or probable violation of criminal statutes. Normally all such information would be turned over to the Department of Justice for investigation and
decision as to prosecution. Occasionally, however, the apparent criminal activities are involved in highly classified and complex covert operations. Under
these circumstances investigation by an outside agency could not hope for success without revealing to that agency the full scope of the covert operation
involved as well as this Agency's authorities and manner of handling the operation. Even then, the investigation could not succeed without the full assis-

tance of all interested branches of this Agency. In addition, if investigation developed a prima-facie case of a criminal violation, in many cases it would be readily apparent that prosecution would be impossible without revealing highly classified matters to public scrutiny.

2. The law is well settled that a criminal prosecution cannot proceed in camera or on production of only part of the information. The Government must be willing to expose its entire information if it desires to prosecute. In those cases involving covert operations, therefore, there appears to be a balancing of interest between the duty to enforce the law which is in the proper jurisdiction of the Department of Justice and the Director's responsibility for protecting intelligence sources and methods. This is further affected by practical considerations.

3. I have recently had two conversations with the Department of Justice, the latter on 18 February being with the Deputy Attorney General, Mr. William F. Rogers. To illustrate the problem I took with me the complete investigation, with conclusions and recommendations, of a case which indicated a variety of violations of the various criminal statutues relating to the handling of official funds. This case arose during the review of a highly complex clandestine operation. The information was developed by the Inspection and Review Staff, Deputy Director (Plans), and even in its completed form would be almost unintelligible to a person not thoroughly familiar with the Agency and its operations due to the use of pseudonyms and cover companies and to various circumstances arising out of operational conditions.

4. I pointed out to the Deputy Attorney General that review by my office indicated that the individual was almost certainly guilty of violations of criminal statutes, but that we had been able to devise no charge under which he could be prosecuted which would not require revelation of highly classified information. Mr. Rogers said that under these circumstances he saw no purpose in referring the matter to the Department of Justice as we were as well or, in the light of the peculiar circumstances, perhaps better equipped to pass on the possibilities for prosecution. Therefore, if we could come to a firm determination in this respect, we should make the record of that determination as clear as possible and retain it in our files.

5. If, however, any information arising out of our investigation revealed the possibilities of prosecution, then we would have an obligation to bring the pertinent facts to the attention of the Department of Justice. I agreed that any doubt should be resolved in favor of referring the matter to the Department of Justice. I also pointed out that even in cases where we felt prosecution was impossible, if a shortage of funds were involved we took whatever collection action was feasible and, in spite of the problems arising out of the covert nature of our operations, were frequently successful in recovering the funds, at least in part. I also mentioned that our investigation sometimes indicated possible tax evasion or fraud which did not involve operations, and that we worked

with the Internal Revenue Service in such situations.

6. Mr. Rogers asked that we follow through carefully on any such case with any appropriate Government agency. He stated that an understanding on these matters could be reduced to a formal exchange of letters, if it becomes necessary, but that he saw no reason why present practices could not be continued without further documentation. I said it had been my recommendation not to formalize the situation unless the matter were brought to an issue either by passage of legislation and a need for clarification thereof or by discussion on specific cases with the Criminal Division of the Department of Justice.

Lawrence R. Houston, *General Counsel*

NOTES

Prologue
Recruitment by Marshall: Warner, pp. 67-75.
Editorials critical of Nussbaum: *New York Times*, February 27/March 4, 1994.
Nixon resignation: Drew, p. 413.
Smoking gun tape: Impeachment of Richard M. Nixon (Judiciary Committee
    Report, p. 53; Drew, pp. 391, 392; Sirica, pp. 313-318.
Coup against Mossadegh government (Iran): Powers, p. 106; Freemantle,
    pp. 33, 168.
Overthrow of Arbenz (Guatemala): Powers, p. 106; Freemantle, 169;
Vidal, p. 120.
CIA-FBI agreement and Abzug cross-examination of Lawrence Houston:
    Hearing of July 23, 1976, House Subcommittee on Government Relations
    and Individual Rights.
Efforts to assassinate Castro and others: Church Committee Report, 1975;
    Hinckle and Turner, pp. 104-223; Freemantle, pp. 168-186.
Kennedy-Nixon concealment of Cuba project during 1960 presidential cam-
    paign: Reeves, chap. 10.
Nixon, Dulles, and U.S. policy in Cuba in 1959-1960: Newman, pp. 113-135.
OSS and CIA recruitment of Mafia members: Hinckle and Turner, p. 289;
    McCoy, p. 34.

Chapter 1
Tip O'Neill on Hugh Addonizio: Breslin, p. 74.
Cornelius Gallagher: Breslin, p. 74; Clancy and Elder, p. 188.

Chapter 2
Washington Post article on Rodino: Drew, p. 114.

Chapter 3
Tip O'Neill on impeachment book: O'Neill, p. 253.

Breslin on impeachment book: Breslin, p. 71.
Morgan's first meeting with Zeifman: Morgan, p. 232.
Morgan on elitism: Morgan, p. 249.
Robert and Spencer Oliver: Lasky, p. 265.
Ervin quotes: Morgan, p. 249.
Ervin-Kennedy colloquy on Senate Resolution 60: Congressional Record,
    February 6, 1973, p. 3552.

Chapter 4
Discovery of tapes: Woodward and Bernstein, pp. 330, 331.
Deep Throat and discovery of tapes: Woodward and Bernstein, p. 333.
Woodward's ties to Scott Armstrong: Lasky, pp. 320.
Hughes's ties to CIA: Morgan, pp. 317-327; Hinckle and Turner, pp. 277-282.
Hughes's employment of O'Brien: Lasky, p. 263.
Colson tape: Morgan, pp. 308, 309.
McLaughlin background: Drew, p. 290.
Drinan threat: Mezvinsky, p. 61.

Chapter 5
Agnew quotes in Speaker's office: Breslin, pp. 57-59.
Agnew speech to Republican women: Drew, p. 25.

Chapter 6
Bittman's background: Fields, pp. 83, 180, 181.
Becker and Bittman's questionable activities: Edwards dissent in Ford
    Confirmation Report, p. 33.
William Cramer: cited in Conyers dissent in Ford Confirmation Report, p. 40.

Chapter 7
AFL-CIO opposition to Nixon: Drew, p. 125.
Tip O'Neill's assessments: O'Neill, pp. 245, 255; Clancy and Elder,p. 142.
Obstruction of justice charge: Mezvinsky, p. 69.
Waldie opposition to McCormack: Clancy and Elders, p. 114.
Lacey appointment: Fields, p. 65.
Description of Cates: Fields, p. 65.

Chapter 8
Doar's decision not to investigate: Breslin, p. 118.
Kennedy amendment to Watergate Committee resolution: Fields, p. 34.
Doar's prior positions: Rockefeller Commission Report, pp. 116,117; Lasky,
    pp. 199, 212-214, 348, 349, 360, 387-390, 390.
Goldwater on Nixon: Drew, p. 151, citing *Christian Science Monitor*

Chapter 9
Cates quotes: Fields, pp. 74, 78.
Charges against Edward Morgan: Jaworski, p. 289.

Chapter 10
Adler quotes: Adler, p. 78 et seq.
Hillary Rodham: Warner, p. 70.
Doar advocacy of "Nurenberg defense:" Judiciary Committee Impeachment
    Report, p. 382, citing Summary of Information 10.
Tip O'Neill on delay: O'Neill, p. 252.
Zeifman threatens to resign: Fields, p. 139.

Chapter 11
O'Neill and Zeifman: Clancy and Elder, p. 140.
Suspicions re Rodino: Drew, p. 114.
Fields quote: Fields, p. 145.

Chapter 12
Status report, March 1, 1974: Judiciary Committee Impeachment Report, p. 8.
Non-investigation by Doar: Breslin, 118; Adler, p. 76 et seq.;
Fields, p. 299.
St. Clair as "stormtrooper": Mezvinsky, p. 121.
Secret extension of deadline: Fields, pp. 148, 149.
Status report, April 26, 1973: Fields, p. 149.
Wayne Hays: Mezvinsky, p. 126.

Chapter 13
Quotes from *Chicago Tribune:* Drew, p. 271.
Quotes from Railsback: Drew, p. 269.
"Case Against the President": Jaworski, chap. 11.

Chapter 14
Cohen quotes: Drew, p. 279.
Flowers quotes: Drew, p. 235.
Charles Morgan quotes: Morgan, p. 232.
Waldie quote: Mezvinsky, p. 151.

Chapter 15
Korff on Nixon: Drew, p. 296.
Eilberg guilty plea: "Congressional Ethics," *Congressional Quarterly,*
    2nd ed., p. 24.
Fields on Brooks: Fields, p. 12.

Chapter 16
O'Neill on delay: O'Neill, p. 25.

Chapter 17
Mezvinsky quotes: Mezvinsky, p. 161, 164.
Cross-examination of Dean: Fields, p. 200.

Chapter 18
Hungate quote: Drew, p. 71.
Doar summary: Fields, p. 215.

Chapter 19
St. Clair quote: Drew, p. 335.
Nixon resignation: Drew, p. 413.
Smoking gun tape: Judiciary Committee Impeachment Report, p. 53; Drew,
    pp. 391, 392; Sirica, pp. 313-318.
Boggs 1971 speech: Congressional Record, April 22, 1971, pp. 11567 et seq.
Boggs's psychological problems and knowledge of Maheu-CIA-Mafia ties:
    Personal interviews with close associates of Hale Boggs.
Johnson's concerns re Robert Kennedy: "Johnson Tapes," *Nightline;*
    Washington Times, April 16, 1994, p. A3.

Chapter 20
Frost interview of Richard Nixon, 1977: Fields, page 296.
Rodham assigned to work with C. Vann Woodward: Warner, p. 70.
Submission of Woodward report to Doar: C. Vann Woodward, Editor's
acknowledgment.
Adler on relation between Church Committee Report and Woodward
Report: Adler, pp. 79, 80.
Jenner quotes re Woodward report: Adler, p. 80.
Conyers quote: Judiciary Committee Impeachment Report, p. 296.
Kennan quote: *New York Times Magazine,* May 27, 1951, pp. 7, 53, 55.
Brandeis quote: *Olmstead v. U.S.,* 1928, 277 U.S. 438, 471-473, 478-480, cited
    in Frankel, p. 162 et seq.

Epilogue
Litigation versus Hillary Rodham Clinton, et al.: Files in U.S. District Court,
    District of Columbia, Case 93-399; Robert Pear, "Misconduct Found on
    Clinton Health Plan," *New York Times,* December 2, 1994, p. 22; David
    Johnston, "Ruling on Top Health Care Aide Brings Worry for
    Administration," *New York Times,* December 23, 1995, p. 20; Paul Bedard,
    "Health Care Task Force Costs Exposed," *Washington Times,* March 1,
    1995, p. A1.

BIBLIOGRAPHY

Official Publications (Government Printing Office)

Alleged Assassination Plots Involving Foreign Leaders. Interim Report of the Senate Select Committee to Study Government Operations with Respect to Intelligence Activities ("Church Committee"). U.S. Senate, 1975.

Confirmation of Gerald R. Ford as Vice President of the United States. Report of the Committee on the Judiciary, House Report 93-095. 93rd Congress, 1st Session, 1973.

Congressional Directory, 93rd Congress, 2nd Session, 1974.

Impeachment of Richard M. Nixon, President of the United States. Report of the Committee on the Judiciary, U.S. House of Representatives. House Report 93-1305. 93rd Congress, 2nd Session, 1974.

Report to the President by the Commission on CIA Activities ("Rockefeller Commission"). June 1975.

Selected Materials on Impeachment. Committee Print, Committee on the Judiciary, U.S. House of Representatives, 93rd Congress, 1st Session, 1973.

Selected Materials on Impeachment Procedures. Committee Print, Committee on the Judiciary, U.S. House of Representatives, 93rd Congress, 2nd Session, 1974.

Books and Periodicals

Adler, Renata. "Searching for the Real Nixon." *Atlantic Monthly,* December 1976.

Boettcher, Robert. *Gifts of Deceit.* New York: Holt, Rinehart & Winston, 1980.

Breslin, Jimmy. *How the Good Guys Finally Won.* New York: Viking, 1975.

Carson, Clayborne. *Malcolm X: The FBI File.* New York: Ballantine, 1995.

Clancy, Paul and Shirley Elder. *Tip: A Biography of Thomas O'Neill.* New York: Macmillan, 1980.

Dean, John. *Blind Ambition.* New York: Simon & Schuster, 1976.

249

Dobrovir, William, et al. *The Offenses of Richard Nixon: A Lawyer's Guide for the People of the United States.* 1973.

Drew, Elizabeth. *Washington Journal.* New York: Random House, 1974.

Fields, Howard. *High Crimes and Misdemeanors: The Story of the Rodino Committee.* New York: Norton, 1978.

Frankel, Lionel. *Law, Power, and Personal Freedom.* St. Paul, MN: West Publishing, 1975.

Freemantle, Brian. *CIA: The Honourable Company.* London: Futura, 1983.

Hinckle, Warren and Bill Turner. *Deadly Secrets.* New York: Thunder's Mouth Press, 1992.

Jaworksi, Leon. *The Right and the Power.* New York: Readers Digest, 1976.

Lasky, Victor. *It Didn't Start with Watergate.* New York: Dial, 1977.

McCoy. *The Politics of Heroin in Southeast Asia.* New York: Harper & Row, 1972.

Maheu, Robert. *Next to Hughes.* New York: HarperCollins, 1993.

Martinez, Eugenio. "Mission Impossible." *Harper's,* October 1974.

Mezvinsky, Edward. *A Term to Remember.* New York: Coward, McCann & Geoghegan, 1977.

Morgan, Charles, Jr. *One Man, One Vote.* New York: Holt, Rinehart & Winston, 1979.

Newman, John. *Oswald and the CIA.* New York: Carroll & Graf, 1975.

O'Neill, Thomas with William Novak. *Man of the House.* New York: Random House, 1987.

Powers, Thomas. *The Man Who Kept the Secrets: Richard Helms and the CIA.* New York: Simon & Schuster, 1979.

Reeves, Thomas. *A Question of Character.* Rocklin, CA: Prima, 1992.

Schlesinger, Arthur, Jr. *Robert Kennedy and His Times.* Boston: Houghton Mifflin, 1978.

Sirica, John. *To Set the Record Straight.* New York: Norton, 1979.

Stein, Jeff. *A Murder in Wartime.* New York: St. Martin's Press, 1992.

Summers, Anthony. *Official and Confidential.* New York: Putnam, 1993.

Vann Woodward, C. *Responses of the Presidents to the Charges of Misconduct.* New York: Delacorte, 1974.

Vidal, Gore. *Palimpsest.* New York: Random House, 1995.

Walters, Vernon. *Silent Missions.* New York: Doubleday, 1978.

Warner, Judith. *Hillary Clinton: The Inside Story.* New York: Penguin, 1993.

Woodward, Robert and Carl Bernstein. *All the President's Men.* New York: Simon & Schuster, 1974.

Wyden, Peter. *Bay of Pigs.* New York: Simon & Schuster, 1979.

INDEX